Praise for *The Heart of Who We Are*

"Collective liberation is first grounded in collective healing. Collective healing starts with the labor of individuals willing to begin healing for themselves. That will open into collective healing. Our future must be a future that centers the work of healing to get free. In *The Heart of Who We Are*, Caverly Morgan offers us a vision of how to do this imperative work through the profound lens of Buddhist dharma, which she has deeply embodied through her many years of practice and study. This book is a part of the canon of work we must rely on to bring about a more liberated future."

Lama Rod Owens, author of *Love and Rage: The Path of Liberation Through Anger*

"Awareness is contagious, and Caverly skillfully encourages readers to harness our awareness to find the peace and contentedness that already exist within. The energy that follows brings healing to our lives, as well as helps us work to improve the lives of others."

Sharon Salzberg, author of *Lovingkindness* and *Real Change*

"Caverly Morgan's writing is immediately intimate, fresh, and friendly—and it goes straight to your heart. She combines spiritual depth with enormous practical wisdom. I loved reading her personal stories, mind-stopping enlightenment zaps, effective suggestions, brief psychological exercises, and gentle, humorous, encouraging guidance. She is a true friend to the reader, a deeply realized being who is utterly committed to your healing and awakening. A gem!"

Rick Hanson, PhD, author of *Neurodharma: New Science, Ancient Wisdom, and Seven Practices of the Highest Happiness*

"Transcendence and transformation. In *The Heart of Who We Are*, Caverly deftly holds two seemingly opposing truths—our shared being of oneness whose nature is peace, and our shared world of apparent separation and its suffering—and invites us to explore how our true nature might find its fullest expression in both ourselves and the collective. This beautiful and courageous book not only provides a way for us to explore who we are and how we are in the world but stands as a shining example of what it means to do both."

Rupert Spira, teacher of nonduality, author of *The Nature of Consciousness* and *Being Aware of Being Aware*

"This book is a masterpiece. It offers the reader a deep understanding of nonduality in an accessible and tangible way, illustrates how to apply this understanding to social justice and cultural change, and offers a path toward realizing freedom together though love, compassion, and awareness. One of the most personally impactful books I've read in a long time."

Kristin Neff, PhD, author of *Self-Compassion: The Proven Power of Being Kind to Yourself* and *Fierce Self-Compassion: How Women Can Harness Kindness to Speak Up, Claim Their Power, and Thrive*

"Drawing upon her decades of experience as a Zen monk and meditation teacher, Caverly Morgan generously shares the practices of deep inquiry and guided meditations that have transformed the lives of thousands of teenagers in the Peace in Schools program in Portland, Oregon. At a time when so many people are discouraged about the future of the world and its inhabitants, her creative teachings can help us see through the illusion of a separate and flawed self, offering the real possibility that individual awakening can become community, societal, and eventually, worldwide awakening."

Jan Chozen Bays, Roshi

"Inspiring and immersive, *The Heart of Who We Are* invites us to access a way of being whole that dissolves the illusion of the separate solo-self, so often taught in our modern culture, and instead come to release what rests beneath that veil—an open awareness from which love, experience, and consciousness arise. The practices and stories of this marvelous book are lessons guiding us in how to live more fully and freely, releasing the life force of love that is the essence and energy of the liberation within these transformative pages."

Daniel J. Siegel, MD, *New York Times* bestselling author of *IntraConnected: MWe (Me + We) as the Integration of Self, Identity, and Belonging*, executive director of the Mindsight Institute

"Caverly Morgan has created a practical guide that will change your life and help you see the world differently. This work moves you from despair to hope, from pain to possibility, all through deep practices, truth, and love. Read this book. You, and the world, will be better for it."

Justin Michael Williams, author of *Stay Woke*

"*The Heart of Who We Are: Realizing Freedom Together* is a game changer. It is a book for spiritual teachers and for students alike. In her practical approach that draws on her successful methodologies, Caverly shows us how to bridge the chasm between spiritual wisdom and social responsibilities. Caverly guides us to understand what we are not seeing as individuals and the impact of our blindness on the collective unconsciousness within our culture. She gives us hope by showing us not only what we can do but how to do it. *The Heart of Who We Are: Realizing Freedom Together* is a significant addition to spiritual wisdom teachings."

Jac O'Keeffe, teacher, author of *How to Be a Spiritual Rebel* and *Born to be Free*

"In *The Heart of Who We Are*, Caverly Morgan has offered our troubled world a wish-fulfilling gem—crystal clear in its transparent honesty, luminous in shining the light of wise compassion on the shame that binds us all in different ways, incisive and unbreakable in its exposing and cutting through the knots of fear-based conditioning that lock us into lives of separation, othering, and harming. Given the urgency of this now—with our individual and collective lives, our spiritual practice, and communities crying for voices that help awaken us from the nightmares of spiritual bypassing and systemic racial and other oppression, her voice is a freedom bell that calls us to return again to our wholeness and to join as one in the act of co-creating the beloved community we all need to truly be together in shared presence, here and now."

Joe Loizzo, MD, PhD, founder of the Nalanda Institute for Contemplative Science, assistant professor of psychiatry at Weill Cornell Medical College

"*The Heart of Who We Are* is a luminous and multifaceted gem of a book, beautifully written and grounded in wisdom from Caverly Morgan's own lived experience as a dharma practitioner and teacher. This treasure store offers us one of the clearest, heartfelt, and most compelling conversations that I've come across on why it is essential for each of us to wholeheartedly endeavor toward mutual and collective liberation. With a voice that is equal measures warm and accessible, poetic and profound, Caverly skillfully guides us in applying Zen teachings and nondual practices to a number of karmically conditioned complexes that hinder our recognition of our fundamental awake nature and the intimacy of our shared being. *The Heart of Who We Are* serves as a wise, encouraging friend and a tremendous resource for anyone yearning to realize—and actualize—true freedom and happiness in the personal, interpersonal, and collective dimensions of their lives. I hope that many will have the opportunity to encounter this truly transformative gift!"

Tenzen David Zimmerman, abbot of Beginner's Mind Temple, San Francisco Zen Center

"We live in a world and times in which we are increasingly confronted by division, uncertainty, and a falling away of things we once took as unshakable. With *The Heart of Who We Are*, Caverly Morgan extends a hand of kindness that coaxes readers to embrace the necessary journey of rediscovering themselves, and the compassion of walking alongside them. She generously offers her hard-earned wisdom—as a monk, a teacher, and a willing student of life—as a practical manual to turn fear into curiosity, confusion into awareness, and separation into love. You will return to this book over and over again."

Rev. angel Kyodo williams, Roshi, co-author of *Radical Dharma: Talking Race, Love and Liberation*

"In this touching and timely book, Caverly Morgan explores what happens when the loving awareness that emerges from seeing through the delusion of the separate self turns towards collective social delusions such as racial superiority and dominance. What happens when a diverse, polarized community feels safe and respected enough to explore their shared Being as so many of Caverly's Portland public high school students learned to do? This book brings the mindfulness conversation to both a deeper level and wider scope by pointing to an inherent wholeness beneath all of our psychological and social wounds. *The Heart of Who We Are* invites us into a vital transformative group or individual inquiry. An inspired, loving, authentic, and original work."

John J. Prendergast, PhD, author of *The Deep Heart* and *In Touch*, Retired Adjunct Professor of Psychology, CIIS

"Morgan is calling us back to our origin, which is to call us towards our innate freedom. She is calling us to our ancient ways of community, wholeness, belonging, discovery, and service. She does this first by dedicating her work to her mother, the one who gave her life and then to her beloved who nurtures it. In *The Heart of Who We Are*, Morgan brings us back to what we know in our bones. If only we are willing to allow such wisdom to surface and spread between us."

Zenju Earthlyn Manuel, author of *The Shamanic Bones of Zen* and *The Way of Tenderness*

the HEART of WHO WE ARE

realizing
freedom
together

CAVERLY MORGAN

sounds true
BOULDER, COLORADO

Sounds True
Boulder, CO 80306

Published 2022

Cover design by Jennifer Miles
Book design by Ranee Kahler

Printed in the United States of America

BK06391

Library of Congress Cataloging-in-Publication Data

Names: Morgan, Caverly, author.
Title: The heart of who we are : realizing freedom together / by Caverly
  Morgan.
Description: Boulder, CO : Sounds True, 2023. | Includes bibliographical
  references.
Identifiers: LCCN 2022017826 (print) | LCCN 2022017827 (ebook) | ISBN
  9781683649229 (paperback) | ISBN 9781683649236 (ebook)
Subjects: LCSH: Mindfulness (Psychology) | Peace of mind. |
  Self-actualization (Psychology)
Classification: LCC BF637.M56 M67 2023 (print) | LCC BF637.M56 (ebook) |
  DDC 158.1/3--dc23/eng/20220509
LC record available at https://lccn.loc.gov/2022017826
LC ebook record available at https://lccn.loc.gov/2022017827

10 9 8 7 6 5 4 3 2 1

FSC
www.fsc.org
MIX
Paper | Supporting
responsible forestry
FSC® C103098

My Moma
for modeling the greatest generosity of spirit
I have ever known

And for my beloved Vineet
for your devotion to Love

Contents

Contents

Foreword

My friendship with Caverly began in one of my favorite vegetarian restaurants in Portland, Oregon. Having lived there for a year before returning to North Carolina, I was back in town for a week to lead some workshops based on my first book, *Skill in Action: Radicalizing Your Yoga Practice to Create a Just World*. Caverly had read it and reached out to me to invite me to break bread with her. We met and talked about our lives and mothers, our love of dogs, spiritual practice, liberation, and about how systems of oppression prevent us from thriving. I left that meeting with an awareness that my life and Caverly's would weave together in a radical and revolutionary way.

We are both deeply committed to collective liberation. We are students of mindfulness and spiritual practice. We are spiritual teachers. We believe we are love and that we must love each other and all creatures more fully and deeply if we want to be free. We know divinity and love are one and the same. We understand that the divine maternal energy of Spirit coupled with the work of our ancestors manifested us into this lifetime to support people in both remembering their divinity and remembering that we are all love.

We are all love.

Love is actionable.

We know that if we remember these two things we can transmute the conditions in the way of us all not being free. We can transmute systems of oppression. Together, we can transmute our individual and collective trauma into a state of peace. If we love out loud and embody love, we can create a world with less suffering and strife and more grace, unity, and connection.

As a collective, we are facing a tremendous spiritual crisis—we have forgotten we are interconnected. We suffer because we have forgotten all the ways we are connected with everything. We have forgotten that the five hearts an earthworm embodies are connected to our own beating hearts. We have forgotten that the delicate balance of the oceanic ecosystem needs to be maintained for our collective survival, just as our own internal ecosystem, mind, body, heart, spirit, and emotional body need to be in balance for our collective survival. We suffer because we believe we are our thoughts and have forgotten that at any moment in time we can engage in spiritual practice to support us in unlearning all we need to unlearn to heal individually and collectively. We suffer because we think we can transcend suffering, which only deepens our suffering. We suffer because we are in our heads and not moving from our hearts. I do not mean this in an esoteric way. I admit there is so much I still don't understand about my own heart, but I do know I feel different in my whole being when I drop into my heart and out of my head.

The Heart of Who We Are: Realizing Freedom Together speaks to the spiritual imperative at this time, which is a call, or perhaps a scream or plea being bellowed from deep in the earth, from the above and below worlds, from the oceans, the mountains, the desert, and cosmos for us to engage in practices and strategies that will bring us back to our hearts and the truth of who we are, to the remembrance of how deeply connected we are to all things everywhere. Practices that will remind us we are connected to all beings, big or small; living or passed on; human or plant species, in the earthly or cosmic realms. Practices that will support us in interrogating and undoing the thought patterns and behaviors that keep us in a cycle of suffering. *The Heart of Who We Are* provides a framework for us to meet this spiritual imperative and a map and pathway to our collective liberation.

Caverly beautifully weaves together anecdotes, personal stories and learnings, metaphysics, divinity, love, spiritual teachings, and contemplative technologies. She masterfully centers love as a practice throughout this beautiful book because love is what will bring us out of the delusion that we think we are separate. *The Heart of Who We Are* models how we must collaboratively and with mutual care practice being in community with one another. It calls us to respond to the spiritual crisis we are all facing by asking us to contemplate how every action we take can be in service to something bigger than ourselves. *The Heart of Who We Are* acknowledges that our collective liberation is not just about the moment we are experiencing right now but all of the moments that have passed and the moments yet to come.

If you choose to respond to the spiritual crisis and imperative of this time, *The Heart of Who We Are* is an essential tool you will need to do so. Each teaching, lesson, question, story, pause, poem, and prayer invites the reader to begin where they are. As they are. This is one of the many gifts Caverly embodies. She knows she cannot force learning, love, or transformation. She understands the power of raising one's consciousness in such a way that cracks open one's heart, allowing one to respond to the call to transform for the good of us all. Allow your heart to crack open in the most soulful way as you journey through this stunning offering from Caverly's heart to yours. Allow yourself to come back to the heart of who you are. May we all come back to the profound and unchangeable truth that we are divine beings with a divined purpose rooted in love at this time and in this place.

Michelle Cassandra Johnson

July 5, 2022

Winston Salem, North Carolina

Author of *Finding Refuge: Heart Work for Healing Collective Grief* and *Skill in Action: Radicalizing Your Yoga Practice to Create a Just World*

Introduction

Our own self-realization is the greatest
service we can render the world.

—Ramana Maharshi

W̶e all long to be happy. Not happy as in glee but deep contentment. We all long to feel at ease, to know that we're okay, that life is okay, to be at peace. And we're deeply habituated to look for this happiness outside us, to grasp and scramble for an experience that, at best, ends up being fleeting, then something we long for again. We forget that this experience we long for is already seated in the heart of who we are—and that it's always here.

Have you ever touched this peace, this contentment, this deep knowing of who you truly are and then struggled because you recognized the degree to which the world around you didn't reflect this experience of our true nature?

Our true nature.
Oneness. Spiritual practice reveals the reality of oneness. Part of me feels called to write about this reality and nothing else. To live quietly. To meditate often. To be still. To perhaps make goat cheese on an island in the Puget Sound with my husband and our dogs.

Another part of me can't write or teach about this reality exclusively. I am propelled by a deep call to address how in so many spiritual practice settings this oneness is named yet is not reflected in our daily lives as practitioners. Not to mention how many report feeling overlooked, excluded, and ignored in prominent spiritual communities, the realities of their lives unseen, even unwelcome.

How can I, a former monk with a lifelong commitment to non-harming, talk about oneness while participating in systems that I recognize as harmful—systems that I can't be teased apart from? How can I speak about this reality of oneness without addressing the ways we often don't act on behalf of this knowing? How can I recognize the privileges afforded to me based on race and class while also coming to terms with the way it is not a "privilege" to be part of a system of domination and othering? What do I mean by "othering"? Actions arising from the perception of separation; behaviors that don't reflect the truth of oneness.

This divide speaks to two realities: the reality of interconnection and oneness—the absolute reality; and the reality of isolation and separation—our relative experience, where we enact the shared delusion that we are fundamentally separate from each other on personal and collective levels.

These are two truths.
The truth of the absolute and the truth of the relative.

The relative—the conventional, the material; things as they appear to be.
The absolute—the ultimate; things as they truly are. Empty.

Empty—not as in a grim void or a kind of nihilism. Not nothingness.
But empty of objective experience. Empty of language. Empty of meaning.
Empty of separateness.

Everything comes from something else.

Everything is connected to something else.
No thing exists in a vacuum.
No thing stands on its own.
Things simply appear to.

Emptiness means empty of limitation.
Emptiness means spaciousness.

Emptiness means openness.
Emptiness—the home of possibility.
The great mystery.

Where nothing is formed.
And nothing is known.

I am called to speak to both the absolute and relative realities, to reconcile these truths, to not omit any part of reality. How can our personal and collective practices be employed not merely to "transcend" the pain of the world but also to help us to accept and be with the pain of the world so we can then transform it? Transforming not only individually but also collectively?

What are the ways that our spiritual practices have been conditioned to have filters? To be by-products of the very distortions we aim to see through? How can we not only directly experience oneness but also apply this experience and understanding to address the impacts of the delusion of separation and pain in the world? Most importantly, to not just address the impacts but also to get to the root issue?

I long to live in a world that reflects the reality of oneness rather than the distortion of our shared delusion. I long to live in a world that reflects the deepest truth of our *shared being*, a term I first heard from the meditation teacher Rupert Spira. I know this world from my meditation cushion in my remote hermitage on the hill, and I know this world from inside the walls of public high school classrooms. What is possible reveals itself in countless ways.

I don't write about anything here that hasn't touched my life directly: teens who struggle with depression and self-harm; an increasing homeless population in the city I live in; wildfire season, now the norm where so many of us live; loved ones who are affected by racism daily; the recognition that we are *all* impacted by racism daily; the pain of seeing how I participate in systems that I recognize as harmful, that we all do. *This* relative plane reality. The reality that so often reflects the pain of living on behalf of the belief that we are separate from each other. The reality where we suffer. How might our experience of oneness be brought to bear on this reality?

It's been painful, yet also freeing, to wake up to the ways I participate in harm. The work of Radical Dharma—based on the book of the same name by Rev. angel Kyodo williams, Lama Rod Owens, and Dr. Jasmine Syedullah—has been particularly supportive of my learning, not only around how I participate but also how I am affected by these systems. How we all are. How none of us are separate from them.

Spiritual practice offers a way to be with this pain. To not run from it, to address it, to transform pain and return to the sanity of the truth of unity. I value being part of collective movements dedicated to the shared journey from the insane to the sane. I know I am not alone in longing for this, in being committed to creating this, in valuing this.

Throughout my life I've received tremendous support from others in my practice to expose and end the suffering that happens within. Everyone deserves such support. We all deserve to know our inherent well-being. We all deserve to be happy. And at the risk of being overly simplistic, if all had such support, our world would appear differently. I have dedicated my practice to exploring how these supports—the tools, teachings, practices that help us end suffering within—can be applied collectively. I've seen it happen in high school classrooms.

I've tasted what's possible.

How can these same practices be applied in an even larger world? I believe the only way we'll find out is through experience, by continually exploring how. I'm inspired by the possibility of the awakening of human consciousness at large. The knowing of our oneness at large, and how that knowing, collectively, might then impact our world.

In my years as a retreatant and in the public sphere, I've learned much about how the ego—the illusion of a self that is separate from life—operates. The revealing of the ego in action—insights about how it functions—has a particular taste, a particular feel. Freedom has a flavor.

I've come to understand how collective systems arising out of the delusion that "we are separate" also have the same resonance as the personal delusion "*I am separate.*" The workings of the ego, which we might think of as operating on a personal level, and the workings of collective conditioning have the same taste. I've had moments of experiencing how and where delusion—*personal or collective*—manifests and ripples through the mind and body in the same way, creating the same feel. And seeing *through* distortion, whether we are seeing through personal or collective delusion, has its own same feel. The feel of freedom.

All that distorts the reality of oneness is, to me, worth seeing, worth naming, worth letting go, on any level, in any realm. And freedom is freedom.

In the societal realm, I continue to learn about how I participate in and am impacted by systemic oppression—how systemic oppression operates and expresses itself through me via my personal and collective conditioning. So I speak about race in this book. But this book isn't meant to be a book about race. Rather, it is a book about spiritual practice, and about truth, that includes an ongoing learning process around race, among other things. A book about practice that doesn't leave behind this relative plane exploration or see it as separate.

I'm clear that I don't have all the answers. I'm also clear that no one person does. I have faith in collective wisdom, collective awareness, collective love.

At the end of the day, my mission is simple: live in a world where we all experience our inherent belonging, our inherent wholeness, and our inherent freedom. Where the reality of oneness is fully expressed in the world we create.

I believe that true and lasting world change depends on knowing ourselves in the absolute sense. This book focuses on this knowing and how to move through the world from this knowing. To move through the world recognizing the truth of our shared being while not ignoring all that can appear to get in the way within our relative world—our families, our communities, our society. The relative world of our personal and collective conditioning. True change occurs not just when we know who we truly are or have a direct experience of our shared being but when we act in the world on behalf of this truth, this knowing.

This book is about the *act of being* (a phrase that has been used to encompass many knowings and philosophies, from the Catholic philosopher St. Thomas Aquinas to Mullā Ṣadrā, an Islamic mystic, philosopher, and theologian). It's about knowing a happiness you can't explain because you have no reason to point to. The joy of pure being. Of knowing who you are, resting in presence, and acting in the world on behalf of this deep knowing. This book is about the pleasure of being aware of being aware, seeing what gets in the way of this—personally and collectively—and learning how to let it go, to undo, to realize freedom together.

I'm not going to begin with the story that this book is going to give you what you need to finally become "the right spiritual person." My hope is that it doesn't feed the story that if you could only [*fill in the blank*], you could finally be free.

Rather than starting with the assumption that you need to work hard to become free, we begin with a focus on *what is already free*. Already and always.

You are invited to join me in an engaged way, a personal way, a way that doesn't leave the heart behind. This book is meant to be a journey. It's written with the personal and the collective in mind. My first Zen teacher often said, "It's not what, it's how." That became an important guiding principle in my training. While I hope the content of this book—the *what*—will provide benefit on its own, *how* you engage with this content is what will matter the most.

This book is about practicing being in touch with the heart of who we are and how being grounded in the heart of who we are changes not only our personal lives but also our relationships, systems, and how we move through the world. Here we take what can be a somewhat floaty idea of "oneness" and ground it in actions that create tangible change both personally and collectively.

The contemplative technologies in this book will support your experience of being awake in the world: creating an intentional place to practice, seeing and naming negative self-talk, cultivating the compassionate mentor within, exploring how we learned to survive our lives, recognizing the conditioned mind, just to name a few. We'll explore how each tool applies not only to the creation of personal suffering but also to the suffering that plays out in the larger world as well. In other words, we'll focus on what gets in the way of truth. We'll also focus on truth itself, on presence, on oneness. This book is about you, but perhaps more significantly it's about *us*.

The tools in this book are not supports to become something better or something you are not. These contemplative technologies arise out of the understanding that you are inherently whole, that you are unbreakable. These tools are offerings of remembrance.

As we remember what is true, we touch the reality of the absolute—that we are not separate. Our world then changes when we bring this truth to bear on the relative plane of reality—in our churches, our schools, our communities, our society. Our world changes when this truth completely saturates our mind.

You may choose to read this book on your own. You may choose to read it in community. Whether you read it alone or with a group, I hope this book will serve you and your longing to know who you truly are and to live from this understanding.

Reading this book with the support of a collective can take countless forms. You may read it with family members, a church group, your meditation community, a collective of friends who have a shared focus on freedom.

At the monastery where I trained, we were always encouraged to be grateful for the support of the other monks as we practiced being awake in the world. That didn't just mean "when they are supporting me the way that I want to be supported." That also meant "when I'm head cook for a huge retreat and another monk is late bringing the groceries. It's clear that the meal isn't going to be on time and suddenly I'm gifted with the opportunity to practice patience." If you choose to take this journey in direct relationship with others, I invite you to learn from the bumps and the rubs that might arise in this context. All of it is ground for learning. Each chapter includes individual guided practices and ends with suggestions for collective practice.

This book stands on the premise that we *all* long to know Love with a capital *L*. We long to rest in it. We long to know in the depths of our being that we aren't separate from it. We long to recognize ourselves as this Love itself. Ultimately this book is about returning to Love individually and collectively. Acting from being. And finally this book is about realizing that freedom lives here: mine, yours, ours, the world's.

Welcome. I am so very glad you are here.

Chapter One

Return to Community

Creating an Environment of CARE

The next Buddha may be a *sangha*.

—Zen Master Thich Nhat Hanh

D uring my eight years as a monk, my thirst for freedom was so intense I valued it more than I valued my own life. There was a problem, though: I didn't really know what freedom was.

I knew what I thought it was.

I came to Zen because I knew there must be something more to life. I knew I was suffering within. I knew intuitively that the suffering was something I was creating. That, in some sense, made it unreal—or at least not fundamentally true. I also had a deep intuition that the internal suffering I experienced wasn't required.

I had no concept or framework for the way out of suffering, though. Growing up in the Episcopal church where my mother also grew up provided some rhythm and consistency, in spite of the fact that we only went to church when the University of Virginia students were in town (because my mother enjoyed seeing the young men in bow ties).

Most Sundays I skipped Sunday school with my buddies only to gallivant around the shops stealing jelly beans from the bulk bins. (I was a blue-eyed blonde girl in the South, so even if I were caught shoplifting it would at worst have merited a cute, feigned slap on the wrist. I did not understand the injustice inherent in this at the time. I was a thrill seeker who preferred jelly beans to Bible study.)

When it was time to rejoin our parents in church, we'd slide back in, take part in Communion, hear a few songs, and then it would be done. In my sugar-induced hyperactive state, church could never go fast enough. I had trouble being still, which was always scornfully noticed by my mother and grandmother.

I have only one memory of glimpsing a person doing something I can now describe as being in relationship with God. Something more alluring than the thrill of raiding the bulk bins. His name was Mr. Hollison. He always sat in the same pew, close to the priest, facing the central altar. During some songs, he'd lift his arms up in the air mid-verse. Like a child before words calling out to be picked up, his whole being would cry to be held. Head tilted back, singing. A baby bird beckoning to be fed. The longing and the Love were palpable. Though I had no words for it at the time, I knew this longing.

And this Love.

For as long as I can remember, I was offered the model that you were what could cry for God, but there were no guarantees that you would be heard. And pretty early on I figured out that whether someone picked up on the other end had something to do with your behavior. Likely God doesn't answer the phone for little thieves that can't sit still. But maybe if I worked a little, changed my behavior, cleaned up my act . . .

I had few models of unconditional love. I had no experience of inherent belonging. The belief: we are each born needing improvement, like the newest doll that needs batteries to operate yet doesn't come with them. On a deep subconscious level, most of what I did was in response to this framework, which I never questioned.

This book stands on the premise that we inherently belong. All of us.

In Love there is only belonging.

I assume that if you are holding this book, you, too, long to know this Love. That somewhere in the depths of your being you know that it's possible to end suffering, though you might not always be clear about how. That you, too, long to be happy, to be free.

I trust that you, too, long to know that change is possible—individually *and* collectively—and that our actions and our world can reflect our deepest understanding of Love and truth. I trust that you have a thirst for freedom—to be freed from the traps laid by the conditioned mind—yet you don't always know how to reconcile the abundant approaches available to us. That perhaps you even question what the heart of freedom actually is, what it really means to be liberated from suffering. I am with you. This book is for you.

LIBERATION

I want to state my position in this conversation very clearly: I am a white dharma teacher who has been exploring and teaching meditation practice for over twenty-five years. Over time, I've learned a lot about how the mind gets shaped, or conditioned, by thoughts and society. These shaping stories all arise from the mind of separation. I know and have seen over and over the power that is unveiled when conditioning melts away. This book is about how to access this power. To recognize what is real, what is true. To see through what is *not*. To liberate ourselves and others.

Liberation means freeing ourselves from our attachment to our story lines. If we can release ourselves from our story lines, we have freedom to move through the human world with ease, trusting in the innate goodness of all.

In this book I refer to liberation in several ways, personal and collective. I also speak to our capacity to free ourselves from delusion; to liberate ourselves from habits and systems in the relative world while recognizing that liberation is ever present on the ultimate level. In other words, I'll point to liberation as the everyday act of freeing ourselves from internal and external story lines and systems that oppress us—on the relative plane of reality—all while knowing liberation is inherent, our natural state of being, what's here behind all the veils. The ultimate truth of liberation.

Always here. Always now.

I don't think we need more books about self-improvement or that feed a sense of separateness in the name of "spiritual advancement." I'm also not drawn to write about spiritual liberation and oneness in a way that denies the reality of the systems we live within—systems that do *not* reflect freedom and oneness and, in fact, result in the opposite lived experience for so many: living in other-ing, oppression, hierarchies, exploitation. We need books that give us tools for freedom, and remind us of freedom. We need words that return us to freedom.

NO INNER, NO OUTER, NO OTHER

It wasn't until years after I left the monastery that I began to question why, in my training there, we never mentioned race. We never spoke of systems of oppres-sion. It's as though there was a silent (no pun intended) understanding that those things were of no business to a monk or any sincere spiritual practitioner for that matter. In fact, I believed then that having my attention on such things was a distraction from the *real* work of awakening.

As monks, we focused on *personal* process—exclusively. How one thought leads to another. How beliefs and assumptions keep the illusion of a separate self in place. How identifying with various aspects of the personality can maintain a felt sense of inadequacy or superiority. How attending to such conditioning could liberate us from it. When I left the monastery, as I experienced the realities of the outside world, this approach became more and more curious to me. Within the framework I'm describing it makes some sense: "It's your process, it's your suffer-ing," was the approach. Still, I reached a point in practice when this didn't satisfy my thirst for truth. It felt like a nice start, but simply a door opening.

This "I" that suffers is a creation. I knew this to be true. I also had learned that it was enormously helpful to be able to see clearly the processes that keep the sense of "I" in place. Recognizing that you are identified with the conditioned mind, for example, can open an experience of tremendous choice: through prac-tice, you can disidentify with the habits of your conditioning. Returning to presence can happen through choice. There is authentic power in this. It brings a sense of empowerment that I believe we all long for.

I saw something else, though. I saw that what plays out in our society, system-ically, directly reflects these so-called inner processes that lead to suffering. For example, internal processes that lead to othering, such as identifying with the inner critic, mirror external processes that lead to othering, such as systemic racism.

I saw that, in fact, there is no inner and outer at all!

Then my true learning about how I participate in systems that do not reflect the truth of our shared being began. In the same way that at the monastery I learned how the activity of the ego veiled truth, I began to see the myriad of ways that I participate in these societally systemic processes without being aware of it.

A burning passion to uncover these places of unconsciousness has consumed me for years now. How can I teach about freedom, about being awake in the world, without being aware of the ways that I participate in societal structures that I perceive as causing harm? While my own ignorance about my privileged identities creates an experience of othering? While I, too, am affected by these structures arising out of distortion? If I'm going to question beliefs and assumptions about myself that keep a limited and small sense of "I" in place, why not *also* question how these patterns play out in society at the same time? How they manifest collectively?

It seems clear to me that there is actually only one process at play here. The illusion of separation is a process of activity within the conditioned mind. This mind isn't mine or yours. It's ours. Our very being is shared. I know this to be so based on my experience.

There's more, though. In this wildfire query I began to see that in my monastic training, *it wasn't a coincidence that we omitted an exploration of the collective from our practice.* I began to recognize this omission as part of a larger system—a reflection of a shared process that, collectively, keeps an experience of "other" in place. I don't have a single memory of a Black person visiting the monastery where I trained. I understand more now about why this was the case.

In a way, this book is an opportunity for reconciliation and to explore this reconciliation in community with others. Thank you for picking it up. For being in this conversation. For saying yes to this relationship. It is my hope that this book is a shared exploration. It cannot happen without you. Like all good relationships, may we all benefit.

So, ultimately, what is being reconciled?
All things.

The heart of truth can be found in all things, in all circumstances, in all times. This book is about acting in the world on behalf of this truth. It's about reconciling our personal desire for truth and freedom with our desire to relieve suffering in the world. Our suffering is not separate from the suffering of the world. Our liberation is not separate from the liberation of the world.

Our liberation is the act of being.

Our liberation is Love itself. Why capital *L*? To distinguish that I'm referring to a love that's not tied up with personal conditioning. It has nothing to do with causes and conditions. It isn't bound by time and space. This Love excludes nothing. This Love embraces everything—unconditionally.

In Love, all is reconciled.

Here we reconcile various approaches to practice. We reconcile experiences that seem to contradict each other. The truth that we are one with the manifestation of a reality in which this oneness is not reflected. This book doesn't simply accept what has seemed to be irreconcilable. It celebrates that in truth, in the absolute, all is reconciled.

While I know this in my bones, and teach from this recognition, I am also a student continually learning. I've realized that it's important that these two roles not be seen as separate. A teacher who cannot learn cannot truly teach.

As a society, we are deeply conditioned to place teachers on pedestals. To view them as having completed their learning, thus qualified to offer something to others. This view is dualistic and doesn't honor the collective mind—the shared field in which growth occurs. This book honors this collective field.

FROM THE ABSOLUTE TO THE RELATIVE

Here is a relative truth: I am white and cisgender (meaning my gender identity corresponds with the sex I was assigned at birth. I use the pronouns *she* and *her*). I am a US citizen by birth, able-bodied, and have proximity to societal power. I did not grow up identifying with the experience of being marginalized. On a material level, I've always had everything I needed to survive. I did not grow up in a family with parents who lived paycheck to paycheck, and I've never wondered where my next meal will come from.

In conversations about freedom that includes our everyday world, I hope to be clear about not only the seat I'm sitting in but also how this seat impacts my participation in the dialogue. If I were only writing about the ultimate truth, the experience of oneness on the most absolute level, many might suggest it's not important to highlight my identity. But in this book we'll be in conversation about our relative world as well. The material world where we experience trauma, the world where systemic oppression exists, the world where we perceive ourselves to be separate and act out of this belief.

Why mention these highly complex topics at all?

Because my spiritual practice has been deeply affected by learning how I play a part in systems of oppression and domination. I've learned that no one is free in these systems, and I long to live in a world where we all know our inherent freedom and we can collectively move through the world from this recognition. Where we can create from this recognition. Love from this recognition.

I'm in the seat of the student when it comes to learning about racism—a lifelong process I'm committed to. It's not lost on me that I have a choice to learn about racism while some have no choice but to live it. We are all impacted by it, but the impacts are different.

It seems clearer than ever to me that it's important for those who share my positionality, my position of unearned benefits, to turn our attention to creating a world that reflects the deepest truths regarding the liberation that is inherent—a society where we are all free. In fact, historically, white people are the predominant group that has *not* been focusing on this. Given that white people hold more perceived power in the form of wealth, property, and influence in government, for example, if we truly wish to live in a world that reflects the truth of interconnection, it is deeply necessary.

I have learned from teachers such as Rev. angel Kyodo williams that depending on where we are situated, our roles are different in the movement for collective liberation. I am constantly exploring what my role can be. I hope we can do this together. I hope we can lean into our shared caring.

FREEDOM THROUGH COMMUNITY

For me, focusing my attention and actions toward liberation for all has been most impactful within community. In fact, most of my learning has happened within community, by being in relationship. I've learned when others have lovingly held me accountable, when I've brought everything I have to the table; when I've fallen down, crashed, leaned into others, gotten up, steadied myself, and begun again. The most impactful learning has occurred when I've encouraged others to do the same, to be in the game, to show up together.

It's not lost on me that even when I decided to focus on a very solitary practice that was held in the silence of a monastery, I chose to do it *with* others. In fact, I've lived in some form of community my entire adult life. I moved from a college community to the home of Innisfree, a life-sharing community with disabled adults; to the community of Penland School of Craft, where I slept, created, and worked with other CORE fellows for several years. I then moved to the monastery and from there into the creation of the community that at the time was called One House of Peace, the nonprofit I founded that eventually birthed Peace in Schools, which created the first semester-long, for-credit mindfulness course within US public high schools. More recently I've been focused on Presence Collective, a community of cross-cultural contemplatives committed to personal and collective transformation.

Being so drawn to community is clearly not everyone's path. And I'm certainly not suggesting that it's the right and only path. It is the path I know, though.

For this reason, I'm inspired by the vision of folks moving through this book as a collective. But, as mentioned in the introduction, it is not required. If you wish to make your way through this book as part of a group, you might find it helpful to spend time exploring what creating conscious community for your shared exploration could look like.

CREATING CULTURE

The staff of Peace in Schools spent a year moving through Michelle Cassandra Johnson and Kerri Kelly's Race and Resilience training. Our team found their approach for being in community useful. I appreciated that in the training Kerri said, "We need to be in a practice of creating culture or culture will create us." It can be fruitful to intentionally create culture that allows for new ways of being in relationship with each other, ways that differ from how we are conditioned to relate with each other within the dominant culture.

One of the many things I value about my Buddhist training is how I learned to be in relationship with other sangha members. The word *sangha* means to "bring together" into a group; it is the general word for community in both Sanskrit and Pali. It can refer to a herd of cows or a flock of geese, but within Buddhism it primarily refers to the community of people who practice together.

As monastics, we didn't relate to each other as personalities. I trained for over eight years with many of the same people and never knew anything about the content of their prior lives—their occupation, marital status, hobbies, favorite TV shows, and so forth—unless they revealed something in one of our regular group sessions.

I'm certainly not suggesting you relate to people in your practice group in this fashion. I'm simply naming that there was something profound about removing this layer of knowing from the equation. It can be quite transformative to have what unites your community be a shared longing for freedom above all else. The content of our lives intentionally dropping to the backdrop rather than remaining at the forefront.

If you've ever lived with someone you're close to, perhaps you know the intimacy of what gets shared in the silent moments, simply being in the presence of each other. The way they untie their shoes after a long day, or quietly hum when sliding into a warm bath, or the quality of silence they hold. This intimacy isn't contingent on the surface layer of the personality—our likes and dislikes, the baggage we carry from childhood, what we do for a living. It's a subtle and quieter knowing. A knowing of each other's being.

Should you choose to create a book collective, regardless of how you create it, you are invited to be conscious of how you relate to one another. Allow yourself and the members of your collective to flesh out the specifics together. This is important. It's your group. And if you read this book on your own, I encourage you to pay attention to how you relate to yourself and to those around you as you do so. Just because you are not part of a book collective doesn't mean you can't do practices aimed at dismantling stale, limiting beliefs that manifest collectively, seeing through distortions and barriers that affect us all.

If in a group, I invite you to practice meeting each other essence to essence. What does that mean exactly? If we were attending a stuffy cocktail party, many of us would be habituated to mingle wearing a theatrical mask of sorts—the mask of identity. "This is what I do for a living, this is who I am, this is what I want you to see about me." Essence to essence is an invitation to remove the mask to the best of your ability, to consciously disarm.

This will likely take time, and that's okay. Naming the intention to do so is key. It gives everyone the same permission. All are invited into the same pool at the same time. Some will be more comfortable than others when it comes to consciously disarming. Some will dive in the deep end headfirst. Others will tiptoe in. That's okay too. I appreciate the phrase "Move at the speed of trust" that I first heard in the context of the Black Lives Matter movement. Let it be like that. This act of acceptance is itself an important aspect of creating conscious community, together.

If choosing a solo journey, ask yourself, *What might support my experience of disarming, revealing my soft underbelly to myself—perhaps more completely than I am habituated to?*

CARE

Before we even teach basic meditation in our Peace in Schools classes, we create an environment of CARE. (A special shout-out to the teens at Ida B. Wells High School who created this acronym with me.)

Confidentiality—respecting another's experience by not sharing it inappropriately. (What's said in the room stays in the room.)

Acceptance—resting in our inherent capacity to be with what is.

Reverence—respect tinged with awe.

Empathy—recognizing and understanding the experience of another.

If you think about it, it's pretty radical that within the walls of a public high school, teens are agreeing to be in reverence together. It's pretty radical to create a community of CARE at all.

Before designing the class, I knew it would be important to create an environment, a container, out of which the tools of the curriculum, the contemplative technologies, could arise. I knew that we, as a group, would need to create conscious community. I had no idea *how* important it would be, however. Many who take the class report that the tools offered in the course benefit them deeply. Even more speak to the environment of CARE they experience in the classroom—an environment where all commit to the practice of seeing and releasing the mind of judgment, where all are encouraged to be themselves, and where people speak to each other with respect, owning their own experience rather than assuming and/or projecting.

The environment of CARE is a consciously designed environment where a deep sense of belonging is cultivated, an intimacy that has nothing to do with the personality. This, in and of itself, is healing. This environment becomes precious to students, I could even say sacred; and it's not uncommon for them to defend the environment of CARE if something arises that creates a breach.

A Practice: Your CARE Journal

If you are reading this book on your own, you can explore what creating an environment of CARE *within* might look like. I encourage you to get a journal that allows you to be in relationship with yourself in a mindful way. Allow the journal to be an expression of CARE. Within its pages, pledge to yourself to:

Hold confidentiality. Allow this space to be just for you, sharing only what you consciously choose.

Practice acceptance. Lovingly embrace all that arises for you in this journey.

Express reverence. Honor your experience and even meet it with wonder and awe.

Embody empathy. Allow yourself to have kindness for yourself and others as you make your way through this journey.

As your first entry in this journal, I invite you to engage in an exercise that students in many Zen groups have been exploring for decades. I like to do it at the beginning of establishing a culture of CARE: write your *Way Seeking Story*. If you are drawn to a book like this, I assume that you, too, long to know Love with a capital *L*, that you value consciousness, and that perhaps you've been exploring awareness practice as a way of knowing yourself and the world. Your *Way Seeking Story* is the story of what led you to contemplative practice, what led you to seek freedom within.

There is no right or wrong here. You might simply comment on what led you to this book, what you hope to learn from it. This is simply a chance to explore your own experience. See if you can get clear about what might allow you to feel safe to be honest with yourself, to explore without judgment, and to feel held by your own loving attention. What drew you to contemplative practice? Did you resist at first? Did you struggle against the call? Or was there never doubt? Did you know you were "home" the minute you learned about meditation or awareness practice? Have the same reverence for yourself, for your own experience.

Allow your *Way Seeking Story* to be written and received in this caring and mindful context.

My *Way Seeking Story* starts like this:

Deborah Eden Tull, a dear friend from college, gave me a little book titled *That Which You Are Seeking Is Causing You to Seek* by Cheri Huber. The book made a deep impression. It was unlike anything I had ever read. Everything about it felt true.

It never occurred to me that perhaps the person who wrote the book was still alive. Perhaps I could even meet her. When Eden ordered the book for me, I was added to a mailing list, and one day I received a flyer in the mail for a retreat that was happening in North Carolina. The retreat was led by the author. I was quite excited indeed.

I was in Crozet, Virginia, working as a live-in caregiver in a community with people who have disabilities, and my vacation days were the exact days of the retreat. I talked two of my girlfriends into joining me for the adventure. I had no idea what we were getting into. Read: none.

Somehow I missed the fine print that it was a silent retreat. And I knew nothing of Zen. "Retreat" (in this extrovert's mind) meant a fun but also meditative, of course, getaway with my girlfriends. Think: a conscious party.

There was a snowstorm, so we borrowed my mother's four-wheel-drive car. I drove it off the road on the way down. None of us was hurt, but we were many hours late. We had plenty of tunes for the drive and even more beer for our time away. (And no, I wasn't drinking when we slid off the road.) About this whole Zen retreat thing: we were clueless. To this day I don't know why I didn't inquire what the schedule would be. If I had read it, I likely wouldn't have signed up.

When we arrived we were met by a lovely woman who approached us and spoke in a whisper. Had someone died? She didn't make eye contact, and I found myself wondering if she had some form of social anxiety. I had not read the fine print that suggested that not only would the retreat be held in silence but that folks would be encouraged not to make eye contact as a way of keeping the attention inward rather than on each other. The host told us that the evening group had begun and that she'd need to check with the teacher to see if we could enter. Before she parted, she bowed to us.

I turned to my friends, slack-jawed, "Aw man, they're bowing and shit. We are outta here." But of course we didn't leave . . .

I had never faced myself the way I faced myself on that retreat. I had never known what it was like to be with myself, with no distractions, in this fashion. It was horrifying and liberating all rolled into one.

As the days of the retreat unfolded (and because I had never been as present as I was on that retreat, time unfolded and it felt like weeks, not days), I was beginning to see myself and the world differently. I'll never forget a particular moment when I was gazing at a raindrop hanging from a leaf. (And you should know that as an active extrovert who didn't have a history of ever sitting still, the sheer fact of that sentence is noteworthy on its own.) This raindrop was magnificent, mesmerizing, and contained the universe. I understood something about my place in the world that I couldn't describe. And I saw the inherent brilliance of all things. I tasted and knew something that I had been habituated to overlook.

Toward the end of the retreat, every time the teacher passed, I remember bursting into tears. I had never been around someone who modeled presence like she did. I had never had someone tell me that there was a *way* to have this experience—consistently, not randomly or as a fluke. I knew that however she learned to access this, however she trained to master the art of being present, I was going to do as well. I didn't care if she had joined the army. I was ready. Sign me up.

Of course, in my mind at the time, this did not mean becoming a monk. I spent a few years resisting that idea. Until one day I was sitting in a guidance appointment on a Zen retreat and . . .

No two *Way Seeking Stories* are the same. Each is to be honored. It's not the content of the stories that matters so much but rather the quality of listening—whether you are listening to others or consciously listening to yourself. It's about meeting yourself in the most authentic way possible. It's about meeting others essence to essence.

If you are working with a group, you may also appreciate creating group guidelines. I've found this invaluable in many circumstances. Allow your group to feel into what suits.

Whether you are working with a group or making the journey on your own, gently ask yourself, *What do I value having in place to support the process of disarming, feeling held by a group or held by myself, and leaning in rather than away? What allows a space to feel safe for me?* If you are having trouble accessing this, consider where in your life you've felt most comfortable being yourself and reflect on what allowed that to happen. Let whatever feels true to you, be true for you.

If we use everything in our experience to see how suffering is caused, everything will enlighten us.

If you choose a book collective, think of it like a little lab for the larger collective. Your group is your opportunity to create a model for the enlightened society we seek, one that hinges on mutual responsibility and collective care—taking care of ourselves and taking care of each other while consistently returning to the knowing of our inherent wholeness.

If you choose to read through this book on your own, it's still a lab. How are you in relationship with yourself as experience unfolds?

Pay attention to everything. Notice process. Remember, it's not *what*, it's *how*. Pay attention to how you create structure. Who, if anyone, tends to be the most dominant voice? Pay attention to who might not speak up and/or be heard, internally or externally. Bring consciousness to group dynamics. Pay attention and cultivate a conscious space where naming patterns is normalized. Practice naming them lovingly, with an intention to return to an experience of unity versus clinging to the notion that someone or something is "wrong." Watch for the conditioned temptation to fall into righteousness.

I believe that we need this kind of pattern recognition and naming on an individual level as well as a societal level. When an event like the 2021 storming of the US Capitol happened, what if we were able to collectively acknowledge the patterns? Imagine commentators on the most widely broadcasted evening news emphatically stating that white people had attacked the police without, for the most part, legal consequences, in stark contrast to the violence enacted upon Black Lives Matter protestors in the same year. Naming this manifestation of the unearned benefits that come with being white. And what if they went on to acknowledge the distortion such conflict arose out of? A public recognition of how collective experiences such as these reveal the sometimes severe and violent manifestation of the perception of separation. What if we had, on a mass scale, conversations about this aspect of what unfolded?

If we wish to be free, we must begin by facing the mechanism of separation.

This is the ground for true community.

Lastly, and most importantly, I want to underline the value of you and/or your group centering around contemplative practice. This is key. Countless people tell me they struggle to find the time or space to bring mindfulness practice (or any kind of meditative practice) into their lives. We live in a dominant culture that values *doing* over *being*. Our struggle is understandable given our collective values.

Here's a critical shift we'll be making together in this journey:

You will learn to bring your life into your practice versus your practice into your life.

This distinction is foundational. From this approach, everything in our experience is an opportunity to practice being awake, to remember and know our inherent wholeness, to lean into our interconnection and to turn toward Love rather than suffering.

Allow your shared practice to be an opportunity for remembrance, not achievement. Like a loved one who reminds you of your inherent goodness when you feel lost, allow your group to be this for each other. And practice offering this to yourself.

Lean in.

Dip a toe in.

Dive in.

Even if in the beginning it's difficult to fully sense, trust the unity that is inherent. Trust what called you to practice. Trust how this book made its way into your hands.

There is no need to fall for the story that you have to suffer on your way to ending suffering.

Allow yourself to enjoy the ride. Whether in a group or on your own, look for ways within the collective movement from I to we that the joy of belonging sings. And if joy is nowhere in sight, don't worry. We as a conscious collective have boundless room for this too.

Collective Practice: Moving from I to We

Each chapter of this book ends with a section called "Collective Practice." You do not need to be moving through this book with others to engage in the collective practices. In many cases, these practices are simply ways to take the tool, or the highlighted teaching, in that chapter and apply it to the wider community rather than have the practice simply stay in the realm of what you might think of as "your personal practice." All of these practices are optional, of course.

Part of what we're undoing in this journey together is the notion that practice has to be difficult. And the notion that we are alone. Much of this book focuses on seeing through the personal and collective conditioning that creates suffering. Even if difficulty arises in these practices, allow yourself to remember that realizing freedom together can be an inherently joyful process. Practice giving yourself permission to lean into this joy, to feel it and express it.

It's all well and good to just read these practices. Something shifts, though, when we deeply engage with them, when we allow ourselves to be vulnerable—with ourselves and each other—and we give ourselves wholeheartedly to the experience of practice. Not practice in the name of trying to get something right but practice as a recognition that we have the power to transform our lives. And that there's a way to do it. This book offers *one* way. I hope these practices support you in finding *your* way. Trust yourself.

If you are moving through this book on your own, share your *Way Seeking Story* with one other person. See how it feels to stretch yourself and share with someone who you haven't shared with in this way before (or at the very least, see how the thought of doing this affects you). Create an opportunity to connect with someone—perhaps in a way that you don't usually. Invite them to do the same. Treat it like a gentle experiment. What do you notice?

If you are moving through this book with others, take time to set up your group. Create a ground for the journey that feels right for you all. Do it together with one voice no more dominant than the other, to the best of your ability. Here are some other things to consider:

- When your group assembles, it can be important to begin by getting to know each other a bit. I like to start with basic introductions that include pronouns and positionality (like I did at the beginning of this section).

- This can be one friend, a few family members, a church group, and the like. It's entirely up to you. Decide if you wish to create guidelines, how often you'd like to meet, and discuss whatever other structure you'd like the group to have. You may decide to establish a container of CARE. In our Mindful Studies classes, this is not something that happens in one session. Take your time with this. Really find out what you and your group need for this to be a mindful and compassionate space that allows for vulnerability and deep exploration. And commit to shared meditation practice as a central component of your journey together.

- Next, share your *Way Seeking Stories*. Allow space for these narratives to unfold. Allow each person to share without being interrupted. In a sense, you're finding out how each unique and precious person in the group heeded the call to know truth to the fullest extent possible. And to end suffering.

Chapter Two

Return to Truth

Giving the Gift of Attention

If a person does not know to which port he
is steering, no wind is favorable to him.

—Seneca

I buried my dog last week. He had been by my side for eleven and a half years. He wasn't just a loyal companion; adopting him was the start of a new era in my life. He represented the end of isolation, the start of relation. I had been a silent monk for over eight years. As monks, we didn't relate to each other socially—ever. When I left the monastery and adopted Bankei, everything changed.

Bankei was named after the seventeenth-century Japanese Zen master whose Buddhist teachings had been pivotal to me. When Bankei the dog came into the picture, my life pivoted again. Suddenly I was in a relationship in a completely new way. A certain flavor of intimacy that had been entirely absent, appeared. My spell of isolation was broken. I still recall the joy of feeling released from this bottle.

A few weeks ago, Bankei began limping after a small fall trying to hop into the back of the car. My husband and I took him to the vet. The diagnosis: soft tissue damage. The remedy: anti-inflammatories and rest. We were diligent with medication and protocol and were surprised when things worsened.

The memory of the specialist delivering the results of the MRI will be forever burned in my brain. It was like being in one of those Charlie Brown cartoons where the words run together as indistinguishable sounds, as if delivered by someone with marbles in their mouth—except for a few select phrases: "inoperable tumor," "malignant cancer," "degradation to the vertebrae," and "you could do chemotherapy."

By this point Bankei had lost use of his hind legs, so we were clear that we weren't going to put him through chemo. By the end of the conversation, more came crashing into clear view. Though we thought that, following an MRI, we'd be putting Bankei through minor herniated disk surgery, we were actually going to have to put him to sleep—that day.

After his death, the purity of searing grief consumed us. It had particular weight given that my husband and I were in shock—for days. Shortly following Bankei's death, "Great Mender," a Chinese medicine we had ordered just days before to support his inflammation, arrived in the mail.

We thought the issue was inflammation. We were unaware, even the night prior to his passing, that he was nearing the end of his life. We were clueless that cancer was causing this inflammation. The package of herbs is still sitting by the front door. Unopened.

Since we buried Bankei, I've been present to the movement of my attention. Over this last week, which in some ways feels like an eternity, I've been particularly aware of the mind's conditioned temptation to gravitate toward regret:

> *Why didn't I catch that he was sick?*
> *How did I miss his signals to me?*
> *Did I express my love for him in the fullest way possible?*
> *Was I attentive enough?*

IDENTIFICATION WITH THOUGHTS

It's not that self-doubting thoughts are inherently bad or wrong. When such thoughts go unrecognized, however, it's easy to identify with them, to see things through the limited perspective of those thoughts. If we're fully identified with them, it then becomes easy to spiral into further story-making. And spiraling into further story-making is spiraling into suffering. It's in moments like these that I'm infinitely grateful for awareness practice.

It's taken practice for me to recognize such thoughts as creations, to see that when the attention is fully given to them they become a "reality" of sorts. They masquerade as truth. This "reality" keeps one thing in particular in place—the illusion of a self that is *separate from life*. A self that *could have done more*, that *should have seen more*. A self that believes that *whatever I do, it's never enough*.

Over the years, that's the most common block I've seen when working with others: *Whatever I do, it's never enough*. It's a Shakespearian tragedy. The hanging carrot that can never be held and eaten, only chased. The belly of the hungry ghost that is forever empty. The only result of such a constructed "reality" is dissatisfaction. It can be no other way.

DIRECTING THE ATTENTION

Learning to place our attention where we want it to be is step one on the path toward freedom. Without this skill, our attention habitually moves from object to object, searching for something it will never find. It is key to discover that we can redirect our attention when it's habitually starting down the slide of suffering.

In the case of Bankei, for example, without practice, my conditioned habit would be to focus on regret, to intensify it, to drown in it. That regret would rob me of the intimacy of grief—the purity of it, the heart of it. For it's clear to me that this grief is a deep expression of Love.

There's something exquisitely beautiful about resting in this Love. I don't take it for granted. It's worth drawing my attention back to this experience again and again. Why would I miss it? And at what cost?

Years ago, Allyson Copacino and I were offering yoga and mindfulness tools to teens after school in Portland, Oregon. Before I taught them basic meditation practice, I offered a lesson that revealed the habituated way our attention moves. So often we are not conscious of the way our attention is conditioned to bounce from thing to thing to thing. Moving from object to object—seeking, longing, grasping, resisting. Getting lost in experience.

The teens were palpably stunned when we played a collective game around directing the attention. A student would choose an object to place in the center of the room. Then all the students in the group were asked to direct their attention to that object and simply raise their hand when they noticed their attention wander. Most were deeply surprised to learn how quickly their attention went from attending to the object, to thoughts of the past or future, to an internal story, or to another object entirely.

The game continued. The students were instructed to consciously direct their attention back to the assigned object when they noticed their attention wander. They were asked to work that muscle of placing their attention where they wanted it to be, to practice doing it without judgment and to notice what tends to get in the way: "Does anything make this practice seem difficult? If so, what?"

What surprised me most about this game was to see a clear theme emerge: **students felt empowered.** They felt empowered by directly experiencing two things:

1. Seeing clearly how habituated the attention is to wander about without direction.
2. Seeing that they have the innate, internal capacity to place their attention *where they want it to be.* To redirect. To have a choice about something they had no idea they could be in choice about.

The teens and I didn't talk about the findings of this game until after they experienced it. That is not accidental. Though I'm writing to you about this now, I hope that you, or you and your group, will try this out on your own. I am inviting direct experience. Theory doesn't engage me much, but experience does. Theory may interest you, but

Your direct experience will be the ultimate test of reality.

Stop. Pause.

Set a timer for five minutes and simply notice where your attention goes during this time. Notice *how* it moves. Choose the breath, sensations in the body, or sounds around you as an anchor. When you see that your attention has wandered, gently bring it back your anchor.

Where is your attention habituated to go? When your mind is left to its own conditioned pattern of activity, what is revealed? Do the grooves of your attention patterns lead toward suffering or away from it? What happens when you redirect your attention to presence, to the experience of being here, now? Or to the Love that is here, now?

This is an exploration. To the best of your ability, gently watch for any conditioned tendency to merely give the "right answer." The right answer, on its own, won't serve you. Exploring through a nonjudgmental practice of inquiry will.

ENERGY FOLLOWS ATTENTION

Consider how this notion might be true in your own experience. How does energy, or life force, follow where your attention lands? I'll offer an example. I encourage you, with your group or privately, to find your own examples of your energy, or life force, following your attention.

If my attention is constantly directed toward the conditioned standard that suggests that I need to be thin in order to be loveable, for example, then energy is bound to follow. Imagine a mind filled with thoughts about the importance of being thin, comparing myself to others, judging myself for gaining weight. It's not hard to imagine those thoughts leading to behaviors—perhaps obsessively working out or even developing an eating disorder. Energy follows attention.

Picture a flashlight. The beam of light illuminates whatever it lands on. Now imagine that this light isn't being consciously directed. Perhaps instead it is on autopilot, shifting from object to object, bouncing randomly and quickly. We might think that our experience is varying a great deal, based on the fact that these illuminated objects appear to be different. Light landing on a chair is different from light landing on a dog.

Now consider objects that are less neutral. Imagine the light of your attention landing on an internal story about not being good enough. And now the light is landing on longing for something that will never be. And now it has shifted to regret. What, in your experience, is the result of this?

Again, we might think that our experience varies a great deal based on the variations of thoughts, but ask yourself, what is the outcome of this *process* of thinking?

Once you've noticed where the attention lands, then consciously redirect it to something here and now. Perhaps the feeling of your breath rising and falling. Perhaps the sounds in the room. Maybe the sensation in the soles of your feet. What happens?

I'm not suggesting that if your attention lands on something negative, you should simply redirect it to something positive, or that redirecting your attention equals getting rid of thoughts. This is about bringing attention to the present moment as thoughts arise.

What we are unconscious to silently governs us.

This practice is about seeing where our attention habitually lands, noticing the effect of this, and consciously redirecting it to what's real, to the present moment, to what is true. It's about realizing that the flashlight is in our hand. It's about realizing that *we have choice*. We can choose where our attention lands and thereby where our energy will be directed.

The quality of our lives is dramatically affected by the focus of our attention.

In this practice of directing the attention, the mind becomes steady. Personal narratives that feed the illusion that we are a self that is separate from life fade. Presence is revealed. But those are just nice ideas until you test them out for yourself. Again, I encourage you to do so. I can't underline enough that your experience will be your greatest test of reality, your greatest proof of what's true.

YOU ARE NOT YOUR THOUGHTS

One day, while I was teaching the teens after school, the principal came by to observe what we were offering. It wasn't the first time, and I had started to recognize my inner dialogue around whether he had concerns about what we were teaching.

I knew what we were doing was radical. We were teaching teens to recognize conditioned thought patterns; to unhook from the stories about themselves, each other, and life; and to explore who they truly are beyond who they've been conditioned to perceive themselves to be. There's something deeply subversive about this.

As the principal hovered, I recall remembering to practice what I preached: noticing my thoughts; recognizing them as creations; consciously redirecting my attention to the breath, to "I don't know mind," to presence. I saw that there was no way for me to know if my stories about why he was there were "true." "I don't know mind" could be trusted. It was based on reality. It always is.

Returning the attention to reality, to the moment, allows us to be freed from the story that the world revolves around us. It frees us from looking through the habituated lens of limitation. It allows us to rest in being, to trust.

The principal, Brian Chatard, pulled me aside. It turned out that his response to what we were doing was far from a raised eyebrow. There had been a suicide in the school the year before. I learned that, though Brian knew little about mindfulness, it was clear to him that we were offering the students a form of wellness the institution lacked, and he wanted to reach more than a large handful of teens at a time. He saw a dire need to do so.

I knew that there was no way we'd reach more students as an after-school program, so I asserted that the class would need to be offered *during* the school day, just as any other credited elective course was. Having been a monastic and having never worked deeply in the belly of public education, I was unaware that this had never been done before. To me, it simply made sense.

Brian invited us to offer demonstration classes for tenth graders, to give them a taste of what a semester-long course in mindfulness might feel like. He said that if twenty to thirty students expressed interest in the class, he'd figure out how to weave it into the school day.

We were placed in the high school gym. I still don't know why, but I didn't question it. I recognized it as a grand opportunity. And on one particularly stunning spring day in 2014, students entered the gym dressed to play basketball, only to find yoga mats and meditation cushions in a circle.

We offered two days of demonstrations that included the attention practice. Somewhere near the end of each ninety-minute class, I dropped the phrase "You are not your thoughts." The silence was profound, especially given the number of young people gathered in one place. You could almost hear their silent self-talk—the internal dialogue that often runs in the backdrop of our minds:

If you aren't your thoughts, then who are you?

Their interest was piqued.

Brian called me several days later. "We've created a monster," he said. "Over three hundred teens have signed up for your class and I have absolutely no idea what to do about it." In the fall of 2014, we launched three sections of the first for-credit, semester-long mindfulness course in a public high school. Years later, our program is in eight Portland public high schools, offers trainings for adults, and continues to grow. And our curriculum still offers lessons about learning to direct the attention, taught before we dive into teaching formal meditation.

What's one of the most important themes of the lesson focused on directing the attention?

Energy follows attention.

FROM THE PERSONAL TO THE COLLECTIVE

Dr. Daniel Siegel, the bestselling author and cofounder of the Mindsight Institute, tells us, "Where attention goes, neural firing flows and neural connection grows. This not only helps us understand how psychotherapy and parenting work, but also how our societies shape our minds as well."

Let's widen our focus now and imagine what would shift if we applied ourselves to a collective practice of focusing on what's real versus what's created.

You may have noticed that when you're focusing on created thoughts like *I am not good enough*, you are *perceiving* yourself as separate from life. This results in *feeling* separate from life. In redirecting your attention to the present moment, you are freed from experiencing yourself through a limiting lens. You move from believing you are at the center of the universe to recognizing that you, of course, are not at all. You taste reality. What is this reality? What is this truth? It's the reality of our interconnection, that we are not isolated egos, the truth that we are something more than this. Thankfully, we are something more than this.

INTERCONNECTION AND INDIVIDUALISM

I'm writing this while adhering to the shelter-in-place policy in response to the onset of the COVID-19 virus. It has been a time when I've watched potent messages of our interconnectedness come to the surface. Viral narratives have spread as readily as the virus itself. In this environment, we don't have to look far to find support for narratives flooded with fear.

As our collective attention moves from fear to the perception that we're being attacked to the frantic attempt to control what cannot be controlled, our stories that we are separate from each other and from life are given megaphones. It's no surprise—when this perception pervades our culture—that we see disastrous results.

With the rise in confirmed cases of the coronavirus, for example, I've witnessed a steady increase in expressions of racism. It's been heartbreaking to bear witness to the reports of Asians and other People of Color throughout the world being the subjects of harassment and attacks, to be present to our collective conditioned tendency to blame.

Collectively conditioned inequities are not new. COVID-19 seemed to lay them bare in a particular way, the virus amplifying preexisting social inequities tied to race, class, and access to quality health care. While anyone can be infected with COVID-19, certain populations are far more vulnerable to contracting and experiencing severe cases of it, with Black, Indigenous, and People of Color more likely to die from it. Lack of access to quality health care and the types of jobs that tend to vary based on race increase exposure to the spread of the virus and hinder the ability to cope with it. This inequity is not an expression of *we*, and to realize freedom together we must begin by moving from *I* to *we*.

My longing to live in a society that reflects the reality of "*we*" was heightened as I watched Black and LatinX people being put at greater risk in their day-to-day lives during the pandemic. As I noticed the structural reasons at play—long-standing economic and health disparities between white people and BIPOC (Black, Indigenous, People of Color). In addition, the pandemic shone a light for me on the depth of our ageism, as we watched nursing home residents die in astounding numbers because we were not in positions to adequately protect them. Our disabled populations were particularly vulnerable as well.

All of this is the result of *our collective attention being directed in a particular way*. We are conditioned to have our attention directed by society, or more specifically, by dominant culture. According to Oxford Reference, "Dominant culture is one whose values, language, and ways of behaving are imposed on a subordinate culture or cultures through economic or political power. This may be achieved through legal or political suppression of other sets of values and patterns of behavior, or by monopolizing the media of communication."

In the very same way that my attention is conditioned to move from thought to thought to thought, resulting in a felt sense of being separate, the collective conditioning of the dominant culture also affirms the story that we are separate. Our collective conditioning supports a process of othering based on race, gender identity, sexual orientation, class, physical ability, and so on. It perpetuates the story of individualism.

In the same way that a teen experiences a sense of empowerment by discovering that they can direct their attention to the moment versus a conditioned internal story, we have the capacity to do so collectively—to redirect to truth, to reality.

The result: *collective empowerment*. When we are practiced at seeing where and how the attention moves personally, internally, in the privacy of our own minds, it becomes easier to see how our attention moves and is directed collectively—in our schools, our communities, our culture, our world.

When we learn to direct our attention personally, we experience greater levels of freedom from our conditioned mental patterns. When we learn to direct our attention to truth collectively, our collective experience of freedom opens. What is revealed is the truth that we are interconnected; that what hurts one of us, hurts all of us; that we need and belong to each other.

Dominant culture is constantly reinforcing the notion of the individual. As a collective, dominant culture is not habituated to focus on the collective. One particularly striking aspect of COVID-19 was that in every other collective issue of my lifetime, there was a clear *us* and *them*. In a global pandemic like COVID-19, we've had the opportunity to realize that there is only *us*. We've had the open door to more fully step into the reality of *we*, the truth of *us*.

As mentioned, the pandemic highlighted a preexisting class and race disparity for me, as well as the persistence of racism against Asians and Pacific Islanders. Along with such injustices arising from the perception of "other," our habitual *us/them* view manifested through labeling the virus as the "enemy." Us on one side, the virus on another. With sides comes the potential of war.

Yet the beginning of the pandemic was the first time in my life that I witnessed global consciousness take the form that it took as nations and individuals worked together to overcome the effects of the virus. It was striking thereafter to see those glimpses of cohesion eclipsed by conditioned habit, to, over time, become something less cohesive and quite polarizing, reverting to *I, me, mine*.

Even with the threat of death on a massive scale, the ingrained paradigm of us versus them, of scarcity, overtook the impulse for cohesive action in many cases. We regressed to perceiving ourselves as separate. More apart rather than more *part of*.

We can consciously redirect our attention to *us*. Every time our attention moves to the story of individualism, isolation, and separation, we can consciously return to *us*. When our collective conditioning asserts that some of us belong while others do not, we can redirect our attention to *us*—all of us.

I want to be careful here. I recognize that this may sound overly simplistic, as though I'm suggesting that if we just redirect our attention, all injustices would be solved. I'm merely pointing out that when I fall for the story that I am a self separate from life, I suffer. When we fall for the story that we are separate from each other, we suffer. When we fear what we see as "other", we suffer. It is all the same process, the same illusion. Catching when our attention is feeding the narrative of "other" and consciously redirecting it is simply one tool within a larger journey that we are taking together.

WHY CONTEMPLATIVE PRACTICE?

As mentioned in the previous chapter, I want to underline the value of you and/ or your group centering around contemplative practice. There are countless expressions of this. Truly no *one* right way. The only requirement is that you create an opportunity for stillness, reflection, and the ease that is here as we place our attention where we want it.

In a world where our attention is so habitually pulled from thing to thing, endlessly getting lost in various objects, it's important to give yourself the gift of noticing *how* this happens.

Give yourself the gift of your own attention.

The teens I've worked with through Peace in Schools speak of mindfulness as "being here and now with kindness." If having a contemplative practice is new for you, let it be that simple for now.

Some of you perhaps have had a meditation practice for years. Others might be new to it. Some of you might be quite accustomed to prayer. Others of you perhaps have an aversion to such practices. There's room in this journey for all of us.

I'd like to suggest that for the duration of this book, you allow yourself to explore whatever contemplative practice you feel most drawn to in a structured way. That might be as simple as ten minutes of meditation a day. Choose something that's a little bit of a stretch without being unrealistic. Perhaps you do this on your own, perhaps it's with a group. It's truly up to you. Find out what's most supportive.

There are many ways to anchor the attention in the present moment—for example, returning to the body/sensation, sound, or breath, just to name a few faves. Again, allow this to be an enjoyable exploration. Receiving the gift of your own attention has quite a different feel than feeding the story that you can control the mind (and then attempting to without avail)!

For now, we'll focus on the type of meditation that helps you practice placing your attention where you want it to be. Think of it like practicing on the straightaways in preparation for the curves. When very little is going on, perhaps in the privacy of your own home, practice building your capacity to redirect your attention when it wanders. As you hone your capacity to place it here and now with kindness, you will be better able to do so when you're in the midst of a chaotic moment or even a crisis.

This is the first of many meditations sprinkled throughout this book. You may prefer to listen to them in the audiobook. You may wish to record them in your own voice and play them back. You may wish to simply use them as opportunities to slow down and access the mind of spaciousness as you read along. Allow yourself to be as experiential as you can be with these, in whatever way works for you. You can return to this practice any time.

A Practice: Directing the Attention

Begin by letting the attention rest on the breath.

Perhaps taking three of the longest, deepest inhalations and exhalations you've taken yet today.

Notice the process of breathing. Feel the air as it enters and leaves your body.

Notice the motion of your body as you settle into stillness—your chest expanding and contracting, the movement in your belly and shoulders.

The movement in your spine.

We tend to struggle when the mind pulls us off into thoughts about the future.

We tend to struggle when the mind drags us off into a review of our past or emotions such as regret, fear, or anger.

We can also find the place, the refuge, in which we're fine and life is fine.

This refuge we experience when the attention is in the present moment. Touching our inherent fineness. The okayness of what is.

Resting here.

So simply allow the attention to rest on the breath, our anchor, here and now.

Simply breathing.

Allow yourself to enjoy the breath.
We so often take the breath for granted.

It's okay to enjoy breathing. The simplicity of it. The beauty of it.

It's okay to enjoy simply being.

If the breath is difficult to enjoy, try a different anchor such as the sounds around you.

Sounds, always arising here and now. A reliable anchor, in a reliable refuge.

When your attention wanders, when suddenly you are caught in a story, swept up in emotions, or identified with thinking mind in some other way, gently and lovingly notice this and come back. Redirect the attention. Come back to your anchor.

Return.
Here and now with kindness.
Come back to being.

Collective Practice: What Is Shared?

PRACTICE 1: DIRECTING THE ATTENTION

- Place an object in the center of the room and set the intention to focus on it completely. Be with it fully.

- Notice the movement of your attention. When your attention wanders from the object, make note that it strayed by raising your hand. Then return. Strengthen the muscle of returning.

- Share what you noticed in your journal. If you're practicing this as a group, share your observations with each other.

PRACTICE 2: WHAT IS SHARED?

- Choose one way your attention habitually maintains the story "They aren't like me." *They* could be anyone you're habituated to see as different from you—for example, someone who holds different political beliefs or is from a different cultural context or generation.

- If working with a group, journal individually and then come together to share your responses. Explore: What beliefs make *They aren't like me* "true"? Write them down. Make a list of what you believe about "the other." (For example, if reflecting on someone with different political beliefs, you might write, "He/she/they are narrow-minded.") We'll be coming back to this list later in the book.

- How does it leave you feeling to maintain this narrative?
To be identified with it?

- As a practice, consciously direct your attention to seeing
and naming what you *share* with this person. What
happens within when you look for and focus on what you
share? There's information in this process.

Please note that sharing qualities is not the same as having no
difference. Just because the daffodil shares the same essence as the
iris, it doesn't mean we should overlook the distinct brilliant colors
expressed in each. And certainly, because this essence is shared does
not imply that all flowers are planted in the same soil, offered the same
access to water and sun, given the same encouragement to thrive.

Now take this practice out in the world and into your interactions, internally weaving in this question: *What do we share?*

- As a practice, direct your attention to what is shared,
fundamentally and collectively. Notice where your
attention habitually goes, what story lines you follow.
Consciously redirect back to the core question—*What do
we share?*—when your attention wanders.

- What do you notice? What shifts when you direct your
attention in this way and focus on what is shared instead
of allowing it to habitually slide down the road of fear?
For example, what changes when you direct your attention
to Love?

I invite you to notice when the mind of differences arises and
to use this practice as an opportunity to redirect your attention.
This practice of noticing where your attention is conditioned to go,
then consciously redirecting it, can shift how behaviors manifest
in the world.

When you return to your group, share your experiences and
observations.

Racism, implicit bias, or any other form of discrimination can only exist within the distortion of *us* versus *them*. What changes when we consciously direct our attention to the truth of *us*? To the reality of *we*? How does our world look different?

Remember, energy follows attention.

When the attention habitually strays, return to the truth of *us*. Return to the truth of interconnection.

Chapter Three

Return to Wholeness

Recognizing the Conditioned Mind

Why are you unhappy?
Because 99.9 percent
Of everything you think,
And of everything you do,
Is for yourself—
And there isn't one.

—Wei Wu Wei

I was assigned to clean the outhouses. Eight of them spread throughout the property. A bucket of cleaning supplies in one hand, a bucket of lime in the other, I headed off, albeit grumbling. I was a monk, so whether I wanted a particular task or not was irrelevant—deeply irrelevant.

One of the gifts of being a monk is that whatever your task seemed to be wasn't what your task actually was. Yes, there was an expectation that the outhouses would be cleaned by the end of the work period. However, there was a much greater expectation that you would be paying close attention to your experience as you went about your task, no matter what your task was. There was an understanding that you would be practicing directing your attention to the present moment, noticing when it wandered and, specifically, where it went. Then consciously returning your attention to now.

I remember where I was on the cedar chip path—outhouse #1 to my right, outhouse #2 to my left—when I got it that the tape loop playing in my mind was just that: a tape loop. (This dates me, doesn't it? If you weren't alive in an era when music was recorded on cassette tapes, then hang with me here. What's great about the analogy of a tape loop, what's most significant, is that the same songs repeat over and over and over. They'll play until you turn the machine off, the batteries run down, or the tape breaks.)

On this blistering summer outhouse cleaning day, the voice of the conditioned mind was clear:

If only it weren't so hot.
If only I had been given an indoor assignment today.

If only it were Sunday. (Sunday afternoons, which we called Holy Leisure, were the only unscheduled times at the monastery.)

In a flash of insight, I got it that "if only" was a scam. I got it that "if only" implies that the external content of my life was responsible for my internal state of being.

I recall putting the buckets down, hands on hips, pausing. For the first time I recognized a pattern with the voice that had previously been in the background of my experience—like the background music in a shopping center that you don't notice ... until you do. I had recognized my internal dialogue before—the chatter that prior to awareness practice I had assumed was simply "me." However, I hadn't caught on to the *pattern* of the chatter. It's as though I had noticed the songs that were playing but, though they felt familiar, I hadn't noticed that they were on repeat—over and over and over.

As the test of reality, one reason I value experience over theory is because my experience cannot be argued with. It's not debatable. No one will ever be able to convince me that any internal conversation that begins with "If only ..." will lead anywhere promising—ever. If you haven't already, test it out for yourself.

Be curious.

Open.

Find out.

To be clear, there's value in an insight that comes in the form of a creative solution to a problem. That's not the "if only" thought I'm referring to, however. I'm referring to the voice of the conditioned mind that is continually asserting that you should be different; that life should be different; that if X, Y, or Z would change, then you would *finally* be happy. If this book is in your hands, it's likely that you recognize this story line as a trap.

This story line belongs to the conditioned mind. When we first introduce the notion of the conditioned mind in our Mindful Studies classes, we ask the teens to describe what they think that term might mean. Young people are quick to describe it as the mind of limitation. The mind that has been shaped and influenced by parents, school, society, culture. The mind that is habituated to think in a particular way. The mind that believes what we were taught: *This is how I'm supposed to be. This is how life is supposed to be.* The mind that regrets the past and worries about the future.

Have you ever rescued a dog, cat, or horse? It's really common for rescue animals to be more fearful. This is because sometimes they've been conditioned to be that way based on their previous experiences. They're just trying to survive, right?

It's the same for us. The conditioned mind isn't bad or wrong. It's often just how we are trying to survive. Underneath the masks we put on is often a deep desire to belong. One way we could talk about our conditioning is that it's how we've learned to try to achieve belonging. So while the conditioned mind isn't bad or wrong, it can be really limiting. It assumes, for example, that we don't inherently belong. That's why we also talk about it as "the mind of limitation." Even when this animal is in a new and safe home, it might not be able to fully relax and enjoy the experience because of its conditioning; it's limited by the imprint of its past experiences. Over time, and with practice, this can change.

When we identify with the conditioned mind, we believe what this mind of limitation asserts is truth. So, if I'm conditioned to believe that the grass is always greener on the other side, and I identify with that "if only" conditioning, whatever the mind asserts simply feels real and true—especially when I'm in the midst of it. For example, it might seem real and true that "things never work out for me."

We are conditioned not to question our conditioning!

FROM THE PERSONAL TO THE COLLECTIVE

Consider for a moment how we collectively identify with "if only" conditioning. Our capitalist structure is born of and thrives in an "if only" environment. From a very young age, we are conditioned to believe that "if only" we had [*fill in the blank*], then we'd be happy. This perfectly sets the stage for us to believe that our sense of well-being depends on objects. (And by "objects," I mean conditioned standards, such as being my "ideal weight," and/or circumstances in general— how much money I have, if I have the "ideal partner," and so on). This way of thinking assumes that our well-being is intimately tied to the content of our lives: happiness is an outside job.

If only I had a new car, I'd be happy. If only I had a new partner. A different job. More money. These objects, within consumerism, are placed on a pedestal. They become props in the play of our longing. Within consumerism, this "if only" view keeps us purchasing, bound in the role of the consumer. This conditioned creation of consumerism thrives off our personal and collective perception of lack. It requires it.

In the same way we've inherited *individual* conditioning (I am conditioned to believe that in order to receive love, it's important to get things right, for example), we also inherit, absorb, adopt *collective* conditioning. The two are so intimately woven that they cannot, with accuracy, be called "two." The fish does not exist as an alive being outside the water it swims in. If the water is polluted, the fish will be ill. It can be no other way.

THE LIMITATION OF INDIVIDUAL CONDITIONING

Consider the various ways you've been conditioned—by parents, school, society, community, culture. Consider the set of beliefs and assumptions you refer to in your mind, perhaps in order to touch an experience of wholeness. You might make a list in your CARE journal. Consider your positionality as you go. My conditioning as someone from the American South, for example, is quite different from the conditioning of someone who was raised in a different cultural context.

The great thing about this kind of list making, or journaling, is that if you can write it down, you have some distance from it. Writing is an opportunity to get a belief or assumption an arm's length away. If you can write it down, you (at least intellectually) can recognize that what you are writing down is not you.

This step is critical in any form of awareness practice, to recognize yourself as the observer of your thoughts and beliefs rather than the thoughts and beliefs themselves. Writing can be freeing for this reason. It can assist in the disidentification process.

One way you can access how you've been conditioned is to respond to the prompts below. Should you take this on, be sure not to edit yourself. Remember, you want to reveal the conditioning that is often lying quietly in the backdrop of your experience.

Again, what we are unconscious to silently governs us.

A Practice: Fleshing Out Our Conditioning

We are intentionally pulling what's been in the backdrop of experience to the forefront. We want to see what's been in the shadows. Write without editing, without indulging internal commentary.

Some prompts to get you started:

In order to be loved, I need to . . .

During times of conflict, I should . . .

My parents always taught me that . . .

I deserve . . .

I'll be comfortable when . . .

I'll be happy when . . .

I know I should avoid . . .

If only . . .

Other people would be happy if I . . .

It's best not to . . .

I'm usually afraid of . . .

> To feel successful I need to . . .
>
> The thing I should most watch out for is . . .
>
> I never seem to be able to . . .

Obviously you can keep going with this. If you are in a group, you could even have each person in the group offer a different prompt. The point is to begin to get a map of your conditioning. This map, this opportunity to have your conditioning at an arm's length, creates a concrete way for you to disidentify from the conditioned mind, to recognize yourself as more than the mind of limitation.

You are *aware* of your conditioning.

You are *not* your conditioning.

Disidentifying from your conditioning is key on a path of liberation. The most beautiful part? Disidentification is a *contemplative technology* that can be practiced. It's a tool that can be used in moments when you're suffering. As a practice, it becomes more and more refined. Over time, your capacity to catch the subtleties around disidentification increases.

For example, when you're new to the practice, you might catch that you're identified with the conditioned mind *after* you've raked a family member over the coals and really given them "a piece of your mind." With practice, you'll catch the identification as it forms rather than in the aftermath. You'll feel your body tighten in a particular way. You'll notice an internal energetic shift. You'll catch a change in the landscape of the mind. You'll notice the quality or tone of your thoughts shift. With practice, you'll be able to step off the train of suffering sooner and sooner—until eventually you won't be called to board.

WHY "CONTEMPLATIVE TECHNOLOGIES"?

For me, contemplation means loving dedication to understanding the nature of reality. Just as scientists conduct experiments with technology, contemplatives conduct experiments using perception—with and through awareness. We are conditioned to ascribe validity to scientific study, but Western dominant culture places less validity on contemplative exploration. The results found in each approach are not customarily treated equally.

In a "learning to trust your own direct experience" approach to practice, I like blending "contemplative" and "technology" because it challenges the notion that our direct contemplative experience cannot and should not be relied upon as fully as a scientific one. Putting the two together softens the created perceived duality.

LOSING THE TASTE FOR OUR CONDITIONING

Having been raised in the American South, I have a lot of conditioning around the importance of politeness. Now sprinkle that on top of already being an extrovert who loves people. My husband, Vineet, still teases me about the morning we were walking our dogs to the park for a quick potty break before I had to head off to work. I recall saying to him, "Now let's not stop to talk to anyone, please, because I really don't have a lot of time today." We both knew this comment was for me, not him. (He's a deep introvert who rarely initiates conversations with people he is only tangentially connected to.)

Not five minutes into our walk I was waving at a neighbor at the park who then approached us to get an update about something happening on our street. As we said our goodbyes, I could feel Vineet's quiet internal chuckle. I defended myself before he even said anything: "But we made eye contact and I didn't want to be rude!" We both had a good laugh.

I use such a benign example for a reason. Of *course* there was nothing life-threatening about being perceived as rude at the park. But for the part of me who is conditioned to believe that in order to be accepted, and therefore loved, I must follow the social code of conduct called "politeness," it wasn't an option *not* to engage.

Have you ever tried to go up against your conditioning? While your life may not actually be under threat, part of you may well *feel* that it is. This isn't simply a mental experience. It's often a deeply somatic one. Practice gives us a way to see our conditioning as it arises, to be with the sensations, thoughts, and feelings that are present as we notice our conditioning and consciously choose not to engage it.

Through practice we don't end suffering forever; we lose our taste for it.

And what we don't enjoy the taste of, we tend not to eat.

BEING WITH DISCOMFORT, CULTIVATING COURAGE

An important part of my own journey has been learning about the distortion of internalized white superiority. I did not grow up with an awareness of how indoctrinated I was into this mindset, this collective conditioning. I did not grow up seeing that even when white people know intellectually that we are not superior to people of other races, we often don't recognize how we play out this distortion. When we actively deny the conditioning we've been indoctrinated into, we are stuck with it.

Without seeing through and uprooting our conditioned beliefs, we cannot be free.

And we cannot let others be free.

Often the most harmful conditioning operates under the radar of our conscious awareness. Here's where practice becomes our lifeboat. We practice not only seeing the unseen but also being with the discomfort that arises as we confront our conditioning.

Knowing how to fully be with discomfort allows for openness.

In openness, transformation is possible.

Resistance to discomfort shuts us down.

Avoidance makes us small.

Have you ever met anyone who is comfortable admitting that they are racist? Or that they think of themselves as superior? It seems to me that in most cases, the conditioning of racism is so embedded and ingrained, and so deeply upheld by our conditioned systems at large, that many white people don't even see it. We've been conditioned not to.

In the same way that at the monastery I was trained to see how my personal conditioning manifests, I've more recently been steeped in seeing and learning about all of the collective conditioning that I did not grow up recognizing.

We cannot admit to something that we do not see.

Step one is to see.

In my experience, to even begin to see how we are all impacted by racism, that we all absorb and perpetuate racism, brings about tremendous discomfort for most white people. Then, of course, there's the conditioned process of denial that serves to ensure that we can avoid such discomfort. Ironically enough, we are deeply conditioned to go through great pains to avoid discomfort!

While starting to see how such conditioned systems like white supremacy have been absorbed can be uncomfortable, we can't release what we can't see. Conditioned systems that create harm can only be maintained in a landscape of ignorance. There is a lot of collective conditioning that supports the eyes staying closed.

What I value about the Buddha and countless other spiritual heroes is that their eyes were open. They were awake. Our heroes commonly do not describe waking up as a comfortable process. We can learn to accept this—even embrace it. In discomfort there is often growth, a particular aliveness.

There's a wonderful story about the twentieth-century Surrealist painter Salvador Dali in which he apparently went to a restaurant and was offered a seat that had a sharp metal spring pushing up through the cushion, poking his thigh. His friend took notice and requested that the chair be switched out. I've been told that Dali responded with delight, something to the effect of "No, no! Please. What a nice little gift this is! Here to keep me awake to a lovely meal and precious time with my friend—none of which I wish to miss!"

I can't confirm the truth of this little anecdote (and have embellished it slightly with my choice of adjectives) but it illustrates a perspective that differs from the one most of us are conditioned into. Most of us are conditioned to go to great lengths to be comfortable at all times.

Ask yourself, what is the cost of this?

Awareness practice teaches us how to embrace discomfort rather than try to avoid it. In fact, my first Zen teacher, when speaking about choosing things that go against the grain of our conditioning, used to say, "When you feel that red light within, the one that suggests that you go no further, it is often your conditioned system simply feeling threatened. Take it as a sign to go forward."

Please be sure to hold this conversation within the context of ending suffering. I've worked with adults who are in unhealthy relationships and who use this pointer to suggest that perhaps they should sustain the abuse because they now believe they should "face their discomfort"—all in the name of spiritual practice. That's not the lesson here.

Also, for those of us who have experienced trauma, it's important to note that this red light within could be inherent wisdom that tells us when something isn't currently supportive to us. Again, it's not *what* but *how*. Here's the important takeaway:

Practice teaches us how to cultivate courage.

It takes courage to be with discomfort.

Courage fuels the letting go of what binds us.

Courage is what allows us to stand on our own two feet.

It takes courage to go up against personal conditioning. It also takes courage, of course, to go up against collective conditioning. There's a tremendous momentum that keeps personal conditioning in place. Now multiply that by the masses when reflecting on collective conditioning. This momentum is one of the many reasons collective change can be slow. To transform personally and collectively, we must show up, see how we've been conditioned, witness our habit to avoid the discomfort that may arise as we seek truth, and keep our eyes on wholeness all the while. Returning to wholeness again and again when we forget.

Our lighthouse is liberation.
The freedom we realize together.

COLLECTIVE EGO: SUSTAINING SEPARATION

The ego—the illusion of a self that is separate from life—is not actually a self at all. It's simply the activity of the conditioned mind. When we identify with this activity, follow this story line,, we feel separate and therefore behave and act in the world as if we are separate.

The same is true collectively. We have a collective ego that also asserts its apparent reality, though in both cases these "egos" can be found nowhere. Again, the ego is just the activity of the conditioned mind. Our identification is what gives it apparent reality.

In the same way that the personal ego "fights for its life" when threatened, so does the collective ego. We have seen this in the United States with the destructive delusion of white supremacy battling for its survival. White supremacy is a collective ego. Patriarchy is a collective ego. These collective egos assert separation and deny interconnection. They demand domination. They can only exist within the distortion of conditioned hierarchy. They have no life in the truth of inherent wholeness.

RETURNING TO WHOLENESS

Awareness practice offers us a way to expose the falsehoods of the ego—personal and collective—and return to wholeness. It can be difficult to return to the direct experience of wholeness when you're in the midst of believing the story of separation. It can be even more difficult to return to wholeness when you don't realize that you are caught in the story of separation. The story simply feels real and true. This is how delusion works. It's like a movie that has you enthralled, and the idea of getting up and leaving would never occur to you.

Sometimes we're so steeped in the delusion of separation that it takes a direct experience of wholeness for us to realize that there is an alternative.

I adored my Mindful Studies student "Isaiah." Still do. He loved the community and was always quick to support someone struggling. Isaiah took the class repeatedly, and I never thought much about this . . . until the day his guidance counselor came to our classroom and suggested that Isaiah go to the office. Right. Away.

Isaiah asked if I'd come with him. It was in that cubbyhole of an office that I learned that Isaiah was not actually enrolled in Mindful Studies and that he hadn't been all year. I was as perplexed as Mr. Jones, the guidance counselor, though less agitated by the unfolding of events. He turned to Isaiah with a glaring eye: "You have taken Mindful Studies four times! All year you've been enrolled in Economics for first period. You haven't been attending because you've been crashing Mindful Studies instead. You know that means you're failing Economics, right?! Why on earth are you jeopardizing your graduation in this way?!" Mr. Jones was far from impressed.

Isaiah didn't hesitate. He sat upright, and I was struck by the quality of his assuredness. I could see, even before he spoke, that no one was going to argue with his experience. "Mr. Jones," he said, "Mindful Studies is the reason I come to school. It's what gets me out of bed. This class is why I'm sober. It's why I'm here at all."

All fell silent. Truth had been spoken. The mic had been dropped. Neither Mr. Jones nor I wondered what Isaiah meant by "It's why I'm here." I was flooded with the image of the young girl, a well-loved soccer player at the school, who had died by suicide the prior year.

As Isaiah and I walked back to class, he shared more about his experience. He told me how much he valued the class and how important the community had become to him. What struck me most about this was that his community had been continually shifting. Every semester a new set of thirty students showed up, aside from the handful that had room to take the class more than once.

I realized that the conscious container of the class provided a consistency that Isaiah could lean into. Unlike any other class he'd ever had, this class made clear it wasn't "cool" to judge others. Getting "on top" wasn't rewarded. In this class, everyone recognized and named identity as a creation of sorts. Elsewhere you might be labeled the "jock", "the class clown", or the "nerd who aces everything." Within these walls, none of this mattered. Very intentionally, none of this mattered.

In Mindful Studies, he wasn't told what to think. Rather, he was consistently asked to explore his experience. And his fellow students trusted that he was adequate to this experience, whatever this experience was.

In this class Isaiah knew that he was whole. He had a direct experience of this wholeness and he learned to value it. Not only did he recognize the importance of it—he even went to bat for it under pressure.

One of the most impactful aspects of working with teens has been witnessing when the story of separation is washed away, even if just momentarily. I've seen that often this has to do with the proper context. Such as this case where Isaiah was able to experience that he has always belonged and that saved his life. Wholeness is personal—you feel that nothing is inherently broken within you; it's also collective—we belong wholly as one human family. It can take practice and awareness to remember this basic truth.

Though I've lost touch with Isaiah, I hope that his experience of wholeness will be with him for the rest of his life. The specific techniques of sitting meditation might fade, the language around the conditioned mind and the specifics of the contemplative technologies the class provides will perhaps blur, but once we've tasted our inherent wholeness, once we've remembered it, it's rarely completely forgotten. Traces of this experience are left behind. Its perfume lingers timelessly.

Wholeness is foundational, fundamental, and primary. You are not the ego that busies itself with activity to become whole. The reason self-improvement never works is that there isn't actually a separate self to improve.

All feelings have a certain validity to them, however, and it's valid to say that we feel separate sometimes. Perhaps often. It's valid to express that separateness is our felt experience. It is our felt experience when we identify with the conditioned mind. Ego *feels* like it doesn't belong. It *feels* like a fragment of an experience that can take many various forms: believing you're unlovable, feeling superior and therefore other than, perceiving that you're less than and therefore unworthy. We could also call the conditioned mind "the mind of comparison."

The good news? We don't have to get rid of the conditioned mind in order to experience our inherent wholeness. The conditioned mind isn't bad or wrong. It's a creation.

What is created can be dismantled.

It's because you are whole that you know the whole range of human experience. Don't shy away from what you are conditioned to believe makes you broken, even if it sparks discomfort. Perhaps especially if it sparks discomfort!

Identifying with the mind of limitation leads to suffering. Remember, if you can see that you are identifying with the conditioned mind, then you inherently have some distance from the experience. You are aware of it; you are not it.

A Practice: Disidentifying with the Conditioned Mind

These simple steps are a way to practice disidentifying with the conditioned mind:

1. See it. Notice the suffering as it arises.

2. Name it. Recognize it as conditioning, a learned or inherited response. Label it as such.

3. Let go. See that this conditioning isn't you, that it's impermanent, and release it. (But how do we let go? How do we drop the story? Through step 4!)

4. Return. Direct the attention back to the moment, to your experience of wholeness. Return to presence.

IDENTIFICATION CREATES DISTORTION

When my mother was diagnosed with cancer, I took a sabbatical from the monastery to be with her as she began treatment. I remember standing in front of the bookshelf my father made me when I was a child. It was filled with countless handmade journals containing stories, photos, articles, notes from friends, poems—all the things that might fill a girl's journal from when she was old enough to write until her midtwenties.

A part of me struggled so very much with being a monk. The silence. The schedule. The strictness. In my mind, there was one prevailing problem: my inability to let go of identity. That, surely, was the source of my suffering.

The journals became a representation of "the problem." On one hand, I saw them as beautiful expressions of the experience of growing up. On the other hand, even that appreciation of them was evidence that I clung too much to identity. (At that point in time, I wasn't questioning what was up with the aspect of the personality that wanted to get rid of identity; it simply felt real and true that "I need to let go.")

Journal after journal, I threw the full books into heavy-duty garbage bags, knotted them closed, drove them to a nearby dumpster, and shoved them in.

That night I floundered in bed as if physically ill. Sleep was impossible. I wondered, *What if someone finds my journals? I wanted to let go of these expressions of my past, of the personality, but what if all that is kept alive through someone else's ownership of these books?*

There was an ache too. Deep down, I felt it was disrespectful to have thrown all this history in the trash. *Clearly,* I thought at the time, *I need to create a more reverent way to get rid of myself.*

I leapt out of bed, drove back to the dumpster, fished out my past, hauled it back to my wood cabin in the woods of Virginia, and placed each journal carefully, one by one, into the consuming flames of my woodstove. *There. No more identity. I'm free.* (Cue hands wiping clean in front of a fire.)

It took me years to see that only the illusion of a separate self would try to get rid of the illusion of a separate self, to see that this was not how to know freedom. It took me years to get it that all this efforting was a spiritual form of self-improvement.

"Letting go" isn't truly letting go when we're identified with the ego. When we're identified with the ego, any activity can become an activity that reinforces the hologram of separation. Remember,

In awareness practice we aren't creating wholeness; we are returning to the wholeness out of which the ego arises.

We can do this every time suffering occurs.

We can do this on our own. We can do this as a collective.

We must disarm and disidentify with the ego, personally and collectively, to imagine something different from the conditioned reality that we are accustomed to. From wholeness we can dream and imagine. From wholeness we can create.

Collective Practice: Undoing Collective Conditioning

- Begin with some meditation.

- Then, in your journal, move through the Fleshing Out Our Conditioning prompts from page 47 if you haven't already. Share your observations first in pairs and then with the whole group. As always, give yourself permission to keep your observations private if that feels most honoring.

- Ask yourself these questions and together as a group explore:

    What's the cost of my personal conditioning?

    What's the price on my body, my mind, my energetic system?

    As a practice, what is required of me to stay with it?

    What is required of me to not fall for the habit of turning away?

- Next, recognize places of collective conditioning. Things might come up around collective conditioning of your gender, family structure, or the region in which you were raised.

    *What is the **cost** of this conditioning?*

- You may choose to reflect on some of the same prompts that were offered in Fleshing Out Our Conditioning, but now reflect on them in relationship to a collective you identify with.

Please note, however, that this exploration has the potential to be triggering. It's important to approach this with tenderness, gentleness, and kindness. Explore this to whatever degree feels useful, fruitful, and illuminating. If some discomfort arises, you might find it useful to practice with it. To sit with it and explore it with nonjudgmental inquiry. To see it, name it, let it go, and return.

If you move beyond discomfort into overwhelm or the kind of anxiety that doesn't allow information to be absorbed, gently back off. This is not a contest.

- Share your observations if you choose to. As you share with each other, practice listening without interrupting. Practice nonjudgment. Your group may still be getting to know each other. Allow this practice to be an opportunity to continue to build trust. Honor the inherent wholeness in each of you as you speak and as you listen. Let nothing get in the way of this.

As the author and recording artist Justin Michael Williams says, "We must own and acknowledge that we, as individuals and as a collective, see things through a certain lens, or perspective. And if enough people agree on a certain perspective, then that perspective becomes our collective reality and belief." Here, together, we are exploring the impact of these beliefs and assumptions. Unpacking them. Bringing them into the light. Allowing for undoing. In the name of liberation for all, allowing for undoing.

Chapter Four

Return to Inquiry

Releasing Negative Self-Talk and Shame

It is hard to fight an enemy who
has outposts in your head.

—Sally Kempton

Forget about enlightenment for a moment. Let's talk about how different the world would be without self-hatred.

I should start by acknowledging that when I went on my first Zen retreat and heard the teacher speaking about self-hate, I truly believed that I didn't have any. How was this belief possible? Because I couldn't admit to something I couldn't see. Truth be told, I simply had no idea that not only did I have a full share of self-hate but, in many ways, the inner critic was running my life, influencing decisions around every bend.

As participants on the retreat revealed their inner negative self-talk in the group discussions, I felt somewhat shocked and horrified. I deeply related to what folks were sharing and yet all of it had been below the surface of my awareness until then.

When I was a little girl, I wanted nothing more than to be a veterinarian. In particular, I adored being around dogs, and my care for them was profound. I always had at least one dog when I was growing up. We were one of those households where dogs were truly part of the family. (Along with the cats, guinea pigs, fish, and yes, even a ferret at one point.)

Whenever one of our animals needed to go to the vet, I'd always accompany them. I liked being there for them during times of stress. I felt called to provide reassurance and love.

I also admired our veterinarian, Dr. Freedman. He clearly loved these creatures like I did, and watching him work was way better than TV. There was an art to how he did what he did, and to me his creations were beautiful. Whether he was helping an animal get well or having to put a furry friend to sleep, he was supporting life. At the clinic there was a reverence for life I connected with. It permeated everything.

I must have only been in middle school when I began asking my mom if I could spend more time at the clinic with Dr. Freedman. He had been the family vet forever, and he had a great relationship with us. My mom brought so many animals to him, for so many years, that he used to joke that she put his kids through college. When my mother called him and asked if I could start spending more time there, he didn't hesitate. (I chuckle about this as an adult. She got free childcare; he got free help—an energetic kid, enthusiastic about even the dirty work. It clearly was a win/win for them—and for me!)

I'd go on many Saturdays and help out any way I could. At one point I even started observing surgeries. Scrubbing in, suiting up, and handing Dr. Freedman tools throughout his procedures. (This was the eighties, y'all, so think: no restrictions.)

I'll never forget seeing the tumor removed from Betty the Beagle. It was miraculous. Here was this sweet, tender being suffering from the pain of a tumor located just behind her right ear, and due to the wonders of modern medicine, she could experience relief—within hours. It was awe-inspiring. I was hooked.

After that surgery I was elated about having found my calling. I was practically breathless when I gushed to my mother that I knew what I wanted to be when I grew up. (That we collectively sometimes overemphasize this question—"What do you want to be when you grow up?"—with children is another conversation about societal conditioning. "Your Self-Worth Comes from Your Occupation" could be a chapter in its own right.)

My mom reacted without hesitation: "Oh, Caverly, that is a wonderful thought, but veterinary school is very, very difficult. You don't test well. You'd never make it through the schooling, much less even get into the kind of college you'd need to get into." Those were her exact words. Years later, she swears she never said, "You aren't smart enough to be a vet," but certainly that is what I heard.

To say that I was deflated would be an understatement. Devastated might be more accurate. Cue the image of a child hanging her head and plodding up the stairs to her bedroom to cry. Soft, melancholic piano in the background.

I can't share this story without being compelled to explain that my mother loves me deeply. Her intention was not to crush my dreams, of course. In fact, she wanted to prepare me. In her mind, she was saving me from disappointment, making sure I didn't get my hopes up, being realistic.

Internalizing this experience was swift. My mother never needed to say another word about it. New internal negative self-talk was born: *I am not smart enough*. It played out in my classes at school. When deciding what to do when school let out, I always chose to be active and avoid things like reading. When it came time to consider life after high school, *I'm not smart enough* was so ingrained that becoming a vet seemed as unlikely and unrealistic as walking on the moon. Not only was it no longer on the table—it wasn't anywhere in the kitchen. No argument, just forgotten. Not even an internal debate. I left high school and moved to New York to become an actress. It was simply real and true that I wasn't smart enough to do anything else. I had reset my eye on what *did* feel possible.

IS THAT TRUE?

It did not occur to me then to practice inquiry. "Is that true?" wasn't a question in reach. In fact, it didn't even exist. We don't inquire about things we assume to be true. We are habituated not to question our beliefs. Having a practice that allowed me to see negative self-talk as something other than me was revolutionary.

To be honest, when I first started to question my inner negative self-talk it freaked me out. It was creepy. "Who *is* this voice inside my head?!" I found myself asking. It was like I was in a bad sci-fi movie. There were the obvious psychological conclusions: "Oh yes, that's the voice of my dad. Yep, there's my internalized mom." But with just a bit of exploration I quickly saw that things were more complicated than that.

I saw that I had negative self-talk that had nothing to do with my childhood. I saw that some of the roots of what I told myself couldn't be traced to anything logical. In fact, I saw that this negative self-talk actually wasn't "mine." It didn't belong to me; I had simply always claimed it.

And here lies one of the greatest gifts of practice—the capacity not to take personally what you've always assumed to be yours—in fact, not only what you've assumed to be yours but what you've assumed to be YOU. Remember, you are not your thoughts or the voice of the inner critic.

This is intensely important personally, and it's imperative collectively. We can't disidentify from negative self-talk when we claim it as ourselves.

We must inquire into the way in which that is not actually so.

We must question it.

EXCUSE ME, WHO SHALL I SAY IS CALLING?

One way I support practitioners in being able to question the voice of their negative self-talk is by externalizing this voice. Pause to picture this now.

How would you respond if a person were following you around in your life, commenting on your every move, most commonly with criticism or, at minimum, veiled judgment that serves to "help, protect, support you in being realistic"? How long would you keep this "friend" around?

For many of us, the journey from negative self-talk to an experience of full-blown self-hate is short. And self-hate is a glue of sorts—holding the structures of the conditioned mind together. Imagine looking at the world through tinted glasses and continually assuming that it is reality. In meditation practice, the glasses come off. We see the tint as something that belongs to glasses rather than a reflection of truth—rather than an experience of reality. But we must begin by inquiring about what we've been looking through.

If you're constantly being bombarded by a voice that suggests that *you are not enough*, that *there is something wrong with you*, you become so busy defending against this voice, agreeing with this voice, fighting this voice, that often there's little energy left to inquire into the nature of this voice, and little space to ask who this voice is even referring to.

The ego takes everything personally. It's a masterfully designed self-referencing system. Everything comes back to "me." And self-hate keeps it all in place. Remember, the ego isn't real. It is the activity of the conditioned mind. Think of it like a hologram. There's nothing solid about it. It can't actually be found when you look for it.

THE INNER CRITIC AS CLOUDS

My first Zen teacher used to say that true spiritual practice can't begin until self-hate ends. My experience is not so linear. Yes, it can be helpful to name some basic steps of practice, which can be viewed in a linear fashion:

Step 1: See it. Recognize that the voice of the inner critic exists.

Step 2: Name it. Cultivate the capacity to say, "Ah, there's the voice of the inner critic again."

Step 3: Let go. Further inquire into the illusory nature of this voice to disidentify, to release the grip.

Step 4: Return. Align with *awareness* of the voice rather than the voice itself. Return to presence.

However, having taught this process to teens and adults for over twenty years, I have come to recognize that this ongoing practice is shaped like a spiral, not a line. If we cling to the idea that we have to get rid of self-hate before we can get to the "real practice," then we're feeding the distortion that there is a self who needs to get rid of something in order to get somewhere else. This keeps in place not only a limited belief in a separate self but also a linear view of time.

It's difficult to ask ourselves foundational practice questions like "Who am I truly?" if we're mired in conversations about worthiness. And we must be careful not to give too much validity, attribute too much reality, to a hologram, otherwise our practices can easily slide into "self-improvement." Remember:

The reason that self-improvement ultimately doesn't work is that, in reality, there is no separate self to improve.

It's not my experience that, through practice, negative self-talk—the voice of the inner critic—disappears forever. To believe so gives this illusory voice in our heads a solidity it doesn't actually have. It is my experience that through practice we become clearer and clearer about what this voice is and therefore we tend to fall for its shenanigans less and less frequently.

This is not to say it never arises again. We can think of the workings of the inner critic as storm clouds. We could say that over time, with practice, we believe less and less that every time the clouds roll through, the sun has disappeared. We can, absolutely, focus on the recognition that not only does the sun *not* disappear but we are the steady sun, while the clouds do whatever the clouds do. They are transitory. Impermanent.

We are undisturbed.

There is plenty of room for any and all weather patterns in the truth of reality. The reality is that we are not the weather patterns. The reality is that the weather patterns arise in us, pass through us, dissolve in us. There's plenty of room for storms to do what they will as we inquire: *Who am I? Who are we? What is "us"?*

It's liberating to realize that we don't have to get rid of anything to know who we truly are.

When we are identified with negative self-talk, the ego is legitimized. It gets fed. And, as discussed in chapter 1, where we place our attention matters. What we feed, grows. This feeding process doesn't make the ego more real but rather more believable. Practice challenges our conditioned beliefs. And in this challenge, what isn't true dissolves.

Believing negative self-talk keeps us feeling alone, busy, fearful. That we are separate isn't *true*. The more we believe the voice "I'm not good enough," the more likely we are to feel isolated. That we need to get rid of the ego in order to be free, and that there is something wrong with us for having an ego in the first place, isn't *true*. The more we feed this narrative, the more likely we are to continually strive. "Whatever you do, it isn't enough" isn't *true*. When we believe this, we're afraid, unable, and/or resistant to rest in the satisfaction of what is here—now.

A Practice: Inquiring into Negative Self-Talk

Create a list in your CARE journal. On one side of the page, list the negative self-talk; on the other, the result, the impact.

I'll never get this project right	Missing all my deadlines
I'm such a lousy father	Missed opportunities to genuinely listen to my daughter
People are not interested in what I have to say	My voice is not included in group decisions

Now inquire into the illusory nature of all this. Allow yourself to be like a scientist of the self, seeing how it all works.

To be clear, just because I'm talking about it as illusory doesn't mean that it is entirely unreal. There's a particular reality to the felt sense of isolation, isn't there? By using the word *illusion* in this case, I'm referring to how this voice isn't what it appears to be. It's not Reality with a capital *R*. That's what inquiry opens the way for. Questions like:

What is this voice?

What is the impact of believing this voice?

Is this voice mine?

Is what this voice is saying reality?

Does it assert the truth?

Am I this voice?

Where do I look for the answers to this question?

Who am I without this internal conversation?

FROM THE PERSONAL TO THE COLLECTIVE

When we step back from the workings of the inner critic and its cycles of negative self-talk, we see these workings simply as processes of suffering. We have greater clarity about how these processes normalize the absurd.

There's a certain absurdity to believing we are isolated while living in such a deeply interconnected world. There's a certain absurdity to a child having to question their worth based on believing an illusory voice without a body. On a personal level, we are conditioned to normalize the absurd. That's true collectively too.

We have been conditioned to perceive "the other." We have been conditioned to perceive hierarchy—hierarchies that are made up and mythologized, such as hierarchies of race, a made-up concept, and the rigid hierarchies enforced by class. We have been conditioned to avoid seeing how these things came to be, to maintain the status quo, to not question.

We have a collective ego.
We have a collective inner critic.
Neither have reality without the ways our collective attention feeds them.

For some time now I've been paying attention to how we collectively normalize the absurd, a phrase I first heard in a workshop with Michelle Cassandra Johnson. As social and political turmoil has been reaching a fever pitch as I write this book, I find examples of this phenomenon everywhere. So many circumstances, wildly unreasonable yet normalized.

There is a particular absurdity to the way in which, within dominant culture, our expanding homeless population is normalized. Or the prevalence of gun violence. Or the fact that Black mothers are more likely to die during childbirth than white mothers. Or the rapidly increasing rate of species extinction.

Pause.

Watch for any temptation to skim through those sentences. This is part of the conditioned normalization process—to read without feeling, to go numb, to absorb information as if we aren't affected. Or perhaps we are part of a collective that is conditioned to see these things as someone else's problem. Read the above paragraph again and, this time, pay close attention to what happens in your body, mind, and energetic system as you do so.

Our shared processes of avoiding feeling do nothing to dismantle our collective conditioning, which we'll discuss more fully later.

JUDGMENT: A TOOL OF THE INNER CRITIC

For now, let's focus on judgment.

It also plays a role.

Judgment collectively keeps much of the machinery of the conditioned cycles that "normalize the absurd" in place. In other words, the collective inner critic acts like a glue for our collective conditioning.

For example, the collective belief that poor people are only poor because they don't work hard enough and thereby deserve our collective judgment. This judgment keeps a collective "those people" conditioned lens of separation in place. It acts as a glue keeping the *collective* conditioning intact in the same way that judgment acts as a glue keeping *personal* conditioning intact.

HOW SHAME CAN BE A BLINDFOLD

As I've been learning more about the collective conditioning that I've been indoctrinated into, I've paid particular attention to the role of guilt and shame. For many white people, shame pervades most, if not all, aspects of learning about race and the history of oppression. I'm clear that there can be no learning, and therefore no transformation, in a soup that has been seasoned with guilt and shame. And that these two ingredients are by-products of judgment.

Judgment poisons the heart.

The pain of shame prevents clear seeing.

Lack of clear seeing prevents change.

Shame, therefore, is something I've had to practice with, particularly because it's been a prevalent part of my roots. I've debated about whether to share this next story publicly. Upon much reflection, I've realized that many of my readers will likely have different content but similar stories. I share it because I have seen in my family that shared shame keeps a tremendous amount of collective conditioning in place, and that one by-product of such collective conditioning is inequity. Gross inequity.

BILLIE

Her name was Grace Vaughn but everyone called her Billie. My strongest childhood memories of Billie are in the kitchen. I can still smell her ham biscuits, which were divine. (And it's really saying something that I'd describe them this way, given that I have been a vegetarian since I was sixteen. "Divine" and "pork" are not two words I string together lightly!) I rarely saw Billie in anything other than her cleanly pressed uniform and white apron. As a child, I was clear that she was the wisest person in the house. She was grounded, while the whirl of my grandparents' life flitted about like small parasails on the sea.

Billie, a small-boned, shy Black woman from Virginia, raised my mother in the house that my grandparents built in 1950. Slaughter, my grandfather, was the head of otolaryngology at the University of Virginia. Dorothea, my maternal grandmother, played the societal role of the doctor's wife. She was active in her garden and bridge clubs, and by all accounts was somewhat uninvolved in the details of her children's lives. When I called my mother to verify that sentence, she asked me if perhaps I should "tone it down." When I asked why, her response was that it sounded "so heavy." The white Southern conditioned subtext: real is "too intense." Heavy is depressing. One should always smile, be polite, talk about nice things.

Billie did all the housework, all the cooking, and tended to all three children. Her workdays started at 10 a.m. and ended at 9 p.m. My mother, to this day, thinks of her as her mother. She never spoke about it publicly, though, for in her mind it was clear that the sentiment might have offended my grandmother, Dorothea. Even though Dorothea has long passed, I can still feel my mother's deep sensitivity around the complexity of her relationship with these two women. In fact, my name was supposed to be Grace, but my mother was concerned that her mother would be hurt that I wasn't named Dorothea. The solution? Two middle names. Dorothea comes first due to the politics. Billie's middle name follows behind. (Her first name has been changed here.)

Billie signed my mother's report cards, helped with her homework, and inquired daily about her life at school. Billie dressed her and looked after her on all fronts, from scraped knees to celebrating birthdays. My mother claims that

Billie wasn't just a mother to her but also a best friend. I only wish Billie were still alive. I have often wondered how Billie would describe her experience of their relationship. She died when I was too young to ask.

My first trip to Billie's home made a deep impression. I was young. My mother brought me along to deliver some groceries. I used to think that at that age I must have been "too young to understand race and class," but now I'm clear that no one was able or willing to speak to me about these things. It wasn't that I couldn't understand but that the topic was taboo. It didn't fit the Southern, white, conditioned code of conduct. It wasn't "polite talk."

The house was turn-of-the-century old. Wood floors. Thick clear plastic on the couches to keep them nice. Sports trophies from the grandsons on the mantle. What my mother now describes as "a trough that you'd use for animals" stood in the kitchen for baths.

I know now that Billie did not own this house. My grandparents did.

Just to spell this out, my grandparents paid Billie whatever small amount they did for her work, Billie would receive her earnings, and then she would pay rent to my grandparents, her employers.

I was in my midforties when I learned the reason that there are two bathrooms in the basement of my childhood home, which was also my mother's childhood home. The basement holds a bedroom, a living room, and a full bath. And just at the bottom of the staircase that bleeds off the kitchen stands the tiniest half bath you've ever seen. It never made any sense to me, but I didn't think to ask about it . . . until the day my mother was in the hospital after an intensive surgery. Under bright lights, in the lull between nurses' visits and the intimacy of shared history and secrets surfacing in family crisis, I learned that the half bath was built for Billie.

When my mother confessed this through tears, I had to have it spelled out for me. Billie was not allowed to use the other bathrooms in the house. Nor was she allowed to eat with the same silverware.

THE ROLE OF SHAME IN UPHOLDING INJUSTICE

Depending on your lived experience, this story might provoke any number of strong feelings: rage, sorrow, disgust. My mother carries it with guilt and shame. The dark grip of her shame has kept her experiences tightly locked away for a lifetime. She doesn't talk about it. She tries not to think about it.

Shame hides feelings that fester in the dark. When we open the door, the stench can be overpowering.

Many people feel shame about their historic participation in racism or other injustices. On top of this shame is *more* shame about having a lack of understanding regarding how such unjust circumstances came to be. This layered shame is not bad or wrong, but it's not very functional. As I've learned about such history, I've needed to practice with guilt and shame. In this book, I'm not using these words interchangeably.

When you feel guilty, there's a judgment that *something you've done* is wrong. When you feel shame, you believe that *your whole self is wrong.*

In this chapter we're not focusing on whether it's "right" or "wrong" to feel shame. We're inquiring into how listening exclusively to the voice of shame prevents us from learning, growing, or transforming. While the experience of shame may be *followed* by growth, the growth doesn't happen inside the shame. Again, shame, a form of self-hate, is a glue of sorts.

I'm unworthy.

I'm unlovable.

I'm broken.

I'm useless.

I'm flawed.

What are these expressions of shame keeping in place? What's the common denominator?

The "I" that sees itself as limited, separate, cut off, isolated.

As the vulnerability researcher Dr. Brené Brown so succinctly stated, "Shame corrodes the very part of us that believes we are capable of change." This is true individually and collectively. The way many white people react to the history of oppression is just one example of collective shame. While we're defining shame, I should be clear that being present to the pain of harm, or having an empathetic response, is not the same thing as shame.

I'm learning that if we are going to dismantle systems of oppression, we must be unafraid to learn about how they've formed, unafraid of the pain we may feel in learning. How did it come to be that a Black woman, with a child of her own, became the primary caregiver for a white family, got paid close to nothing, was provided no health insurance benefits, and lived in perpetual poverty?

This is not a random arising.

Such circumstances arise *systemically* and, if we're committed to dismantling them, it's important for us to understand how they come to be. But if we are in the grip of our collective inner critic, we can't even look at it, much less dismantle them.

What we are unconscious to silently governs us.

Avoiding our shame keeps us unconscious.

How did "the other side of the tracks" form in towns and cities? How do more Black and Brown people end up imprisoned than white people? How have so many people in our country ended up homeless? I did not grow up learning the answers to these questions. That's not an accident. The not knowing is calculated. It keeps the mechanisms of separation in place. And in addition to systemic, willful ignorance, individuals also take a stance of ignorance, in part to protect themselves from shame.

It is my hope that many of our children today do not have the same story that I do about my education. I do not recall being invited to read a single Black author in high school. Not one. I remember George Orwell, J. D. Salinger, John Steinbeck, Shakespeare—all white men. In fact, I remember when, for the first time, I was asked to read Emily Dickinson. It was practically jarring to experience a woman writer. I didn't know about the brilliance of James Baldwin, Audre Lorde, Langston Hughes, and Toni Morrison in high school. I literally did not even know these people existed. You may have had the same experience of school—it is the norm for education in the United States. If I shame you for your ignorance, will you be more or less likely to seek out books by Black authors?

I am not the voice to articulate the history of race in America. Thankfully there are many educators, thought leaders, and visionaries to support such education. I've benefited deeply from the work of Rev. angel Kyodo williams, Lama Rod Owens, Resmaa Menakem, James Baldwin, and bell hooks, just to name a few.

In order to move into such learning, if you are someone for whom shame arises, I encourage you to practice letting go of the judgment you may have around not knowing. Be willing to inquire with openness and curiosity.

Clarity depends on nonjudgment. Curiosity lights the way.

RECOGNIZING SHAME, OPENING THE WAY FOR GROWTH

As you continue to practice directing your attention, I invite you to be curious about the voice of the inner critic—how it forms, how it operates, and the effect it has. We, too, can be curious about what has been suppressed historically by dominant culture—for example, the kind of shame and guilt that has been present in my family. It is possible to be open to and fascinated by what we don't know. In order to access this, however, we must recognize the shame we might be conditioned to have around not knowing. In practice we have the opportunity to see shame as another aspect of negative self-talk, to recognize the conditioning around not knowing. We must recognize the story line of shame as part of the separate self-illusion if we are to dig into the work of liberation.

Our collective conditioning around not knowing is deep. Most of us were taught to be ashamed if we didn't know something. Dominant culture also teaches us to fear humiliation. Have you ever pretended to know something that you actually didn't know in order to avoid humiliation? Most children have minor (or major) humiliation experiences around not knowing something. Do you have any experiences in which the people around you put forward, "We all knew this, *You* did not; You should be ashamed"? Or "You are stupid for not knowing"? For anyone in modern life to meet anyone else in this hierarchically ordered society and engage essence to essence, there has to be permission, validation, and even celebration of not knowing. It's important for us to collectively disidentify from the shame around ignorance.

We can be liberated from our conditioning around shame.

The path lies in embracing the wonder of inquiry.

If, like me, you are learning about your unearned privilege, it can be helpful to remember that we can learn together. We can embrace not knowing together.

When we defend our ignorance by hiding it or denying it, we are confined by conditioned thinking. One of the tools that allows us to sweep this away is a shameless recognition, a kind embracing, of what we haven't known or been unaware of.

It is freeing to be released from distortion and delusion, not something to be feared.

If, like me, you have internalized shame about "being stupid," for example, then you might sometimes feel trapped in hiding what you do not know. When being humiliated is the consequence for not knowing—say you've been shamed for being clumsy or weak—you might spend your whole life defending that it doesn't matter that you can't run. You defend your feeling of inferiority, which is held in place by negative self-talk. First you're ashamed that you don't know. Then you defend that you don't know. Instead of all this, we can go straight to a compassionate understanding of the way in which *we don't know what we don't know*. With practice, we can bring in tenderness.

Practice teaches us to set the stage for openness and perhaps even excitement around learning. For the love of seeing. The beauty of discernment.

For the joy of waking up.

NEGATIVE OTHER-TALK

In the same way that believing negative *self*-talk about ourselves impacts our actions, believing negative self-talk about others does as well. Thoughts become embodied and then acted upon. When we notice the self-talk we have the opportunity to question it, to inquire. Awareness is first.

I can't question whether I want to continue to abide by the social construct of race, for example, if I can't see what I say to myself about it. Paying attention to our self-talk supports us not only in revealing the inner critic for what it is but also in helping us to see our unconscious biases more clearly.

Awareness practice isn't simply about sitting on a cushion.

It's about paying attention in all aspects of our lives.

Race is a human-invented classification system. In the same way that the ego is not "real," race is not "real." In both cases, we must be careful to say what we mean by "real." We could say, regarding both race and the ego, that in the ultimate sense they are illusions, though they each function on the relative plane in their own way. In both cases, we must underline that simply because something is illusory does not negate the powerful reality that these illusions have. A relative reality.

The ego exploits classifications like race, gender, and national identity. The ego is a deeply ingrained habit. An illusory lens. A distortion that is created by the activity of the conditioned mind. A story line. A meaning-making machine. The aspect of this activity that we think of as "who we are" is illusory. Actions that arise on behalf of the ego have a particular reality on the relative plane.

The idea of race has been critical in the history of America and in the identification of its people. Racial designations have literally marked the difference between life and death in countless circumstances. The assignment of value to race is the issue. What is it that assigns value? The ego. How does it do it? Through its own activity in the mind; through thinking, through self- and other-talk. White supremacy, for example, is a collective ego—that is, a collective delusion that we are all separate. It is a collective egoic stance that presumes white people deserve to be at the top of a hierarchy that is very real to those enmeshed in it and nonetheless completely illusory.

In *Between the World and Me*, the author Ta-Nehisi Coates argues that race itself is a flawed, if not useless, concept—it is, if anything, nothing more than a pretext for rac*ism*. Coates writes, "Race is the child of racism, not the father."

The ancient Chinese philosopher Lao Tzu is reported to have said it like it is: "Watch your thoughts, they become your words; watch your words, they become your actions; watch your actions, they become your habits; watch your habits, they become your character; watch your character, it becomes your destiny."

We can say that there is a particular reality to what unfolds on behalf of the ego while also recognizing that it is unreal. Race is a creation. It is illusory.

You can choose whether to identify with the conversation in your head.

Suffering is a by-product of this identification and is optional.

As you disidentify from negative self-talk, you feel and know your own inherent freedom more fully. As you disidentify from your negative talk about others, others become freer. As we collectively disidentify from our shared conditioned negative self-and-other-talk, we all become more free.

Collective freedom from conditioning stems from this choice to disidentify.

Collective Practice: Unveiling Beliefs, Assumptions, and Judgments

You can do this with your group or individually. In your CARE journal, first spend some time exploring:

What are some groups of people I have negative self-and-other talk about?

What have I been conditioned to assume is "true" about various labeled groups?

What have I been told is "true" about a collective (class, race, gender, occupation, etc.) I identify with?

Make a list of what you believe about these groups of people. (For example, if you're writing about a group of people you work with: "They are afraid of conflict.") Try not to edit. We'll be coming back to this list later in the book.

As the philosopher Jiddu Krishnamurti so beautifully and simply pointed out, "The constant assertion of belief is an indication of fear." Ask, where does fear live in relation to my conditioned beliefs, assumptions, and judgments?

Practice exploring how you know your conditioned judgments are "true." You can do this by considering the origin of this voice. Find out if this voice is a reflection of your direct experience or just a belief. You might journal about it or stay open to insight on the topic as you go about your day.

Insights arise in the mind of spaciousness.

Meditation practice returns us to spaciousness.

Inquire into the ways negative self-talk impacts your actions in relationship with others. How does it manifest in your body? What emotions arise? How does it become embodied? Acted out?

Pay particular attention to whether shame arises. If it does, name it. Flesh it out of its hiding place. What does the voice of shame say? Write down the self-talk. Inquire into the reality of it. Practice seeing, naming, and letting go of judgment as it arises. Inquire into truth. Return to inquiry. Again and again.

If you're moving through this book with others, share your findings with your group. Remember how important it is to do this in a container of CARE (page 18). To do so with great gentleness. It can be tender sometimes to recognize our negative self-talk, particularly when it feels very harsh. Please also remember you don't have to do this alone, and I encourage you to reach out for support if you're having a hard time or getting stuck.

What themes arise? Remember to be openly curious about each other's experience as well as your own. Allow the mind of curiosity, the way of inquiry, to be your guide.

And remember, we can't let go of what we can't see. Allow yourself to experience not being bound by limitation, judgment, constriction, or fear.

Freedom is available in every moment.

Chapter Five

Return to Unconditional Love

Embodying the Compassionate Mentor Within

Nothing I accept about myself can be
used against me to diminish me.

—Audre Lorde

I t wasn't a small mistake. It was one that affected over thirty retreatants and all the resident monks. I was the head cook at the time, and the retreat schedule was unforgiving. Not to mention, this was a *Zen* monastery. Everything happened on time. Exactly. Always.

Do you know those times when something feels so significantly "off" that later the details of the event get blurred? It's as though the mind out of self-protection simply deletes the specifics. I don't even recall the details of the meal. I'm fairly certain that I burned the soup and that the bread was so severely underdone folks might as well have been served firm, warm dough.

What *do* I remember clearly? Knowing that there was no backup meal. The monastery was at the end of a very long dirt road far from town. There was no plan B. I rang the meal bell knowing that what folks were about to eat was borderline inedible (depending on how hungry you were, I suppose). I remember feeling dizzy and being grateful for the silent environment. No one could approach me to complain. No one could yell at me. Of course, no one needed to. The inner critic had that job covered.

Thank goodness I'd been practicing. In fact, this kitchen debacle occurred during a time when I was intensely focused on seeing my own negative self-talk and systematically addressing it through unconditionally loving reassurances. This was a core practice at the monastery, and I had been in the thick of it. I was becoming increasingly accustomed to inquiring into the truth (better said, lack of truth) of the inner critic. I had been exploring where the voice came from, and its effects were not lost on me. I knew intimately the suffering that followed from indulging its stories. This compassionate practice of inquiry, my guiding light.

One of the many gifts of being on a silent retreat, and of monastic training, is that in the stillness the background of our experience comes to the forefront. Sometimes loudly! Not only had I been hearing how obtuse the voice of the inner critic could be but I was now keenly attuned to how cruel it was. I was clear that things were uttered within my mind that I would never, ever, under any circumstance, say to another human being.

Walking back to my hermitage in the dark that night, the voice was pronounced: clear, cutting, cruel. There was nothing to distract me from it. Nothing to drown it out with. I was either going to practice with it or it was going to draw me into hell. I recall pulling out all the stops. I began noticing each thought, questioning it, seeing it for what it was, and offering reassurances to myself that took steam out of the threats. Reassurances that didn't argue with the negative self-talk but instead offered pathways back to truth. Reassurances like "I love you no matter what."

I can't say that I did not suffer that night. I can say that I consciously chose the tools I'd been given rather than feeling completely victimized by the voice in my head. There wasn't anything miraculous about this choice. No bright lights. No rainbows. No euphoria. It was more like an oil change in a car. I was going through motions. It was methodical. I knew by that point in my training that practicing in this way was better than the hell of not practicing at all.

The miracle came the next morning. (Though I'm now clear that this was no miracle but the by-product of a systematic practice. This was no unexplainable event.) At any other point in my life I would have woken up to further internal beatings. I likely would have felt pummeled and done my best to practice with the voice of the inner critic. But this morning was different. Before even opening my eyes there was one clear, direct, embodied, and penetrating conscious thought:

I love you.
That opened the floodgates:

You did the best you could, that's plenty.
So you made a mistake. I doubt anyone died.
I see your goodness. Your goodness has nothing to do with performance or meeting a conditioned standard.
It will be tempting to feel embarrassed when you go to the main building today. I'm with you. If that experience arises, I'm with you. You are not alone.
There's nothing to be ashamed of. You don't have to try so hard all the time. I see you. It's okay.
People came here for a retreat experience, not gourmet food. You are here to be a monk, not a flawless chef. I adore you. I see you.

What felt miraculous about this experience was that it was completely unprompted. I didn't try to bring it about. I simply woke up to Love. I woke up and felt held, seen, worthy. I knew that no "mistake" could take this away. This Love was inherent. It was an experience, not just a thought; a deep knowing, not a theory. In that moment a profound truth about the Love that is at the core of existence became embodied.

UNCONDITIONALLY LOVING REASSURANCES

I've been teaching folks how to craft, practice, and embody unconditionally loving reassurances ever since. Why has this practice become so significant in my teaching? Because I have yet to meet another human being, teen or adult, who does not struggle with some form of the inner critic, and because I know firsthand that the way through this struggle is a practice that is accessible, grounded, and repeatable. It's a contemplative technology that can be relied upon.

It's important to me to distinguish unconditionally loving reassurances from the affirmations prominent in New Age thinking. Affirmations are something that affirm the ego. Imagine a woman staring at herself in the mirror saying, "You *are* pretty." Sentiments like this are simply the flip side of "You are ugly." Ultimately such affirmations are arguments and give validity to our most penetrating internal accusations. Most importantly, they keep in place a sense of separateness that is reduced to bouncing in between pretty and ugly. Fill in the blank with your own: smart/stupid, thin/fat, successful/unsuccessful.

Reassurances, on the other hand, are unconditional. They dissolve the isolation rather than buffer it. They cut to the truth.

Reassurances are *unconditional*.

"I love you no matter what" has nothing to do with whether the soup is burned or gets rave reviews. Reassurances penetrate to the certainty of our inherent worthiness. They are reflections of Love with a capital *L*, which isn't based on performance or conditioned standards. This Love is larger than the ego; it embraces everything—even the distortion of separation.

Most of us have had life experiences that can make this Love feel far away, out of reach, unrealistic, even childish. Yet we all long for it. We all long to know that we are okay, worthy, adequate to our life experience. We all long to know that we are lovable, that we belong, that there is nothing wrong with us.

In practice, we aren't loving ourselves into becoming who we want to be.

We're remembering that we are Love itself.

Pause.

Notice your self-talk.

Does any part of you believe this is just airy-fairy, woo-woo rubbish? Watch for any reactivity to the notion that you are not this conditioned mind. You are not this negative self-talk. In particular, notice any part of you that resists the notion that you are the very thing you long for.

Practice doesn't make perfect.

It reminds you of who you already are.

Most of us have been so indoctrinated into a culture of self-improvement that we've been habituated to question anything that suggests that our happiness isn't based on objects: the car we drive, the job we have, the people we're close to. In fact, most of us cling so firmly to the notion of improving and striving that we fear that were it not for that critical voice in our heads we'd lose motivation entirely.

The opposite is actually true.

It's the negative self-talk that kills our natural tendency to be engaged with life. It dampens our creative spirit. It negates our capacity for childlike, wondrous engagement with the world.

BEYOND POSITIVE OUTCOMES

Dr. Kristin Neff from the University of Texas at Austin, who founded the field of self-compassion research back in 2003, says that a primary barrier to self-compassion is fear of becoming complacent or losing one's edge. Research shows that self-compassion does not lead to complacency and wishy-washy-ness. In fact, it's just the opposite.

Several studies have shown that self-compassion supports motivation and positive change. In a 2016 study, Dr. Jia Wei Zhang and Dr. Serena Chen found that "self-compassion led to greater personal improvement, in part through heightened acceptance," and that focusing on self-compassion "spurs positive adjustment in the face of regrets."

Kristin also found that self-compassion has all the benefits of self-esteem without the downsides. Self-esteem can be built via positive self-talk, affirmations, and comparing ourselves to others or to conditioned standards. But the drawbacks to self-esteem include narcissism and aggression, prejudice, or anger toward those who threaten our self-worth, just to name a few.

Self-compassion is unconditional. It doesn't matter if we're meeting a conditioned standard or not. It requires no outside comparisons at all. Its reference point is Love itself.

Practicing self-compassion can lead to a plethora of positive outcomes. And experiencing these outcomes can ignite dedication to a particular practice of compassion, such as loving-kindness or unconditionally loving reassurances.

Ultimately, though, practicing self-compassion returns us to Love. This isn't about just positive outcomes. This is about liberation. In practice we're dismantling and moving beyond processes of separation and the perception of isolated selves. We aren't building confidence in a fragile sense of self.

This is about Love, the pinnacle of human experience—accessing it, touching it, feeling it, embodying it, living it.

For what is more powerful than Love?

Again, I'm not talking about a Hallmark card definition of love. Not "You give me what I want so I give you what you want." Not "You met my conditioned standards so you get my positive regard—until you don't."

When I speak of the power of Love, I'm pointing to what's beyond the limited, felt experience of "I." Also, to the power that comes from choosing this Love even when the conditioned habit to reach for a form of othering, such as identifying with the inner critic, is strong. Power comes from choosing this Love even in those moments when we feel most compelled to choose *separation* over *connection*.

Choosing Love leads to freedom.

Why? Because choosing Love comes *from* freedom.

When we choose Love consciously, we feel our own inherent freedom more fully. When we choose it collectively, the same thing is true. It's just bigger.

THE MENTOR WITHIN

For years I've facilitated experiences that invite folks to create and practice with an inner "compassionate mentor." Giving a voice to what is mostly deeply true—though is actually without words—is one way to change the habit pattern of self-doubt, self-criticism, self-hate. Again, when practicing with your inner compassionate mentor, you're not just enacting the opposite side of these things or arguing against them but rather shedding the veil of delusion.

I must underline: we're giving this form. There is no separate "inner mentor." It's a play of sorts; a way to embody something inherent, to give form to the formless.

This voice of compassion, this "inner mentor," is the antidote to your inner critic. It is a tool to help you move toward compassion for yourself, toward Love, and to open the possibility of direct experience. Direct experience of what? Direct experience of the truth of universal, unconditional love—to not simply practice it but to know it, feel it, be it.

If touching, feeling, knowing Love with a capital L feels inaccessible, don't worry. There's likely a fair reason it feels out of reach. It's possible to give Love a form, such as the inner mentor, and practice with it. In a sense, you might fake it till you make it. At some point you won't need the form anymore. It may feel mechanical at first, but it won't forever.

Picture the inner critic like a thick cloud. We aren't trying to shred the cloud. We aren't even trying to get rid of it. We're seeing it, inquiring into it, and consciously recognizing that this cloud doesn't change the sun. It may veil its light, but it doesn't diminish the sun itself. Reassurances support us in remembering the existence of the sun. They guide us home to the light in storms. They remind us of truth.

Reassurances don't create an alternate reality. They remind us of reality.

The reality that the sun remains, unaffected by weather patterns.
It shines—always.

KNOWING OURSELVES AS LOVE

In facilitating experiences involving the inner compassionate mentor, one might think that being reassured is the most important element. In truth, the most significant, most impactful, and often most healing experience is one of moving into the seat of the mentor, not the mentee. This shift creates a direct experience of Love through knowing yourself as that which can offer Love, that which can embody it, that which *is* it. What's most impactful is recognizing yourself as Love and moving through the world from here.

From this kind of knowing, even things that habitually appear to create separation are revealed as nothing but distortions. Negative self-talk is a perfect example. I can't count how many times I've facilitated an exercise where participants, through guided imagery, get in touch with the voice of the inner critic and then, following the meditation, expose—often for the first time—what the voice within claims, accuses, threatens.

All in front of others.

Out loud.

A naked reveal.

I only offer this group experience, with teens or adults, when the environment of CARE—confidentiality, acceptance, reverence, and empathy—has been established and always as an opt-in experience with other trauma-sensitive practices in place. When people are feeling safe, and with anonymity at first, the voice is revealed and exposed to them. I will speak to the importance of the container that facilitates these explorations further on. Given this safe container, here is something you can rely on with this exercise:

The notion that you are the only one with such negative self-talk will dissolve.

Isolation ends, even if just very briefly at first. I've witnessed this happen like clockwork. It's particularly poignant with teens: "You mean popular Suzi has the same negative self-talk as the guy who is labeled the class nerd, and they have the same voice in their head as me?! It even says many of the same things?!" It's almost always astonishing to folks. And, interestingly enough, the very thing that appeared to create separation suddenly is connecting. It's a visceral reminder of what we share—that our struggles aren't isolated, that *we* aren't isolated. The inner critic isn't personal and neither is Love.

Love is our birthright.

Love is the soil out of which we've grown. It is the water, the roots, the leaves. It has nothing to do with our personalities, yet it fully embraces our personalities. It has nothing to do with our accomplishments or failures, yet it rejects nothing. Love wants nothing, fears nothing. In practice, we are remembering this Love, not simply that it exists but that it's the heart of who we are. We cannot step outside it. We only think we can. We only falsely believe we can.

A Practice of Love

In chapter two I invited you, for the duration of this book, to allow yourself to explore whatever contemplative practice you feel most drawn to in a structured way. I acknowledged that might be as simple as ten minutes of meditation a day. I intentionally left it pretty open. I invite you now to commit to practicing daily with unconditionally loving reassurances for a defined period of time. Perhaps a week. Perhaps a month. Pick a time frame that feels doable to commit to. Let it be, if nothing else, an experiment.

Start with your lists of negative self-talk. Reread the phrases and pay attention to the themes. What comes up again and again? What are the core threats or wounds? What are the most cutting accusations by the inner critic?

Picture a young version of yourself being subjected to these judgmental statements and assessments. Read the phrases aloud and vividly imagine them being said to a child version of yourself. Practice compassionate inquiry. How do they land? What is the impact? Who does this part of you become in the face of these accusations? What happens? Step in their shoes. How does it *feel*?

Most importantly, what do you need to hear instead? What do you long to be told? To be reminded of? What do you long to know? The crafting of your reassurances comes from here. It's personal, specific to you—your fears, your bruises, your wounds.

Write down these phrases. Then practice offering these reassurances—daily. I'm serious—do it every day, throughout your day. When you are triggered, look for the unconditionally loving reassurance that addresses the part of you that's hurt. The phrases that speak straight to her, him, or them. Phrases that don't mince words. Practice reciting reassurances that remind this part of you that she is whole, worthy. That he belongs. That they are loved. Unconditionally.

Take notes. Which reassurances penetrate your heart the most? Which ones deeply land? What most profoundly affects your body, mind, energetic system? Toss what doesn't. Be sure to stay on the lookout for affirmations. Pay attention to when things suddenly feel conditional. Sometimes affirmations slide in disguised as reassurances. Keep coming back to what's unconditional. Repeat. Repeat.

Let it all be loving. Don't allow the inner critic to beat you up if you forget to practice. Simply return to the reassurances. Reassure the one who forgot. Return.

Every moment is an opportunity for compassion.
Return. In Love. Through Love. With Love.

If this feels hard, keep reading. We'll return to unconditionally loving reassurances in the next chapter.

LOVE AS THE RECOGNITION OF SHARED BEING

I'll never forget the first time I heard Rupert Spira, a nondual meditation teacher, say, "Love is the recognition of our shared being." It was the clearest, simplest, and most direct way to speak about Love I'd ever heard. The words penetrated deeply. Hearing them, I had the experience he spoke of. I felt and knew the truth of the statement in my bones and in my heart.

I thought about lovemaking. Of course we, as people, love lovemaking! For an instant, perhaps longer, the notion that you and I are separate falls away.

Apparently in French there is a popular phrase sometimes used to refer to orgasm: *la petite mort*, or "the little death." What dies? This notion, this belief, that I am separate from you. That we are simply two separate bodies touching, connecting, and that's it. That's all. The death of this idea, the falling away of this felt sense of isolation, reveals our shared being. It reveals that in fact we are more than what we've been conditioned to perceive and that what we are isn't a solitary experience at all. As we recognize this, we experience Love. We experience the very thing we all long for. We realize that "alone" is a figment of the imagination.

FROM THE PERSONAL TO THE COLLECTIVE

In working with teens, I've often been asked what, in my experience, is the core struggle that young people face. Were I to wildly generalize, I'd say a felt sense of isolation. So many of our conditioned behaviors are reactions to this manifestation of the story that we are separate. When we feel separate, we try to remedy the discomfort through connecting in unhealthy ways, checking out, or shutting down. The list of coping mechanisms is long.

This sense of isolation often stems from identifying with the inner critic. The inner critic holds firmly in place the delusion of a separate self. It keeps us from seeing the Love that is inherently at the core of our beings, of our collectively shared being.

When we feel isolated, we also believe in the delusion of "the other": *They can't understand my suffering; they have no idea what I'm going through. "They" are out there, and "I" am in here—alone.* This is where the systematic practice of othering whole groups of people begins. We easily slip from personal delusion to collective delusion. When Love is removed from the equation, isolation, separation, and othering are the results.

To put it simply, any process of othering is a process that does not reflect Love.

Most of the systems and structures created by dominant culture don't reflect the Love we're referring to in this chapter. In fact, they reinforce "other." This is because they arose out of a primary distorted belief of "other."

BEYOND OTHERING

Practicing with the inner compassionate mentor collectively requires a safe container. Though safety can never be guaranteed, this container must still be lovingly cultivated. It took Peace in Schools conscious, sometimes painful work and learning to craft the type of space for teens to inquire together about their deepest conditioning. And the learning is never finished.

I intimately know the power of a practice of Love. It's deeply transformational. I'm enlivened by what happens when such practices are applied collectively. I've seen it consistently in Peace in Schools. This transformation looks like more acceptance, open and caring communication, a deepened ability to trust oneself and others. Transformation ripples from the students in the classes to the school at large. It touches parents and the community. This is the type of collective transformation that I believe can create shifts in human consciousness. And the root of it all? Love.

Consider the average classroom for a moment. (The classroom is just one place we could direct our attention, by the way. We could focus on our prison system, immigration policies, or health-care systems, just to name a few more areas deserving of loving attention.)

In a one-size-fits-all approach to education, many classrooms don't take into account who is in the room or their range of experiences that might make the difference between feeling safe and feeling deeply isolated. For such classrooms to not be responsive to the trauma that might be present is common. Sometimes this trauma is overlooked entirely.

From my perspective, one of the most significant affects of trauma is an experience of feeling othered, whether subtly or dramatically. An experience of perceiving that we are outside Love, cut off from our shared being. Dr. Gabor Maté, a Hungarian Canadian physician who focuses on trauma, has expanded my understanding of trauma by pointing out that it's not the difficult experiences in our lives that are the issue. The real issue arises when we feel alone with what has happened to us.

What does it mean to be responsive to trauma? To be trauma-sensitive? Dr. David Treleaven, the author of *Trauma-Sensitive Mindfulness*, states, "Trauma-sensitive means that we're aware of the unique needs of people struggling with trauma. We're equipped to recognize trauma symptoms, respond skillfully, and prevent retraumatization in our work." To do this, we must direct our attention to what we now understand about trauma and how the earliest traumas of our lives can affect us for the entire span of our existence.

ADVERSE CHILDHOOD EXPERIENCES

Adverse childhood experiences (often referred to as ACEs) are potentially traumatic events primarily arising from disruptions in a child's felt sense of safety and nurturance with caregivers and people they should be able to trust. ACEs include emotional, physical, or sexual abuse, physical or emotional neglect, and loss of a caregiver due to death, divorce, or incarceration. It is sobering to learn that two-thirds of US adults have experienced at least one ACE, and research using the National Survey of Child Health (NSCH) reports that about 50 percent of all US children today have been exposed to at least one ACE. Higher rates are observed for low-income children of color, older children, and children with chronic conditions or special health-care needs.

When not buffered through nurturing and safe connection and skills to manage the stress response, ACEs can lead to toxic levels of stress. Such toxic stress negatively impacts brain development, endocrine/hormone and immune systems' health, and a wide array of social and mental health capacities. ACEs demonstrate a "dose response" effect with strong validation for using a cumulative ACEs score and an array of poor health outcomes both early and across life, including mental health problems, poor social support, heart disease, substance abuse, and much more. The data is clear, says Dr. Christina Bethell, director of the Child and Adolescent Health Measurement Initiative in an interview with ACES Too High News:

> "If more prevention, trauma-healing, and resiliency training programs aren't provided for children who have experienced trauma, and if our educational, juvenile justice, mental health, and medical systems are not changed to stop ignoring or retraumatizing already traumatized children, many of the nation's children will continue to suffer avoidable physical, mental, emotional, and social health problems. Not only will their lives be more difficult, but the nation's already high health-care costs and epidemic levels of mental health problems will soar even higher."

Over twenty years ago, the authors of the original ACEs study, Dr. Vincent J. Felitti and Dr. Robert Anda, calculated that the overall costs of ACEs "exceeded those of cancer or heart disease and that eradicating child abuse in America would reduce the overall rate of depression by more than half, alcoholism by two-thirds, and suicide, [intravenous] drug use, and domestic violence by three-quarters. It would have a dramatic effect on workplace performance and vastly decrease the need for incarceration."

A recent study by Dr. Bethell showed 3.8 times higher rates of adult depression for adults with four or more ACEs and who also lacked "Positive Childhood Experiences" (PCEs) than for those with higher ACEs but who also had higher PCEs. PCEs include having at least one adult you can share feelings with, feeling supported by friends, and a sense of belonging in school or the community.

Now, a quarter century later, ACEs and their antidotes found in contemplative and relational health practices are being recognized as a public health priority. It's becoming clearer to us collectively that ACEs, mindfulness, healthy human development, and social justice are deeply entwined, as leaders in the field, such as the neuroscientist Dr. Sará King, have outlined in the framework she calls "the Science of Social Justice." She explains that social justice and well-being are inextricably linked and that "in particular, contemplative practices that do not directly address the relationship between trauma and identity run the risk of doing the greatest harm in diverse populations . . . because the experience and impact of oppression is an embodied experience. The way people experience their identities in society will have great bearing on whether they are discriminated against, and all forms of discrimination are traumatic.

"If we are to direct our awareness toward our embodied experience with love, compassion, and forgiveness, we must include the parts of ourselves that suffer in relationship to our identities as well."

As I've worked with young people, it's become very clear to me that there's tremendous fallout from not addressing, not seeing, or ignoring adverse childhood experiences. A by-product of not addressing trauma is more suffering. Further suffering occurs as we create, participate in, and maintain systems that don't address it.

Tremendous work is being done in our world by many who aim to prevent adverse childhood experiences. My focus has been on addressing feelings of being othered and alone that accompany such experiences; on collectively applying practices of Love in cases where Love has been forgotten. One might question whether in an enlightened society, where all live in alignment with this Love, would ACEs even arise at all? Would we harm each other in the ways that we have become so accustomed to? While we dive into such questions, I wonder:

What is possible for us collectively when Love is our shared focus, *regardless* of circumstances? We do not need to wait for a society or a future that does not yet exist in order to know Love collectively.

We create what is possible *now*.

THE RELIEF OF SEEING, THE RELIEF OF A COLLECTIVE

When I began Peace in Schools I did not have a true understanding of what a trauma-sensitive and culturally responsive classroom was. In my personal practice I have experienced deep relief when I've seen how and where the ego is manifesting and recognized the distortion, thus opening the opportunity to let go. In the same way, it has been relieving to see how and where my own conditioning reflects and maintains dominant culture. Often it's in ways I don't see—until I do. And if there's one thing practice has allowed me to get really clear about, it's that we can't let go of what we can't see, and that this kind of letting go, though it can have a certain intensity to it, is infused with compassion.

Many of the tools I brought into the classroom from my practice were naturally trauma-sensitive, but I had little understanding of how. Learning the how has been important, as this understanding has provided an opportunity for repeatability and consistency. There's a science behind what allows a tool and a practice to be widely accessible, sensitive, responsive. Tapping into this science has required me to see my own conditioned default settings, to recognize my own conditioned assumptions. Many of them relating to my positionality and to the collective conditioning I've been swimming in my whole life.

When I began Peace in Schools I didn't have any experiential understanding around the importance of leadership in the classroom that reflected the diverse populations of students we were serving. I didn't know—until I did—how vital it would be to tailor the curricula to be accessible to students from different cultures and to seek support from others in doing so.

It's been a relief to be a student in this arena. To shed—within the context of a collective—some of my own myopic collective conditioning and to maintain this direction, this learning, with the many employees and partners who have made invaluable contributions to the organization. My own practice, and the organization at large, has been strengthened as we evolved from a few white teachers with mindfulness expertise to a more diverse organization with different viewpoints, different societal seats, and various backgrounds and identities.

My own learning and the advancement of our curriculum couldn't have occurred without this collective expertise and contribution. Part of my invaluable dismantling, the undoing of limiting beliefs and assumptions, has been shedding conditioning that would suggest that I should be able to do X on my own. Through collective wisdom, we've become more fully able to meet the collective we serve. It's often been humbling learning, and yet it's also been a relief.

EXPRESSIONS OF LOVE

I've come to experience a trauma-sensitive and culturally responsive classroom as an expression of Love. It's a classroom in which each person is seen. Race, identity, and cultural background are valued and embraced. Students have voice. Structures are clear so everyone has the opportunity to feel safe—as safe as possible given that we can never guarantee complete safety.

Any context, group, or learning environment that revolves around truly seeing each other is one that is born of and centers around Love. This is paramount for our collective healing. How can we heal within systems that are unjust? Systems that embody inequity? Systems that reflect a felt sense of separation rather than our shared being?

It's not that it's not possible for these more loving systems to exist, for at the end of the day our ultimate remembrance is the recognition that we are that which is unbreakable, already healed, whole. The very fact that discussions of trauma, its impacts, and its solutions are becoming more prevalent and that programs like Peace in Schools exist and thrive attest that new systems are indeed possible.

That being said, the remembrance that we are whole might feel virtually impossible inside a system that only reflects our distorted sense of separation. In other words, it may be easier for a white male businessperson to feel that he belongs in a work environment that values, praises, and pays him well. Perhaps he gets paid more than his female or trans colleagues who are doing the exact same job or bringing as much value. On the most absolute level, all parties have the same shared being, and in a system that doesn't honor this truth, a system that was created out of the distortion of separation, those who are not part of dominant culture are marginalized. We are all impacted within processes of marginalization. No one is free in such processes, including the dominant culture itself.

Marginalization is a process of othering. Processes of othering always arise from distortion, delusion, a misunderstanding of who and what we actually are.

Rhonda Magee, the author of *The Inner Work of Racial Justice: Healing Ourselves and Transforming Our Communities Through Mindfulness*, has done groundbreaking work in the field of integrating mindfulness into higher education, law, and social change. She invites us to explore the many ways our awareness practice can help us understand the operation of race, racism, and other forms of bigotry and bias in our lives and institutions more effectively, and to move from color blindness to what she calls "ColorInsight."

I've also been influenced by the innovative work of Ruth King, an insight meditation teacher and the author of *Mindful of Race: Transforming Racism from the Inside Out*. Her Mindful of Race Institute advances racial awareness and leadership through mindfulness-based education and group development programs. She teaches that "understanding how we have been conditioned as racial beings to relate to others and ourselves is fundamental to transforming racism and creating cultures of care."

I experience these powerful leaders as pioneers in the movement for collective liberation. For we don't merely need individual clarity regarding these topics. For true structural change, we need collective clarity.

COLLECTIVE PROCESS MATTERS
In the Mindful Studies classes offered by Peace in Schools, students are seen. Their identities are valued. (And valuing identity is not the same thing as assuming that you are limited to identity, that your positionality is the whole of you.) In each class, all voices are invited into the room—and it's always just an invitation. If someone doesn't wish to share, that is honored.

It's also always been important to me and to Peace in Schools that mindfulness is optional and voluntary. I don't believe anyone should be forced to learn mindfulness practice. Too often I've seen cases where an experience of mindfulness is required, and it ends up being another tool in the hands of dominant culture, a way to silence children—particularly those labeled "unruly"; particularly those who are marginalized.

It's not *what* you teach so much as *how* you teach it. The entire environment surrounding what is offered. Process matters.

Our students are always in choice, choosing to not participate in a guided imagery that may trigger trauma, or not making physical contact in an exercise that invites touch. In meditation, students have a choice to have their eyes open or closed, or the choice to not enroll in the class at all. Students, as much as we can make it possible, have options and they are empowered to choose.

This is not merely a trauma-sensitive approach. This is a loving and mindful approach that shows students they can be trusted to listen to themselves, to tune in, to see what is needed, to be empowered to respond. This approach trusts that we are adequate to our life experience and embodying this truth is transformational for both student and teacher.

COLLECTIVE CONTEXT MATTERS

Structures that are truly loving are not one size fits all. What's loving—what leads to an experience of freedom for all—is the creation of structures that reflect the truth of our shared being. They are responsive to what's needed *now*—in this moment, in this time.

For true learning to happen, it's important to be sensitive to the environment or context in which the learning is happening, to lovingly craft it, to tend to it. Environments that reflect our inherent belonging are born of and reflective of Love. We know the result of environments that are not lovingly crafted. They reflect and amplify the distortion of dominant culture. I, unfortunately, have participated in these environments. Many of us have without realizing it, and that's a significant part of the issue.

In skillfully crafted contexts, everyone is given space to fully express themselves, all needs are recognized, and varied life experiences are reflected back. In this way, traumas can be lovingly met and embraced. In this way, a direct experience of Love can be truly accessible to all.

COLLECTIVE EXPERIENCE OF LOVE

I no longer wish to live inside social and economic structures designed to respect and create safety and opportunity for some groups while systematically disregarding others. Yet these structures live within me. They live within all of us. They are part of us, ingrained within our wood.

We have been conditioned to think of trauma as an individual tragedy instead of an event that's interconnected with a larger system of domination that shapes our world. For us to have a system—a classroom, a prison, a health-care system, a society—free of processes of othering, we must clearly recognize systems born of the mind of separation and discern how they operate.

Seeing the delusion of negative self-talk clearly, then having tools that support us in returning to and remembering Love, leads to liberation.

Seeing the delusion of othering clearly, then having tools and practices to undo the structures and collective forms that are born out of this distortion, allows us to create new collective forms that are reflections of truth.

Through new forms we more freely return to a collective experience of Love.

This is true of any distorted views that lead to domination. As the writer and activist bell hooks reminds us, "The practice of love is the most powerful antidote to the politics of domination."

You can only dominate something you see as other than you: domination of the earth, domination over women in the structure of patriarchy, domination of people with disabilities, domination of children. Domination arises out of othering but wears a dirtier outfit. All distortions have the potential to lead to domination. All distortions represent a felt sense of separateness taking form.

We must begin by seeing the distortion. Then we can be creative, forming pathways that return us to Love, to the truth of our shared being. In the same way that at the monastery I learned that I could consciously choose the tools I'd been given rather than feeling completely victimized by the voice in my head, we can collectively turn to the remembrance of the truth of our shared being. As a practice, we can return.

The path to truth *is* Love.

What truth is found?

Love.

Collective Practice: Expressing Love

Compassion is the inevitable consequence of the recognition of our shared being.

Compassion arises out of our innate felt sense of wholeness and oneness.

Either with your group or on your own, create an experience of a collective expression of compassion. Some way to remind yourself and others of the truth of our shared being. Something that goes against the dominant paradigm that reinforces othering. Remember, this isn't just about positive outcomes. This is about freedom.

Let the intention be to help yourself and others remember the truth of unconditional love. Create something from there.

A playful example: In our Peace in Schools curriculum we have a day when students take the reassurances they've been working with, write them up, and distribute them throughout the school in the form of "Love Notes." Phrases like "I love you, keep going" and "I know your inherent goodness" end up taped to lockers, walls, doors. Statements like "Your beauty is not dependent on your appearance" frame bathroom mirrors.

For a short period of time, schools are flooded with collective expressions of Love. While it's powerful for students not enrolled in the class to be met with such expressions, the most palpable power is often to be found in the experience of the messenger, the creator of the phrases, the one whose job it is to shout from the rooftops that everything is going to be okay and that we are in this together. It is particularly powerful to do this as a group.

Get creative. Be playful. You might include song, dance, poetry. There's no right way to do this. Just keep coming back to your intention. Keep coming back to Love.

Bonus assignment: Write a letter to yourself in response to the words of the inner critic. First, on one piece of paper, explain what it feels like to hear these words, the physical responses you had when you read them back, the memories they brought up.

Then, on a separate piece of paper, write a letter as if you were someone responding to this from a place of care. Write unconditionally to the person who is suffering. Tell them what you want them to hear and know. Tell them the truth. Firmly step into the mentor role. Embody the Love that is here in every moment. Express the Love that is ever-present.

Go nuts. Go wild. Be playful or be serious. Share or don't share. Trust yourself. This will become a love letter to yourself, and you can't do this wrong.

Chapter Six

Return to Belonging

Unpacking Our Survival Strategies

Through intimacy and imagination we can consciously
create the world we live in together. Through belonging,
we connect to ourselves, each other, and everything
and, ultimately, remember what we are. We are freedom.
We are joy. We are love. We belong.

—Sebene Selassie

P aulus could, at a minimum, be described as quirky, though some would say he was wildly eccentric. No cell phone. No email account. Making clay pinch pots that he returned to the earth instead of firing and selling, Paulus was a pipe-smoking, barefoot-in-summer-grass, NPR-loving, committed-to-slow-and-savor hermit of sorts. He was a queer artist living the simplest life I'd ever touched—or, better said, that ever touched me.

But Paulus did more than live differently. Paulus revealed new worlds. This world revolved around a profound love of craft, but not just any craft. Craft that centered around connection, belonging, reverence for the earth, and beauty. Craft that was about process over product. The *how*, not the *what*.

When I first met Paulus Berensohn, I was sixteen with a fresh-off-the-press driver's license and a world that could still be packed into my knapsack. I knew nothing of his book *Finding One's Way with Clay*. I knew nothing of his work that furthered the notion that creativity is universal. I knew nothing of the thousands of lives he'd touched through his teachings. To me, he was my fairy godfather (a title he coined and lived into with grace), and he was magic.

His house was full of precious handmade objects, altars, color, music, and stillness. It was here he introduced me to journal making, working with clay, poetry, qigong, and so much more. Spending time with Paulus was like entering an alternate reality. Everything he created and did felt infused with sacredness. His life was a prayer, a poem, a hymn.

Of all the influences he had on my life, what of this new world affected me most? His deep engagement with life and the uplifting joy of his unconditional love. With Paulus, anything felt possible. In experiencing Love, that's how it goes.

In unconditional love, possibility is born. There it sings.

In unconditional love, possibility thrives.

I was at a Gen X Dharma Teachers gathering in the middle-of-nowhere Colorado when I intuited he was dying. A phone call confirmed it. Expectant and heartbroken, I was in the middle-of-nowhere North Carolina by the next day.

As I entered his post-stroke hospital room, I found him in awe. Completely consumed in wonder. Reciting poems without words. Being moved by music I couldn't hear. This wasn't my first experience being with someone who had begun the process of transitioning from this earthly realm, but I had never seen anything like it. Paulus didn't say he had a stroke. He said, "I've been stroked by life!" Eyes open, in every sense of it, Paulus had been stroked by life—and by Love, by awe. He was awake.

I spent the last week of his life with him, over thirty years after our first meeting, and his engagement with life shone more brightly than ever. I will forever be moved by the lack of resistance he displayed as he explored various realms of consciousness with ease and grace. He taught me, even from his deathbed, without words. He taught me about patience and acceptance. Most profoundly, Paulus taught me about Love.

SURVIVAL STRATEGIES

In so many cases, how we do anything is how we do everything. For many of us, as death calls, we can be found clamoring, clawing, clinging to what we know. Grabbing what we deem as "mine." Grasping for what we believe we deserve. Gripping the paper doll of identity. This, of course, is not required.

We are deeply habituated to fear death. Our reaction to death can be a mirror for how we face the challenges of our lives. Do we open? Or do we turn away in moments of difficulty? When love feels scarce—when we feel cut off from our very being—how are we conditioned to survive our lives?

Survival strategies are compensations for the felt sense of separation, the perception of falling from grace, when love feels out of reach or an overall belief that we are lacking takes hold. They are the strategies we develop, the actions we take to not only move away from the pain of a felt sense of separation but also to attempt to return to wholeness. We think we need to *do* something to get love because we have falsely believed that Love is not inherent. That we must *do* in order to belong.

Survival strategies keep in place the felt experience that we are a separate self. There is little thriving here. Plenty of surviving, however. These strategies—thoughts, beliefs, and actions—offer us just enough to keep our head above water as we navigate the circumstances of our lives. Survival strategies arise on behalf of the ego, and much is woven into their fabric. The inner critic, personal and collective conditioning, our traumas—all become part of the tapestry of who we mistakenly assume ourselves to be.

Seeing these strategies for what they are can create pathways for returning, for remembrance, for releasing into inherent belonging—into the heart of who we are.

As Paulus moved toward his death, he displayed an easeful divestment. Gently and with great openness, he shed layers of himself that were not fundamental to his being. When moving through life, he left no stone unturned. Bringing curiosity and inquiry to his experience was his way. As he moved toward death, this continued to be so. He took his time. He listened. He opened toward rather than shrinking away. He didn't rely on survival strategies. Even in death, Paulus chose wonder. He chose Love.

RECOGNIZING SURVIVAL STRATEGIES

As a monastic, I learned to recognize survival strategies. This allowed me to clearly see the ways I learned to keep my sense of self intact in times when my inner critic was at its worst, when I felt isolated, when I felt my survival was threatened—not physically threatened but existentially; when belonging felt inaccessible. This seeing, the recognition of how I survived my life, has been an invaluable contemplative technology for me.

When our survival strategies are revealed, we see clearly that these strategies are actually *keeping* us from wholeness, from thriving. They promise return to what is inherent, but they cannot deliver.

Thriving comes when we are seated firmly in ourselves, when we recognize our inherent wholeness, when we feel and know our inherent belonging.

To use one of my own survival strategies as an example: I learned at a young age that if I did things well, if I got things "right" (according to the conditioned standard around me, of course), I would receive favorable attention. That lens made getting things "wrong" more and more unbearable. That's not simply because I was granted positive attention as I did things well, but also because I perceived disdain, scorn, and rejection as the result of *not* doing things well. Somewhere along the way, "well" slid into a conditioned vision of "perfection" and "failure" became the final nail in the coffin. Not doing things perfectly revealed my innate unworthiness, my inherent wrongness. Again, all this is according to a conditioned standard.

Seeing how we have survived our lives is important because it shows us that maintaining our survival strategies is an inside job. In terms of our liberation, it can be paramount to see this and fully understand how survival strategies—while perhaps sparked by and validated through external events and circumstances—actually live within. They arise out of distortion and maintain distortion from the inside out.

The good news about this?

We cannot control the circumstances and events of our lives.

We *can* have stewardship over our interpretation and therefore our experience.

Consider the Chinese Taoist philosopher Chuang Tzu's empty boat:

If a man is crossing a river
And an empty boat collides with his own skiff,
Even though he be a bad-tempered man
He will not become very angry.
But if he sees a man in the boat,
He will shout at him to steer clear.
If the shout is not heard, he will shout again,
And yet again, and begin cursing.
And all because there is somebody in the boat.
Yet if the boat were empty.
He would not be shouting, and not angry.

If you can empty your own boat
Crossing the river of the world,
No one will oppose you,
No one will seek to harm you.

When we are identified with a conditioned survival strategy, our boat is full. Whether identified with the "perfectionist" in an attempt to know our inherent goodness, or the "helper" we think will make us lovable, or the "achiever" that will validate our worthiness, such strategies have one thing in common: they begin with the distorted view that we are *not already* fundamentally good or right, inherently lovable, and intrinsically worthy.

Each survival strategy is an expression of a limited mental perspective on reality. From this perspective what's inherent has been veiled. The labels "perfectionist," "helper," "achiever" are from the model of the Enneagram, a tool I've found to be particularly powerful for personal and collective transformation. The Enneagram is a useful framework of nine distinct strategies for relating to the self, others, and the world, but survival strategies can take countless forms.

Imagine that if, as a child, you were reprimanded for having needs. You might have learned to survive by showing others and the world that you can take care of yourself. You're self-sufficient and self-reliant. Perhaps, though, you became hyper-independent, at all costs.

Or perhaps you were raised in a "Don't be a crybaby!" environment and you had nowhere to bring your upset. Little opportunity to be seen and held. You might have learned that you need to be tough, to hide your emotions, to push forward no matter your internal experience.

A question for you to reflect upon:

Who did you become in order to survive your life?

As with everything in this book, there's no right or wrong answer here. If you consider the experience of presence, being fully here and now, as being an empty boat, ask: Who did you become in order to manage the stress of life? What form filled the boat? Think of this form (or forms—for certainly there can be more than one) as compensations, forms that came into being as you felt you lost something that is, in fact, inherent.

The same is true of survival strategies. The original impulse to engage in these strategies arises out of our deep longing to connect with what's most primary and most fundamental—our very being. The distortion that we are separate fuels the strategy. We feel cut off. We try to reconnect.

The original delusion is that, on a fundamental level, *we do not belong*.
We cannot experience our inherent freedom and be identified with this
distortion at the same time.

UNMET NEEDS

Beneath every survival strategy lies an unmet need. Consider when you were a child. What kinds of unmet needs were present? And what behaviors did you engage in out of an attempt to meet those needs? Do any of these behaviors continue today?

Some unmet needs that people I've worked with have articulated over the years:

To feel loved
To be accepted
To know that I'm worthy
To be seen and valued
To belong

Take some time to add your own. What's important to recognize about survival strategies is that they are not *you*. Just as you are not your thoughts. Just as you are not your negative self-talk. You are *not* your survival strategies.

In our original training manual for teachers at Peace in Schools, we made this essential clarification:

"This is not a free pass for unjust, harmful, racist, etc. behavior. For example, 'I did that harmful thing but that's not who I am so I'm off the hook.' This just re-creates and reproduces suffering and violence; this is another breach in the recognition of our shared being. The purpose of recognizing that we are not our conditioning is to empower us to bring our actions in alignment with who we authentically are; to have our actions embody the recognition of our shared being and inherent interconnection."

What's also important to recognize is that we're habituated to try to meet our unmet needs through external sources. It's a game changer when you realize you can meet your own unmet needs—that the healing happens within.

COPING MECHANISMS

Over the years, I've found it helpful to distinguish between survival strategies and coping mechanisms. Think of survival strategies as overarching strategies that we apply in a variety of contexts. They all have the same root: feeling cast out of wholeness with a longing to return, to belong. Our attempts to return have different flavors, but the root is always the same. All cases involve seeking and striving, trying to fix, trying to control, fearing failure.

I frame coping mechanisms as behaviors to deal with particular circumstances, stress, or trauma in the moment. They are ways to deal with the pressure that arises as you engage in a survival strategy. For engaging survival strategies always entails a certain pressure. And that pressure builds. And builds.

There are supportive ways of dealing with this pressure, and there are less supportive ways. Distinguishing between them can be helpful. Wholesome ways of dealing with stress—what is known as *approach coping*—are things that make you feel more connected to life and lead to your overall well-being. Think meditating, walking in nature, or making art versus things that reinforce the cycle of separation and leave you feeling worse in the long run: eating an entire bag of chips, consuming alcohol mindlessly to self-medicate, overworking. These behaviors are known as *avoidance coping*. Practicing compassion and accessing Love and presence in tough times lead toward more wholesome coping.

Remember:

It's not what. It's how.

It's about process, not content.

For example, going for a run can be a healthy way to step back from the content of your life, to drop into presence, to move energy through your body. Going for a run can also be a way to avoid dealing with what needs tending to. Or perhaps it's linked to a diet plan that promises to "finally make you the right person." Perhaps you engage exercise in an obsessive way that arises out of, and leads to, further suffering. This is a helpful and important place for inquiry.

Imagine working really hard to accomplish a lot of things to prove that you are worthy. (Perhaps that's not a stretch.) Stress builds. And builds. As this stress builds, what do you do to release it? What behaviors do you engage in? Do they work to meet the unmet need or do they simply serve to reinforce your survival strategies? And then, here comes the fun part. Drumroll . . .

The inner critic is born.

BIRTH OF THE JUDGE

Take a moment to visualize a survival strategy from your life. Pick something juicy, a place you really get stuck. Choose somewhere you habitually abandon yourself or forget presence; a place you find yourself grasping, gripping, clinging, clenching. I'll use my own life as an example.

Scene: Curtains draw back and I'm center stage (where we always are when identified with the ego), trying to get everything just right. A retreat that I'm leading is quickly approaching and I want to be sure everything is perfect. In my tunnel vision, I fixate on perfection. I knock over the set and other people as I buzz about. Nothing slows me down.

My self-talk soliloquy: *Everything is riding on this. I have to get it just right. What if people don't like it? I need to work harder. There's not enough time. I should be doing better.*

In this particular production, let's say I notice the self-talk. That noticing prompts me to pause, to take a breath. Whew. To remember presence. To return to my body, heart, and mind. I consciously decide to slow down. To take a bath after work rather than work some more. To remember that I am not my occupation. To relax and to trust.

What do you think happens next?
(Seriously, though. Ask yourself this question before reading on.)

Enter stage right, the inner critic, loudly, harshly: *I can't believe you are taking a bath right now! You are so self-indulgent. You know you don't have time for this, right?! People are going to think what you've created is a mess! You'll be unprepared. You need to get your shit together!*

Does this sound familiar? (Or am I revealing too much about myself here?)

Were Choose Your Own Adventure books part of your childhood? I adored them. We can choose our own inner adventure.

Next, imagine . . .

Scene: Two closed doors. Behind door A our story is propelled down the road of suffering. With the entrance of "the judge," I get identified with the small part of me who believes every accusation, and I act accordingly. I jump back into the fray. I work harder. I push. I forget myself and hop to it like my shoes are on fire. Remember, self-hate is the glue that keeps the conditioning—and the survival strategy—in place. The sun sets as I ride off, consumed by the cycle. Believing that I'm broken. Longing for wholeness. Fearing I don't belong yet yearning to . . .

Curtains close. Scene.

What's behind door B?

Enter stage left, the unconditionally loving mentor within: *People are coming on this retreat to remember presence. Your primary job is to remember presence. You can let go of this fixation around things needing to be perfect. I love you no matter what happens. I see you. I got you. You are not alone in this.*

I stand on my own two feet. I slow down, embodying presence as I move through my tasks, which allows them to happen with ease. Unbound by time. Remembering my inherent wholeness. In the spaciousness, insights arise regarding small ways to reveal beauty in the process. Urgency and self-consciousness dissolve. I kneel at the altar to arrange brightly colored dahlias for the retreatants who are on the way. I name an intention for our precious time together and whisper a prayer: "May I be of service"...

Curtains close. Scene.

Which adventure do you tend to choose? Which adventure would you like to choose?

As a way of getting a quick sense of what threshold we've walked through (at the risk of being dualistic for the sake of simplicity and understanding), we can always ask:

Is this leading toward suffering? Or away from it?

Is this a movement toward fear? Or Love?

Am I surviving? Am I thriving?

Once we recognize the coping mechanisms and the negative self-talk at play, our patterns can begin to change. When we turn our attention *away* from the inner critic and self-judgment, we can surrender our attention to the unmet need. We can choose which door to walk through. We can rewrite habit's script.

Through the practice of offering reassurance and unconditional love, we can take care of our unmet needs. This is how true healing occurs.

The judge, or inner critic, is born to ensure you enact the survival strategy. For the judge, it's truly a matter of survival. Anytime you step out of the assigned role of being X, the judge is there to say, "You can't be that way." The judge is there to put you back in line. The underlying message or theme that's always present with the inner critic is, "What is wrong with you?" Survival strategies are attempts to "fix the problem."

There is nothing inherently bad or wrong about the inner critic. The judge is simply doing its job, from its distorted view of reality, to help you survive. Again, the judge was born to aid you in surviving your life, *according to* this conditioned system. It's the judge's job to make sure your strategy stays in place so you can survive difficult circumstances. We can recognize, perhaps even appreciate, how it has done that for us.

However, what's important to notice is that while we're caught in any survival strategy, the underlying need *isn't actually being met*.

The survival strategy cannot meet the unmet need. Ever.

Not possible.

Survival simply leads to more survival. It cannot lead to thriving. It does not resolve the tension of perceiving ourselves as separate. In surviving we miss the silent poetry that is forever being sung. We are deaf to what the Quakers call "the still small voice within." We lose sight of our opportunity to rest in our very being.

An example: one of my survival strategies has deep roots in a fear of being wrong—not just having some here or there actions that are wrong, but a conditioned belief that my very being is wrong. When identified with this conditioning, I fervently strive to be right. If you asked my husband about it, he'd say, "All. The. Time." What have I learned about survival strategies such as this one over the years?

You cannot cling to your survival strategy and be free at the same time.

It's not possible.

IDENTIFYING WITH THE INNER CRITIC AND THE UNMET NEED SIMULTANEOUSLY

When the inner critic is on the stage, one of the painful things, besides just getting an internal beating, is that we identify with the inner critic *and* the unmet need at the same time. This is where it gets interesting. Can you think of a time when your unmet need was love or comfort? On the one hand, you're identified with the experience of "I need some love. I need some comfort." But on the other hand, in the very next instant, you're identified with "But I can't show my emotions. I need to be strong, I need to be independent." We thrash back and forth between these two places. This creates pain. This leads toward suffering. Can you relate?

Check out this chart.

MAP OF HEALING

Unmet Need	Survival Strategy	Inner Critic	Compassionate Mentor
When we're stuck in our survival strategy, there is an unmet need present.	*Who we decided we needed to be to survive our lives.*	*When we begin to stray from our survival strategies, the voice of the judge keeps our survival strategy in place.*	*The mentor offers an unconditional reassurance that addresses the unmet need.*
Comfort, safety	Be independent: "The Independent One."	"Don't be a baby." "They wouldn't help you even if you asked."	"You don't have to do this alone. It's okay to ask for help sometimes."
Acceptance, love	Be tough, no emotions: "The Tough One."	"You can't cry. They will see how weak you are." "What's wrong with you? Suck it up!"	"Your feelings are valid. It's okay to feel how you're feeling. I love and accept you as you are."

Security, peace	Be positive: "The Positive One."	"Just be positive! Why are you being so negative? People aren't going to want to be around you."	"I love you no matter what. It's okay to feel negative sometimes; there's nothing wrong with you."
Acceptance, to have life be about more than winning and losing	Be perfect: "The One Who Always Gets It Right."	"You failed again!" "Loser."	"Life isn't about winning and losing. It's okay. You don't have to get everything right all the time."

I'll never forget the day I was showing this chart, in my chicken-scratch whiteboard scribble, to a new group of teens. I was at McDaniel High School. Spring light was streaming through the windows. The students were illuminated and deeply engaged. In discussion with them, I "got it"—this chart was missing one thing: a giant red arrow.

With a dramatic, sweeping gesture, I drew a line from the reassurances column to the unmet needs column. The chart was now complete. I "got it" that these specific reassurances were the very reassurances that could finally meet the particular needs that were never met when we were children—unmet needs that still surface, cry out, beg for attention. This movement is where and how the healing occurs.

It is through compassion that our unmet needs are finally resolved.

When we learn to bring this kind of loving attention to our needs, it releases us from our survival strategies, which all began because *the need wasn't met in the first place*. We are divested from the activity of the conditioned mind. The attention is liberated to rest in being. And in Love.

A Practice: Accessing Unconditional Reassurances

Take time to create your own version of this chart in your CARE journal. The beautiful thing about this as a process is that as you get clear about what the unmet need is, what the survival strategy is, and how the inner critic keeps it in place, you have gathered information about what reassurances are called for so the unmet need can finally be met. The wound gets tended to in a direct way. Healing happens in this practice of reassurance, helping to put to rest foundational distortions that lead us to perceive that we are separate.

We can be really thoughtful about the reassurances we choose to offer ourselves—remember, these statements are truly *unconditional.* Notice how different this feels:

"It's okay to ask for help."

Compared to:

"You should ask for help."

The latter simply sets another conditioned standard: "If I don't ask for help now, I've done something wrong." As you explore this, take your time and ask, "Does this reassurance *feel* unconditional?"

Look to your body for information. Unconditional reassurances invite relaxation, expansion, and openness, whereas conditioned ones tend to leave us feeling small, contracted, isolated.

One way to access reassurances is to ask the part of ourselves that has the unmet need: "What do you need to hear? What do you want to know right now?"

> You are not merely that which can offer an answer.
>
> You—your very being—*is* the answer.

FROM THE PERSONAL TO THE COLLECTIVE

What if we approached collective healing

by *collectively* tending to our shared unmet needs?

What if we did this in a unified fashion?

Hand in hand, seeing, recognizing, addressing

our collective unmet needs?

Can you imagine the outcome?

POWER AS CURRENCY

Rev. angel Kyodo williams and Dr. Jasmine Syedullah led a Radical Dharma Camp at the Shambhala Mountain Center in the summer of 2019. I had the opportunity to assist and will be forever changed by the way in which they made many things clear. One particularly important takeaway for me was this: within a white supremacist capitalist patriarchy, to use a phrase coined by bell hooks, we are collectively indoctrinated into a world where *power* is the currency.

To be clear, we're not talking about the power of Love or the power that we live into when we trust ourselves. We're not speaking of the power of acting in accordance with the recognition of who we truly are or the power of standing on our own two feet. We're not talking about the power of healthy community, the power of being in touch with our cultural heritage. We're not speaking of the power of spirituality or the power of artistic expression. We're talking about the assigned value we place on others according to their assigned position of power. (And I say "assigned" because we don't consciously choose to be born into a marginalized societal position, just as we don't choose to be born into a white, male, wealthy, cisgendered body that, according to cultural conditioned standards, holds the most power.)

Because I had been steeped in the tool of recognizing survival strategies, though focusing exclusively on "the personal" as a monastic, and because I had taught this contemplative technology for years, I recall the lights coming on as Rev. angel spoke. I recall clearly recognizing that this tool could be applied to the collective.

Power as currency is how we as a collective have learned to survive.

In the very same way that a strategy I've used to survive my life arises out of the distortion that *I am separate*, "power as currency," too, arises out of a distorted view of separation. Such strategies couldn't exist without this original delusion of separation—delusion that is shared collectively.

It's no surprise that we're swimming in a soup of shared societal distortions. "Power as currency" is just one *collective* example, just as my fixation on perfectionism is just one *personal* example.

The personal becomes the collective.

The personal is the collective.

The collective becomes the personal.

The collective is the personal.

In Zen, when we speak of oneness, we are not referring to "one" as in singular. Yet we also cannot say "two," as if two objects are completely independent and separate from each other. Zen offers a perspective of "not one" and "not two." It points to a positionless position, where "not two" means freeing ourselves from the dualistic assertion that divides the whole into two parts, while "not one" means not being limited by a nondualistic stance occurring when a practitioner claims the whole as one without complete understanding.

The free movement between "not one" and "not two" is a third perspective that is not confined to either dualism or nondualism—neither "not one" nor "not two."

The personal and the collective are "not one" and "not two."

116

They are not separate from each other and yet they are not exactly the same. When we treat them as separate from each other, we miss the shared root they have. We miss the fact that personal processes of suffering and collective processes of suffering arise from the same distortion, the same veiling of truth.

POWER-AS-CURRENCY AS A COLLECTIVE SURVIVAL STRATEGY

Within dominant culture, we *collectively* become identified with the guidelines dictated by dominant culture. We collectively are conditioned to dominate as a way of getting our needs met. This distorted view is, of course, not a reflection of our inherent wholeness.

In the same way that my identification that I must be "good" to be loved is delusional and does not actually touch my unmet need, the behavior of domination (based on conditioned assigned value) within our society will never lead to freedom. It will never support the creation of a society where we all belong, one that reflects ultimate reality, what is fundamentally true. Both personally and collectively, these distorted views merely reflect the delusion that we are separate from each other, individually and collectively.

In the distorted model of "power as currency," we collectively ascribe to *power over* versus *power with*. This distinction comes from Mary Parker Follett, an American social worker, philosopher, and pioneer in organizational theory and organizational behavior. "Power over" could be viewed in a "one-on-one" sense and in terms of groups of people and/or nations. Based on this distortion, people use dominance and coercion again and again before seeking other alternatives. From this bent view, there is never enough [*fill in the blank*]. Our starting point is competition where one side vies for power over another, at best trying to influence the other to concede its position, at worst using brute force to have its way. In our conditioned world where "power over" is the norm, the distortion of separation is reinforced—continually and constantly.

"Power with" is relational and collective. From this view, new possibilities arise that spring from the very differences that might exist in a group. A premise: differences need not divide us. Unlike brute force, which must be continually reinforced to sustain itself, "power with" emerges organically. And the good news? It grows stronger the more it's put to use.

I've seen "power with" happen in classrooms, when students don't experience teachers using a "power over" approach. Students open; they step out of the story of separation, and a community of belonging naturally arises. All are empowered.

To move toward this empowered world doesn't mean we have to first completely get rid of our current "power over" model. In fact, trying to "outdo" a system of power by overpowering it only serves to reinforce it.

It is critical to remember that what has been veiled—

through survival strategies and/or trauma—

is, in fact, unscathed.

Just as our personal freedom does not depend on our ability to get rid of negative self-talk, the inner critic, or "impure thoughts", our collective freedom does not depend on ridding ourselves of all culturally dominant beliefs like power as currency.

It's our *relationship* to these thoughts and beliefs that allows for the shifting. It's who we see ourselves to be that is transformed. By practicing awareness and observation in how we participate in these systems, in how we become personally and collectively identified with these systems, we can begin to see them for the distortions they are. It then becomes possible for us to see *through* the distortions. We start to recognize what is kept in place with the power-as-currency model, or with any survival strategy for that matter. We can see, feel, and know the pain and suffering that arises within this conditioning. This recognition can invite letting go. And letting go allows us to surrender our attention to something else: shared power and a commitment to not feed, maintain, and perpetuate the conditioned distorted view of separation. Letting go allows us to surrender our attention to Love.

Ultimately, to be free personally and collectively, we must cease feeding all distortions that tell us we are separate. We must nourish the reality of inherent belonging. The pandemic of othering cannot truly end without uprooting this original distortion.

What uproots this distortion?

Clear seeing.

And Love.

OTHER COLLECTIVE SURVIVAL STRATEGIES

Our collective unmet needs are no different than our personal ones. We all have a need to belong. We all have a need for Love. To address this collective unmet need we must release our attachment to the conditioning that reflects the delusion that one group deserves more than another. Ultimately we must free ourselves from our conditioned definitions of "groups" in the way we have been indoctrinated to perceive them.

Some examples of collective survival strategies include:
Rugged individualism
Wealth = worth
The Protestant work ethic
Your occupation is who you are
Perfectionism
What else?

No matter the particulars, what all collective survival strategies have in common is that, as a group, we abandon who we truly are in the name of surviving. We abandon the peace of our shared being. We abandon inherent belonging. This abandonment is the root of all distortions that lead to a felt sense of separation and subsequent othering.

When looking to see other ways we employ cultural survival strategies, it can be deeply illuminating to explore strategies that pertain to any collective you identify with. This might be a broad collective, such as the race you identify with, or something more intimate, such as your family of origin.

I grew up in a family that had a collective survival strategy of avoiding conflict at all costs. Rare expressions of dramatic aggression, countless experiences of passive aggression. Not only did we collectively avoid conflict but we also actively put energy into the appearance that everything was fine, especially when it wasn't.

While I can't say I was traumatized by this shared conditioning, it's fair to say that collective survival strategies such as this leave residue. Tears in the fabric of our belonging. Such moments have ripple effects and lasting impact.

Remember, it's all the same process. When you practice seeing survival strategies in your own life, it becomes easier to see them collectively, and therefore clearer how to not engage in them. In clear seeing we are freed to pursue other options—options that don't arise on behalf of a felt sense of separation. We can choose "power with" and foster loving environments that help everyone recognize we are already whole. This is when communities begin to thrive, when we remember we are already whole. "Not one" and "not two" intertwine to create space for all to remember our inherent belonging.

TENDING TO COLLECTIVE TRAUMA

When we consider collective trauma, we are often habituated to treat what is structural as episodic. In doing so, we neglect to collectively meet the unmet need that could resolve the trauma. The essential medicine for our times is to *turn toward* the trauma, to recognize that this trauma is woven into the fabric of our society. To address this, we must see the collective unmet need and then move *toward* a conscious collective meeting of this need. Our need now is to provoke a shift in collective human consciousness that allows the truth of our shared being to be unveiled rather than obscured.

From 2018 to 2020, Dr. Gia Naranjo-Rivera conducted the first study in the world to directly measure the impacts of a youth mindfulness program by ACEs level (adverse childhood experiences). A public health and equity applied researcher, she chose to study in her dissertation research how mindfulness can improve teen well-being. The study examined what changed among teens who took the Peace in Schools class and what practices and processes led to those changes. In the study, high-needs youth, those who often feel most isolated—including low-income, POC, non-US born, LGBTQ+, female and gender nonbinary, and high-ACEs teens—disproportionately opted into and benefited from the class. The novel study won the 2019 Excellence in Public Health Award from Johns Hopkins University.

Here's a bit from Dr. Naranjo-Rivera about her pilot study:

TRANSFORMATIVE MINDFULNESS AND TRAUMA RESEARCH BY DR. NARANJO-RIVERA

Findings of my research showed that average self-compassion significantly increased by 11.5 percent; and revealed less self-judgment, identification (with the inner critic), and isolation, and more self-kindness, mindfulness, and feelings of common humanity. The "approach" style of coping—including acceptance, positive reframing, and seeking support and information—also significantly increased by 12.2 percent, indicating reduced isolation. Teens also experienced reduced average anxiety (13.6% decrease) and depression (12–16% decrease) with the most improved mental health indicators and reduced thoughts of self-harm (>40%) among female and LGBTQ+ students.

Importantly, students with high ACEs improved most across the six focal areas of well-being and mental health examined, indicating mindfulness can be a powerful antidote to ACEs and isolation. For example, youth with 4 or more ACEs had greater gains in coping skills and the ability to reframe (cognitive reappraisal), as well as reductions in perceived stress and anxiety, than lower-ACEs peers. Furthermore, highest ACEs teens (with 8–14 ACEs) showed a 14.1 percent increase in ability to communicate authentically (reduced expression suppression) and a 22 percent increase in feelings of connectedness. Taken together, these results suggest that the Peace in Schools semester-long curriculum can increase self-acceptance and reduce isolation.

While changes in the measures of well-being examined (which ranged from 11.5% to 40%) may seem low to a layperson, changes of 10 percent or more could be expected to be seen from more intensive, costly, and less accessible one-on-one clinical interventions. While the scales used in the study of Peace in Schools were not intended to be used for clinical diagnosis, the changes observed suggest major improvements in a class delivered universally (offered to all students) and selectively (offered to high-needs students) to diverse groups of public school students for a single class period every other day over a semester's time. Thus, the class holds great promise in addressing mental health issues and enhancing well-being among teens in these settings.

Elements of the class that relieved feelings of isolation and improved well-being were also assessed.

The most important factors of the program design were teachers who embodied mindfulness, the environment of CARE and creation of community, the curriculum depth and duration, and deep tailoring to meet student needs, including trauma-informed, culturally responsive, and equity-based practices. Many teens explained that their self-relationship and relationships with others improved. They became more compassionate and able to support others; more open, vulnerable, and willing to share; and more able to have meaningful interaction across perceived lines of difference.

Tools and practices that students found most helpful included loving reassurances as a compassionate mentor (to counter the inner critic), recognizing survival strategies, and anchors that tether the attention to the present moment.

For example, a student explained, "You don't have to meditate, just hearing the sound of the outside, or focusing on your breath or something like that—just the fact that you can use these things that are always around you to sort of calm down and realize that it's okay and you can just take a step back for a little bit—that's also been helpful to me."

In an assignment of writing a love letter to their future self, another student expressed self-compassion and acceptance around struggles with mental health issues that are commonly linked to isolation: "My anxiety and depression have spiked, and I'm working toward feeling more stable. I know that these feelings are temporary. . . . Being unhappy is okay, it only makes the good times 'better.'"

Students also said they valued being taught to recognize their own survival strategies and having an opportunity to choose differently or shift perspective. One student shared how this exercise impacted a family relationship: "The exercise on survival mechanisms helped me to understand my mom better." Compassion is the natural by-product of such understanding.

Peace in Schools provides potent "power with" medicine to help meet unmet needs collectively, foster belonging, and open people to broader possibilities for thriving and co-liberation.

CREATIONS THAT REFLECT OUR INHERENT BELONGING

In 2019, the US Congress held a landmark hearing on childhood trauma in the House of Representatives. Dr. Christina Bethell, a Johns Hopkins University professor and a leading expert on adverse childhood experiences, said in her testimony,

"Because children develop in the context of a community and need help outside of their homes, we need to ensure quality early care and education, proactively promote and destigmatize engagement in learning about healthy parenting and healing trauma (for parents who carry their own trauma), and foster, support, and evaluate strong school-based approaches such as those emerging in the Gladstone School District in Oregon and the Peace in Schools effort in Portland, Oregon and Tennessee's Building Strong Brains initiative."

It was striking, given the political divide in the United States, to witness both Democratic and Republican legislators at the hearing express passionate support for the need for urgent action in addressing the epidemic of childhood trauma.

It is critical to remember that change is possible. Individually. Collectively.

Remember: what has been veiled—through survival strategies and/or trauma—is, in fact, unscathed. As examples, a personal survival strategy, such as identifying with "the achiever" whose inherent worth is tied up with what is accomplished, leads to the veiling of the inherent rightness of being. On a collective level, our fundamental unity is deeply veiled within the context of any "power over" construct, such as ableism or racism.

While our inherent belonging can be threatened on one plane of reality, our belonging to life, to the universe, can never be diminished.

It is possible to create a society that reflects the truth of our inherent belonging.

This journey is a collective one.

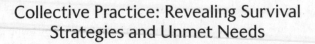

Collective Practice: Revealing Survival Strategies and Unmet Needs

In your CARE journal, with gentleness and over time, explore:

- Where in your life does "power over" versus "power with" manifest? What is the cost?

- What survival strategies were you indoctrinated into within your family of origin?

- What survival strategies can you name that operate on the level of the collective?

Examples of places to look: "We must win at all costs." "We should follow the rules and play the game." "*They* need to be kept in their place lest we lose *ours*." "Don't acknowledge what's really going on, just maintain the status quo."

- What else can you name?

- How do you intersect with these strategies? How do they live within you?

- What collective judgments keep these survival strategies in place?

Personal liberation is being free from the constructs that bind us personally.

Collective liberation is being free from the constructs that bind humankind.

- How would you describe the unmet need underneath these collective survival strategies?

- And what do you envision would meet this need?

- What, for you, brings about the experience of inherent belonging?

- What might invite a direct experience of belonging for any collective you identify with? How might you bring this to form? How might it get expressed personally and/or collectively?

Take your time with these prompts. These questions may take weeks, months, years to truly unpack.

We are conditioned to think that practice has an end.

But practice is an experience of now.

And now is timeless.

Share your observations with a friend or with your group, if you're working with one. Remember, nonjudgment is an imperative ingredient as we end the pandemic of othering.

Acceptance is key.

Chapter Seven

Return to Unity

Seeing Through Duality

> Ultimate reality and relative reality are to be
> understood as two expressions of one truth, two
> sides of one coin. Ultimate reality is often associated
> with the ocean, and relative reality, with the waves;
> ultimate reality is like the sky, and relative reality is all
> that appears and disappears in the sky.
>
> —Ruth King

I n Peace in Schools, our classes take place in a circle. The experience is leveled for the benefit of all. The intention behind the form is to create a reflection of our unity rather than an us/them dichotomy.

Lanh always sat beside me in class. Even though there were no assigned seats in Mindful Studies, Lanh always arrived early enough to claim the cushion to my right. As Peace in Schools teachers, we often shake up the seating. Everything about the class is intentional. It's always been important to me that teachers keep an eye out for cliques that might form. As creatures, we're so habituated to the social pattern of creating them. It's difficult to have cliques without reinforcing an experience of othering—especially in high school.

Usually a particular vibrancy, aliveness, and sense of belonging arises when students are invited to intersect with others they might normally not engage with. As teachers, we do our best to create such opportunities. Of course, there are exceptions to every rule.

I knew Lanh was on the autism spectrum, and I sensed that the regularity, structure, and pattern of having the same seat every class created comfort. For the first semester Lanh almost never spoke yet was never absent. Lanh was Vietnamese American in a primarily white school. It didn't appear that Lanh had many friends. It was clear that, like many other fifteen-year-olds, Lanh struggled with shyness, connecting with others, and social anxiety. Lanh was one of those students who drank up the contemplative technologies of the class and the overall environment as if it were medicine. I think in a way it was.

In every class session we make sure to bring all voices into the room. This philosophy has been significantly enriched by Inward Bound Mindfulness Education (iBme), a nonprofit that offers teen mindfulness retreats. With their permission, we incorporated their "lightning rounds" into our curriculum. At the beginning of a class, as students are getting to know each other, the lightning round creates a way for each teen to be seen and heard. Students say their name, the pronouns they go by, and an answer to a simple prompt. Perhaps something like "What are you present to in this moment?"

Lanh seemed particularly still and notably focused as we made our way around the lightning round at the start of our second semester of Mindful Studies. Sitting beside me as always, Lanh sat up boldly, took a deep breath, and said, "Hi, I'm Lanh. I go by they/them."

Lanh came out as transgender. For the first time. To an entire room of teenagers, most of whom Lanh didn't know.

Lanh went on to say more in the next two minutes than I had heard them say in the entire prior semester. Lanh admitted that they had been struggling with their gender identity for years and that they had never had an outlet to explore anything beyond a conditioned view of male and female. Semester after semester, to my delight, I saw Lanh's name on the roster. Lanh took the class four times before graduating.

THE PERCEIVED DUALITY OF MALE VERSUS FEMALE

Peace in Schools prioritizes an inclusive, responsive environment, but I must confess that when I was first introduced to including pronouns in our initial student introductions, it didn't make sense to me. I had, for years, been steeped in a training that focused on who we are beyond personal identity, and I knew the benefit of this focus in my own life. Deeply.

As a monastic, I was trained to see identity as illusory, not the whole of who we are. While I experienced this statement as true and helpful on one level, it wasn't until I began the work of Peace in Schools that I experienced the fallout from how my conditioned mind equated "identity is illusory" to "identity doesn't matter."

Through working with teens and others in Peace in Schools I've come to understand the value of honoring personal identity, of stepping into shoes that fit. I have been awed to witness the shift that can happen. When these shoes are on, and fit comfortably, we often have more access to the ease and joy of our own being, leading to an ease around accessing being at large.

I've witnessed that this is especially important in cases where identity is marginalized by dominant culture. You don't have to look far to see that trans people are more likely to be the recipients of hate crimes than cisgendered people, and that this violence has significantly risen in the last decade.

In the world of relative experience, identity matters.

At the monastery where I trained, we were not required to shave our heads. Not long into my training, however, I decided to do so and kept it shaved for quite some time. I knew that I derived a strong sense of self through my long blonde hair. Through being feminine. Through identifying as a woman. Shaving my head was a way to challenge this conditioning, to feel what arose when I let go of this external definition of who I saw myself to be. And who I thought others saw—but most importantly, who I thought others valued. It was a deeply freeing experience to have no hair, to let go of some of my conditioning around gender and sexuality.

I have experienced directly how many people, like Lanh, feel deeply boxed in by the binary construct of gender. Because I am steeped in the practice of recognizing duality, it's clear to me how conditioned we are to perceive reality through the lens of right versus wrong, good versus bad, black versus white. It isn't a huge leap from there to see how and why it might be valuable for someone to question what they have been conditioned to believe about themselves regarding their gender, especially when I reflect on the freedom I felt in challenging my gender identity in the monastery. And, potentially even more valuable, to challenge the limitation of seeing gender dualistically altogether rather than as existing along a continuum.

Over the next three semesters I saw Lanh engage fearlessly with other students. Lanh went from being a student who rarely spoke to a student whose sense of humor surfaced with ease. Others began to know Lanh as someone who paid attention to those who might feel left out, always quick to guide them home to community, to a sense of belonging. When I first met Lahn, other students might have experienced them as somewhat invisible. That invisibility ended. Lanh was seen, accepted, loved within the community of the class. I witnessed Lanh come to terms with the sexual trauma of their childhood, join a recovery group, come to grips with and challenge the internalized racism and transphobia that they had been conditioned into, and stand firmly in what they described as a more fitting way to identify themselves—as trans.

Eight years after Lanh's first Mindful Studies class, they now rarely miss one of my meditation groups for adults. Lanh has spent extended time in retreat pursuing meditation practice, and serves on the board of directors for Peace in Schools. They went from being a student any caring teacher might have worried about to an adult who is actively and confidently engaged in life. Lanh went from having a primary residence of fear to having a home base in a practice of presence.

This is what contemplative technologies offer us: seeing the limitation of dualistic thinking, seeing how it is structured and how it operates, stepping away from the game of polarity, becoming free, seeing through us versus them and right versus wrong, opening a door into a more authentic experience of ourselves and a more authentic expression of who we truly are.

THE UNBORN MIND

What does it mean to recognize the illusory nature of identity? And to hold both relative and absolute truths about identity at the same time?

My first show-stopping moment around gender came when exploring the teachings of Bankei, a Japanese Zen master who lived in the 1600s. I even remember where I was sitting when I read about a woman who brought him her suffering. It was a weight she could no longer carry on her own. She was living in an era and a cultural context in which it was believed that a woman could not know her true nature, could not experience enlightenment, until she was reborn as a man. She had been inconsolable. This woman wanted nothing more than to be free. Instead of merely explaining to her that her belief was not true, Bankei asked her a simple question:

"When do you become a woman?"

This can be a helpful question for all of us. When do you become [*fill in the blank*]? A woman, Vietnamese American, blonde, someone with an eating disorder, a person who was abused as a child, to give just a few examples of forms we can identify with.

When, in our minds, do we leave the undifferentiated experience of being? (I specifically state "in our minds" for that is the only place this leaving occurs.) When, in our minds, do we attach to the notion "I am [*fill in the blank*]?" When do we latch onto and fixate on a specific identity? The moment we do, the perception of duality appears within the play—the production that we are a finite self.

I am broken. I need to be healed.

I am fat. I should be thin.

I am a failure. I long for success.

Bankei referred to our vast, unlimited being as "the unborn mind," or Buddha Mind. It is the mind before the thought of identity. Before any thought! This unborn mind is the same in each of us. In fact, it is not that we each have a separate unborn mind—minds that are similar or share the same qualities. There is simply one unborn mind, one shared being, one consciousness, and within that one consciousness many appearances arise: The appearance of a woman, the appearance of a man, the appearance of a trans person. When do you become any of them? When do you grab hold as if that identity is the totality of who you truly are?

Who are you before identity?

A Practice: Exploring Duality

One way we can home in on this question is to bring further attention to who we are not. To bring attention to *what* we are not. Doing so can guide us to our inherent freedom—the freedom that exists prior to the appearance of duality.

Visualize a time in your life when you felt stuck in a particular duality.

Really.
Pause.

See yourself in a moment when you can recognize that while identified with one side of the duality, you believe X, and while on the other side of the duality, you believe Y. Say, for example, you are struggling with "Should I stay or should I go?" (And you get extra points if you sing this line, by the way.) Perhaps the duality has a light emotional charge (Should I stay home or go to work today?), or perhaps the duality has tremendous impact (Should I stay in this marriage?). It's fine if your scenario involves another person, but if it does, just focus on your own inner process for now.

Column A	Column B
I Should Stay	I Should Go

Visualize yourself identified with the part of you who wants to stay. What do you say to yourself about why you should stay? Write down all your self-talk when you're identified with this side of the page. Things like:

"If I leave, I'll be a coward."

"There really are no good reasons to leave."

"I'm afraid to leave."

"It's better here."

Next, see yourself on the other side of the duality. Write down the self-talk you are present to when you're identified with column B; in this case, "I Should Go."

Things like:

"If I stay I'll be a coward."

"There really are no good reasons to stay."

"I'm afraid to stay."

"It's better there."

Simply brain-dump all the things you believe to be true when you're identified in each way. Remember two things:

1. It's not *what* but *how*. Recognize the process. Take a step back from the content.

2. Writing these things down is in and of itself a process of disidentification. By letting these beliefs be at arm's length, you can recognize they are not you.

Remember, you can do this with anything. It need not merely be stay/go. You might flesh this process out with "Was I right or was I wrong?" "Is X worthy to pursue or is X futile to pursue?" "Should I have [*fill in the blank*] or should I not have [*fill in the blank*]?"

Dualities are endless. Why?

Because when we look through the lens of duality,

everything seen appears to be dualistic.

What's important about this exercise is to see what you say to yourself when you're on one side of the duality, then explore what you say to yourself when you're on the other side of the duality.

The perception of duality is maintained through self-talk. A dualistic view cannot be kept in place without it. Recognizing this self-talk helps us recognize when this perception has taken hold.

Note that, in the above example, I specifically wrote down self-talk that is simply the flip side of each argument. How often is it like that within you? Maybe not at all. If your columns don't appear like this, no worries. It doesn't mean you did it wrong! Pay attention to whether the right/wrong binary is arising as you make your way through this exercise. *How you do anything is how you do everything.*

Often we are so identified with one side of the duality, specifically with the content on that side of the duality, that we miss the *process* we go through when bouncing from one side of the duality to the other.

To take this beyond the recognition of self-talk, or merely belief, read column A aloud and notice what happens in your body and within your energetic system. In other words, pay attention to how these thoughts affect not only your mind but also your body and energy.

Then see yourself on the other side of the duality. Read column B aloud. Notice how these thoughts, these beliefs and assumptions, affect you on the level of sensation.

What happens energetically? Can you explore this without getting sucked into the content but rather simply experiencing the result of being identified with this side of the duality?

Now, like a drone, zoom out to get an even broader view. You've brought attention to what it feels like to identify with each side of the duality. Now bring attention to what it's like to bounce from one side to the other rather than strictly focusing on the result of identifying with each side of the duality.

What's the result of pinging between the sides? Of seeking and resisting in this way? Of identifying with a separate self that flings back and forth?

That's what it's like, isn't it? We thrash back and forth. What would shift if we remained on one side of the duality all the time with no resistance? I'm not suggesting that freedom lies in simply choosing one side of the duality, but it can be a fruitful inquiry to play with. Would we suffer if there were no resistance? Would we suffer if there were no comparing?

Freedom lies in our capacity to disidentify from the created duality.

To return to a direct experience of unity.

From this direct experience of unity, we are able to accept and embrace what is. In complete acceptance, is there any residue of dissatisfaction? With nothing to compare our experience to, nothing to hold up against it, how would we suffer? Where would the issue be?

We suffer when we create an alternate reality that does not exist.

We suffer when we compare what is to what could be or, according to the conditioned mind, what *should* be.

Can you see the part of you who gets flung around in the bouncing back and forth? What if, with a sense of play (remember: we're making all of this up), you saw this tossed-about part of you as a young person you love. Would it be easy to recognize the battle they get caught in? To see the suffering that results? What would you want to say to this person? Would it feel easy to access the way this whole drama is . . .

created?

not required?

not helpful?

Would you be able to see this person through the eyes of compassion?

INTERNAL SUFFERING IS OPTIONAL

My student Olivia came to me after class with tears streaming down her face. We had just experienced the exercise above.

"I've been struggling so much with this internal debate about whether I should go to college. My grandmother really wants me to go, and I have all this self-talk about that. But my friends are telling me I should follow my dreams, and I've got all this self-talk about that. I hadn't seen until today how much all this freaks me out. How spiraled into stuckness I get. I hadn't named how shitty I've been feeling all the time. It hadn't occurred to me that I could step back from this internal argument. Like I didn't know I could listen for something else. Like I could listen to something beyond the voices."

"Yes," I replied. "We feel cut off from possibility when we are stuck in the conditioned mind, don't we? And it's true, the result of this stuckness, and this kind of self-abandonment, is feeling shitty. I hear you."

Olivia began weeping. Everything in her seemed to soften. It felt as though if I listened hard enough, I might hear something cracking within.

Fortunately, suffering is optional.

As the saying goes, pain is inevitable, but suffering is optional.

As humans, we see things that we label "external" through a dualistic lens: "This group of people is good; that group of people is bad." "These decisions are right; those decisions are wrong."

When we're identified with the conditioned mind, our attention is on the content that's filtered through this lens. We don't stop to consider the lens itself, the role it plays in generating, forming, and shaping the content.

Our liberation depends on our capacity to question the lens we look through.

Ultimately, our liberation depends on our capacity to ask:

"What is looking through this lens?"

For now, however, let's continue to explore the impact of identifying with the perception of duality. When we're looking through the lens of duality, we see a divided world. We see a divided world because we experience ourselves as divided. From the seat of division, from the throne of the ego, everything is split into a subject/object relationship.

"I am the subject."

"You are the object."

Pause. Ask yourself what this might mean:

What is the result of being the subject, with the world being the object?

What is the fallout?

We cannot expect to see anything other than division when we're viewing life from the seat of division. That's all division knows how to see: more division. From this seat we spend our lives perpetuating the division.

There is nothing inherently bad or wrong with this dividing process. We suffer when we confuse this perception with reality. For example, the human construct of time is a by-product of this process. Time is not bad. We suffer, however, when we forget that time is a creation. That it's a human construct that serves the human experience.

In the unborn mind, there is no time.

In the unborn mind, there is only now.

When I am identified with seeing myself as the subject, I exist in time. I have a particular identity and I view this identity as "me." It appears to be the whole of who I am. Anything that threatens this identity is something to fight with. *It* opposes *me*. *I* need to oppose *it*. There are sides. Teams. From this seat I become an "I," a limited self that experiences myself as separate from life. What isn't me is "over there," somewhere else. I like it or I don't like it. I want it or I don't want it. I avoid or I cling.

I. I. I. in relationship to You. You. You.

I. I. I. in relationship to It. It. It.

Sounds like a good little jingle, eh?

When we're identified in this way, we're stuck forever seeking and forever resisting. Those are the primary activities of the ego. That is its nature. Seeking and resisting. Seeking and resisting. When identified with the ego, back and forth we go! There's no freedom in this process.

A Practice: The Cost of Subject/Object

Pause. Make a list.

What is the result of being identified with the subject within a subject/object relationship?

How about:

I see myself as this body. This body has a start date and an end date. Therefore I have a start date and an end date. Death of this body means death of me. So I fear death. I resist signs of aging because they are reminders that I will die.

How about:

The earth belongs to me. It's mine to do what I want with. I can take what I want, when I want it. I am not inseparable from nature. Nature belongs to me. I seek to possess it.

How about:

I have a particular set of beliefs. *That* group of people has another set of beliefs. My beliefs are right. Their beliefs are wrong. I need to get rid of what I deem as wrong. They are the problem. I need to get rid of *them*.

Keep going on your own. Write down your insights. If you are working with a group, compare notes later with others. Be as dramatic as you want with this. Of course, if you're reading this book, you're unlikely to be a probable candidate for starting a war. That said, can you relate to seeing yourself as separate, judging others, wanting to get rid of what you see as other than you?

Or control what is other than you?

Or possess what is other than you?

Be honest with yourself about what you see.

Notice judgment when it arises. Direct the attention back to presence.

Stay in the mind of curiosity. Commit to not leaving.

THE DISTORTION OF SEPARATION

The subject/object relationship is the ultimate myth.
It is the ultimate distortion.
Liberation is freedom from this distortion.

Every war that is waged arises out of
this distortion of separation.
Every act of violence stemming from
the delusion of supremacy arises out of
the distortion of separation.
Every experience of harm to the earth occurs
within the sea of delusion that is
the distortion of separation.

To heal, we must address the root. The root?
Faulty perception. A mythical story that we are separate—
from life, from each other, from ourselves.

THE DANGER OF BAD

Judgment, like duality, only lives in one place: the conditioned mind. When you judge something, you remove it from yourself.

"But what about when I judge myself?" you might ask.

When you judge yourself, you are reinforcing the story that you are other than yourself—that you are cut off from being. Remember, judgment is like a glue that reinforces a felt sense of separateness. The inner critic underpins that you are "other than."

This process of judgment as a distancing device plays out collectively as well. As an example, as I've been learning about how systemic oppression functions, I have had countless moments in which I, as a white person, have seen racism as "bad," only to be followed by resistance to exploring how racism manifests in me. How it impacts me. It's bad. It's over there. It's not me. In particular moments I've even found myself wanting to distance myself from "other white people," the ones who "don't get it," as if creating that mental separating device will keep me safe. The only thing such mental separating devices actually do is keep us feeling separate.

For those of us living in the United States, we are swimming in a four-hundred-year-plus sea of systemic oppression. I am not going to escape this by placing it "over there." Relegating racism to "a few bad apples," but not me, will not free me. The psychotherapist Resmaa Menakem's work on Somatic Abolitionism as well as the work of Radical Dharma has helped me see that all are harmed in any system of domination, not merely the ones thought of as "oppressed."

When we are viewing the world dualistically, we are habituated to avoid what is "bad." When we are not attached to avoiding bad and to seeking good, when we meet everything with the mind of inquiry and curiosity as practice encourages us to do, we are better able to investigate all the ways that we participate in and are impacted by collective conditioned systems, such as racism.

When we recognize that duality is illusory, we see that what appears to us as polarized is not in fact polarized at the deepest level. Repeatedly returning to the experience of our essential oneness becomes a tool to undermine the habit of separating and polarizing. Recognizing the illusory nature of duality, seeing it like a hologram, then, allows us to bring the truth of oneness to bear on relative-plane experiences that *appear* as polarized. Therefore:

The process of recognizing the illusory nature of duality is not some sort of free pass to a world without injustice but instead an essential tool for building one.

I was one of the facilitators for a series called "Race and the Self" through the Science and Nonduality conference some years back. It was surprising to me, yet an important learning experience, to see how common some version of this feedback from a white participant was:

"You just want me to feel bad because you feel bad about being white."

The depth of this conditioning around avoiding "bad" was sobering. This was not simply *my* conditioning but *collective* conditioning. The year prior I had participated in a panel titled "Are We One?" at the same conference. Konda Mason, Dr. Sará King, Orland Bishop, and I engaged in a conversation about the way that, in our shared desire to focus on the absolute—or the unborn, or true nature—we sometimes ignore our participation in systems of oppression on the relative plane. Again, I was surprised to witness the level of resistance we experienced from white participants. It should be noted that my BIPOC friends and colleagues were not surprised by this. My surprise simply revealed my lack of lived experience and my lack of understanding of how prevalent such resistance is. One statement, regarding some of the sentiments I shared, stood out glaringly:

"She's trying to get me to hate myself for being white."

To be clear, there was absolutely nothing in our presentation that suggested that white people should feel bad for having white skin, and certainly there was nothing that pointed to the benefit of hating oneself. These displays of resistance revealed to me the level of investment white people, including myself, are conditioned to have around aligning with what is "good." Not wanting to be seen as "bad." It runs deep.

When I buy into this type of dualistic thinking, I become trapped. Within such a dualistic process, none of us can be free. We've all been indoctrinated into the same collective story of "other." We all carry the germs of this pandemic. Because of this, even as we try to get free of this plague of othering, we often find ourselves developing new variants.

Consider the wellness industry for a moment. How many times have you been encouraged—through wellness marketing, your yoga teacher, a spiritual guru—to *focus on the positive, transcend the negative, manifest what's good, focus on love?* How often have they promoted that *love is good, indifference is bad, hatred is bad; turn away from the dark, turn toward the light?*

It obviously can be compelling to part of us; it wouldn't be so prevalent if it weren't. But . . .

Being compelling and arising out of truth are not the same thing.

If we see good as the opposite of bad and bad as something we don't want to get tangled up in, it's no surprise we end up incessantly striving after what we've labeled *good.* And, again, we must keep what's bad away from us—at all costs.

From the perspective of awareness practice, examining such intense resistance can provide illumination into how the conditioned mind is structured, how duality is maintained, and how judgment—which belongs to the conditioned mind—keeps it all in place. In recognizing process in this way, we who are examining our participation in systemic oppression can practice not taking any of it personally, seeing all of it as conditioning versus who we truly are.

THE PERCEIVED DUALITY OF POLITICS VERSUS SPIRITUALITY

The good/bad binary tied to being white was not the only duality that surfaced in the conference that year. The very notion that social justice could even be discussed within a context where we were all "here to focus on oneness" triggered a lot of resistance. This resistance took many forms. The most common feedback:

"Politics should be kept out of spirituality."

In the same way that resistance arises when the personal ego feels threatened, I took note of this response as collective resistance by the collective ego that has a deeply vested interest in maintaining a system that reflects *it*: the mind of separation.

I want to address the perceived duality between politics and spirituality because it keeps so many perspectives of othering in place. This particular duality can often go unquestioned in spiritual settings, and I see this as an opportunity to challenge what does not reflect our collective heart.

This duality is yet another way we get trapped by the false deity of separation. We get caught in the conditioning of our particular camp. We stagnate in defensiveness of this conditioning instead of living in the enlivened knowing of the truth that these things are not exclusive of each other. When freed of the yoke of duality, we can ask questions like: Where do we see activities associated with the governance of our country void of the recognition of spirit? Of our shared being? Is my spiritual practice so focused on enlightenment, so focused on transcendence, that I ignore the suffering that exists on the relative plane?

When we are freed from the duality of politics versus spirituality, we can ask these questions and begin moving forward from the knowing of ourselves as shared being. We can move in any direction we choose. Nothing has to be excluded from our practice. When we move beyond binary thinking, good and bad are no longer the guiding forces of our decisions. We are free.

What does it mean to be free?

To know the reality of all things.

To know the truth of who you are.

The truth prior to the arising of duality.

Then, from the knowing of reality, to do what you will.

To move how the heart calls.

To move from the heart of who we are.

THE TRUTH BEFORE DUALITY

We get stuck perceiving emptiness as the opposite of form. If we are all various forms arising in the same unborn mind, then it must be the case that the same unborn mind can be found in all things. I am reminded of the Heart Sutra, a widely studied Mahāyāna Buddhist teaching:

Form is emptiness, emptiness is form, form does not differ from emptiness, emptiness does not differ from form. The same is true with feelings, perceptions, mental formations, and consciousness.

In other words, our feelings, perceptions, mental formations (concepts), and sensory consciousness (including thought process) are what we take to be the "self," which in truth is merely a composite of conditions arising.

The fundamental reality of all things is the same.

The fundamental reality of all things is emptiness—

The emptiness that is not the opposite of form.

"Emptiness" here does not refer to an utterly blank, nihilistic void. It means empty of the projections we place on things, that the ego places on phenomena—things that the ego identifies as separate, solid, going on forever without change, owned by us, dominated by us, dominating us, as other.

Emptiness describes how things "are." From a Zen perspective, emptiness describes the reality that no existence has an inherently existent "self" or essence, that every "thing" comes about only in dependence upon something else. Furthermore, there is not a "thing" or substance called emptiness.

Form is simply all things, all experience, all life. It emerges fully and yet is not owned by anyone. It is not other. It arises by virtue of emptiness, and its true nature is one of emptiness. When dualistic projections fall away, this is not an emptiness that obliterates what is. What is *shines* with emptiness—the emptiness that is not the opposite of form, the emptiness that is pure consciousness itself, the truth prior to duality.

EXPRESSIONS OF DISTORTION

We are living in a time in human evolution when there is tremendous polarization in every direction. Who is the victim and who is the perpetrator? Are you on top or on bottom? Are you awake or are you asleep? We can often see this polarization in politics, with different parties engaging in "power over" dynamics of right/wrong, good/bad. You can even notice how much polarization exists within "the same side." How much spatting there can be. Arguments over the correct language to use within a particular movement. Fights erupting over terminology and approach. To be clear, this isn't to suggest that any of this is inherently bad or wrong. This is to point out the limitation in the construct.

When you become embattled, everything becomes a battle.
If all you have is a hammer, everything you encounter is a nail.

Because we are accustomed to existing within a dualistic frame, we are conditioned to perceive that our options are stay in the battle and fight or "transcend" the battle and avoid it.

You can't choose for others whether they fight and fight and fight. But you can choose the alternative for yourself. You can choose to see the hologram of duality clearly, to not engage. The world has its collective delusion. If you are clear enough to see that it is delusion, it becomes possible to decline and not dive in—not because you *should* keep your shoes dry but because you can.

When we condition our brain to follow certain neural pathways, everything is seen in a particular way, with its own slant. Through practice, we can notice what our prejudgments are, our unconscious biases, our collective perceptions and conditioning. We can see through the veils of these distortions.

I don't have to look far to find places in my life where there has been a perceived threat of some kind, most likely a perceived threat to my felt sense of belonging, that has been met with a conditioned attempt to dominate. In particular, I can see where this has arisen in certain circumstances involving men and, particularly, circumstances that reflect the social construct of patriarchy—circumstances in which I've felt clear that if I had been male, the treatment of me and/or the circumstance in relationship to me would have been handled differently.

In my own history, I have at times felt under the boot of someone exhibiting dominating behavior and reacted with some version of believing I must get on top of the boot. To try to gain power during a time of feeling like power has been taken away, I must become domineering. In moments such as these, haven't always been able to name this behavior. These are often unconscious processes. Sometimes it wasn't until later that I could see how within this framework of *under the boot* or *on top of the boot*, there was seemingly little way to proceed other than the way I have been conditioned to proceed—the way of duality, the way of subject/object, the way that reinforces "other."

It is the ultimate symptom of systems of othering and domination that we've been conditioned to believe we can only meet injustices through the lens of duality.

I have harmed and I have been harmed. We all have—not just in this life but throughout lifetimes. We have played all the roles. We aren't going to stamp out harm with more harmful behavior. Healing involves undoing these conditioned patterns all together.

Healing arises when we've had a direct experience of what's most primary: the unborn mind. Healing actions are actions that are on behalf of the truth of who we truly are.

HEALTHY INTERDEPENDENCE

In her book *We Will Not Cancel Us*, the activist and Black feminist adrienne maree brown beautifully writes about an alternative way:

"I have a vision of movement as sanctuary. Not a tiny perfectionist utopia behind miles of barbed wire and walls and fences and tests and judgments and righteousness, but a vast sanctuary where our experiences, as humans who have experienced and caused harm, are met with centered, grounded, invitations to grow. In this sanctuary we feel our victory, where winning means an intimate healing. Where winning isn't measured by anyone else's loss, but by breaking cycles of abuse, harm, assault, and systemic oppression. Where winning is measured not just by the absence of patterns of harm, distrust, and isolation, but by the presence of healing and healthy interdependence."

Healthy interdependence is our birthright. It is not born of the perception of right/wrong, good/bad, black/white. Healthy interdependence is an expression of the unity of being. Why say an *expression* of unity? Because in truth, "interdependence," dualistically perceived, implies the existence of separate objects that are dependent on each other, and that's not entirely accurate.

The pandemic of othering can only exist in a dualistic view, and within it we lose our capacity to see each other and the earth as beloved. We lose our capacity to know ourselves as each other. Interdependent, beloved, and made of the same being—the same unified being. Remember:

People confuse power with domination.

True power lies in our capacity to love

and to know ourselves as Love.

Consider the interdependence we see expressed through the natural world. Just one example: Milkweed depends on the soil to anchor its roots. It needs the sun, rain, and air to make its own food; and it depends on pollinating insects (e.g., bees, butterflies, tussock moths) to make seeds for reproduction. In turn, the monarch butterfly depends on the milkweed's nectar for food and water. It uses its leaves for food, water, shelter. And the insects, bees, butterflies, and moths use the oxygen (made by plants) to turn their food into energy.

These beings need each other. We need each other.

These life systems depend on each other, and they cannot exist

in the same way without each other.

We cannot exist in the same way without each other.

We cannot exist outside the whole we arise out of.

Because all things are "empty," they inter-arise;

they inter-arise because they are empty.

Remembering our interdependence, our wholeness, our being, is what exists beyond the distortions of dualities. Beyond polarity is where the truth of our humanity resides. This is where the movement toward healing and healthy collective begins, where the content of the dualities of our lives and the distortion of "other" can fall away. Beyond dualistic thinking is where the context for loving connection across all lines of perceived difference can arise. This is where loving across lines of difference can thrive.

Collective Practice: Dreaming Beyond the Dream of Duality

If you have done the practices in this chapter on pages 128 and 134, share with a friend or with your group what you've noticed about how dualistic thinking manifests in your personal life. Share the cost. It is expensive. Unpack this.

Now explore, together if you wish, the collective. Allow yourself to be inspired by the words of the poet and Zen priest Zenju Earthlyn Manuel, who said, "A society that does not examine itself is an unenlightened one."

What are the ways duality is expressed in your family? And/or in your community? Society at large? How about in any other collective you identify with? How does dualistic thinking manifest? How does it take form? What is the fallout? Unpack this.

Next explore and unpack the places in your community where entire *systems* arise out of collective dualistic thinking (e.g., educational systems, or the school-to-prison pipeline). How does dualistic thinking take form in these systems? And, again, what is the cost?

Ask. Explore:

What do we collectively have to let go of in our specific family and/ or any group to return to the experiential understanding that there's something prior to the illusion of a dual world of opposition? Allow yourself to dream into the alternative.

What would a society that was an expression of our direct experience of unity look like? Feel like? We've never experienced this before. Ignite the imagination. (If you start thinking something like "This is silly, Pollyanna, unrealistic," consider letting that go for this period of reflection. We can't bring about what we can't first envision. Even if we don't get all the way there, the very act of imagining can stir and propel us. This exercise isn't actually about an imaginary future that doesn't exist. It's about *now*. This practice is about dreaming beyond the dream of duality *now*.)

Need I mention that there is no right or wrong way to do this? Need I underline that this isn't about success versus failure?

Simply pay attention.
Allow yourself to see.
Invite clarity to guide you.

Chapter Eight

Return to Presence

Knowing the Heart of Who We Are

That which is unborn is the Buddha Mind; the Buddha
Mind is unborn and marvelously illuminating, and, what's
more, with this Unborn, everything is perfectly managed.

—Zen Master Bankei

When I first decided to be a monk, I didn't decide to be a monk. The unique opportunity to not be a monk presented itself as I was finishing a work-study fellowship at the Penland School of Craft. At the same time, a seven-year relationship with a man I had assumed I would marry was also coming to a close. Up until then, I had a solid belief in my future life as a married artist with kids and a career. That belief, too, was coming to a close. More than ever before in my adult life, the unknown unfurled itself in front of me, seemingly endlessly.

By this time I had been studying with my Zen teacher for years. Practice was more central to my life than anything else. Without my having ever stepped foot in a monastery, practice had already become so paramount that almost everything I did, almost everything I experienced, revolved around it. Life's daily activities—walking, sitting, eating, drinking—were all moments for practice. The more I committed my life to a practice of presence, the more I felt free, fully alive, engaged and in love with the experience of living.

My teacher suggested I come to the monastery for a period of time. I recall excitedly responding that I was in—as long as that didn't make me a monk. That's where I drew the line. I loved practice, but practice fit into my life, not the other way around.

I recall thinking that my time at the monastery would be an extended "period of practice." *This will be just like going on a really long retreat, right? At the end of every retreat where I've focused exclusively on being present I've always felt more awake, happier, lighter, more vibrantly alive. This is just going to be like that, times a lot . . . right?* Whatever it meant to live in a monastery and devote myself completely to practice was all good, exciting even, as long as it had an end date. As long as I wasn't actually "a monk."

I committed to six months. Then I'd go off and live in an exciting city somewhere. I recall thinking that perhaps I'd fall in love with a dancer. That I was going to have a light-filled apartment and a dog named Dakota. (Random, I know, but such is the mind of fantasy.)

Inevitably, not long into being at the monastery, I realized that I was in fact a monk. The shattering of what I thought my life was going to be was severe. I pretty much had a nervous breakdown, not only because I saw the vision of my life slipping through my fingers but also because of the debate between the different parts of me that raged within. The deafening silence of being a monk gave space for all my inner demons to surface. Because of my internal landscape, this silent monastery was the loudest place I had ever been.

Part of me was ready to let go, to fully embrace having no idea where this whole monk thing would lead, yet still deeply called to find out.

And then there was the rest of me, the one who wanted a shiny life in the city. Restaurants, bars, dancing. And what about Dakota? The part of me who wanted a partner, to have children—several, in fact. *(What do you mean part of being a monk is celibacy?!)* The want-to-be-a-mother part of me was *not* on board with this whole "being a monk" idea. Here we go again, just like my first retreat. *Why didn't I read the fine print?*

But something much deeper was pulling me. I felt it and feared it all at the same time.

Two months in, I realized I hadn't had my period. *Great. I'm going to be the first monk in history who shows up to a monastery unknowingly pregnant. Who does that?!* I wrote a note on the board to the head monk—that's how communication in the silent environment happened—explaining that I needed a pregnancy test. I was mortified. She took me to the doctor. And then I waited. And waited.

When the results came in, the head monk didn't post a note. Instead, she sat me down on a rickety wooden bench in the dining hall. *Great. I'm going to be the first monk in history whom the head monk has to talk to about pregnancy options.* The mortification deepened.

She proceeded to tell me that, in fact, I wasn't pregnant. The doctor's assessment was that I was . . . wait for it . . . I was . . . stressed. I was stressed, y'all. That was my diagnosis. I was relieved, of course. But perhaps more importantly, I got to see how much my internal debate had been affecting me. The physical changes in my body forced me to come to grips with how much I had actually been suffering.

Seeing clearly the process I had been in and the affect it had on me rendered it limp. It no longer had the same stronghold. I really got it that all the debating had nothing to do with the present moment. It was all fantasy—belief in an alternate reality that didn't actually exist, the whims and whirls that maintained a false sense of identity. I got it that none of it served me and that none of it *was* me.

That didn't mean that the internal debates between the various aspects of my personality never came up again, but certainly they didn't consume my reality in the same way. I had a newfound capacity to step back and find the whole process fascinating, to watch the conditioned mind's part in all of this. How else did the processes of my mind, and my identification with them, affect me, even so much as to interrupt the workings of my body? My interest in seeing how suffering was created and how the whole process worked on a minute level deepened, as did my commitment to seeing.

Some months later, one of the notes I pulled off the board asked for clarification regarding my upcoming commitment date. Now that my end date was approaching, what did I want to do? I recall sitting outside the meditation hall, listening. Listening for the still small voice within.

The part of me who claimed *Okay, I've been really in the moment for months now. Can I have that old fantasy back?* rushed forward. Yet simultaneously there was a quiet recognition that I hadn't even scratched the surface of what training had to offer, that I was still in chapter one of what was possible.

There were monks at the monastery that carried money, but at that time I never carried any. As I sat quietly, listening, I noticed a shiny coin shimmering in the light by my feet. Without hesitation I picked it up, took a deep inhalation, and flipped it. Heads, I leave. Tails, I stay. As I exhaled, the coin spinning, midair, I recall realizing that if it suggested that I should leave, I'd give the game two out of three.

In that suspended moment in the space between my breaths, the space between my thoughts, the answer was clear. It wasn't until I was freed from the pressure of *Should I stay or should I go?* that I could clearly hear the truth of my heart's deepest longing. The act of giving over to a coin flip, stepping outside my limited debate of monk or city girl, quieted the inner argument enough to allow the truth to come forward.

ASPECTS OF THE PERSONALITY

A contemplative technology that has been invaluable to me over the years is recognizing aspects of the personality. This tool is a way to acknowledge that we have different forms of our psyche and that each has its own set of beliefs, assumptions, and fears. It's a tool that can create a lot of space. This contemplative technology helps to lovingly invite the questions

Who am I?
Who am I truly?

When we're identified with any of the various forms of the conditioned mind, who we perceive ourselves to be feels solid, fixed, even permanent. When we're identified, it leads not only to treating *ourselves* in a particular way but also to treating *others* in a particular way. The conditioned mind is quick to grab onto ideas and beliefs as if they're unshakable, as if they are *reality*. In this grabbing we lose the remembrance of who we truly are.

With this contemplative practice, we notice that we have a *part* of us who might love a certain something, another part of us who might resist that same thing, and yet another part who doesn't care about that thing at all. This overall awareness of the various parts of ourselves allows for an experience of harmony that isn't possible when we are bouncing through various experiences of total identification with these different aspects of the personality.

If you can see clearly that you have a part of you who [*fill in the blank*] and another part of you who [*fill in the blank*], then you're not fully identified with believing that either of these parts of you are, in fact, the whole of "you." They are *aspects* of being. They are *expressions* of being—each a wave in a vast ocean among many waves.

You are the ocean.

How does your experience of yourself shift when you recognize that you are not one limited, contained, constrained wave? What constructs about who you might have previously seen yourself to be begin to crumble? What is the result of recognizing that you refer to all these various parts of yourself as "you"? What is the result of seeing that you *experience* all these various parts as "you"?

WHO ARE YOU?

When we look beyond our identification with all the different aspects of the personality, throughout the shape-shifting and changing, what remains?

What is constant?

What has been the same throughout your entire life?
So much has changed form. What was the same when you were five years old, ten years old, fifteen, and now?

What has remained untarnished?
What has never been broken?

What is actually unbreakable?

This is inquiry. It's not about the conditioned mind figuring out the right answer. It's not about noodling. Let these questions be prompts that guide you to your own direct experience.

Let yourself find out, in your own direct experience, what is always true—in all times, in all circumstances, in all spaces. In a world in which everything is always changing, what remains the same?

THE VEILING OF BEING

When we are identified with the ego, we seek externally. As we look outward for peace or contentment, our true sense of self gets mixed up with the content of our lives. We believe we'll get to experience contentment once we [*fill in the blank*], or once we have [*fill in the blank*]. Many different aspects of the personality get ignited in our search for what we all long for: peace, contentment, happiness, ease. Coping mechanisms kick in. Survival strategies cloud the sky.

No aspect of the personality is bad or wrong. However, when we're identified with any given aspect, our experience of life becomes limited. When identified with one of them, who we truly are is veiled. As you learn to recognize when you are identified with a particular aspect of the personality, you have the opportunity to remember that this singular experience is not the whole of you but rather one wave in a larger sea. When we disidentify with an aspect of the personality, we are freed to recognize and remember ourselves as the ocean.

How do we disidentify from an aspect of the personality?
Through Love.

Every aspect of the personality has a different set of characteristics, beliefs, assumptions, fears. And they are all longing for Love and searching for happiness. Even if it doesn't appear that way, the wanting and the seeking are always the same at the core. At the end of the day, all these seemingly separate expressions of the personality long to return to being.

How we relate to ourselves, each other, and the world depends on "who" we are identified with. For example, I have a part of me that my husband, Vineet, nicknamed Justice Judy. This part of me has very dogmatic views about what's right and wrong. Justice Judy wields a weapon; she is unafraid to stand up for justice and has no fears about the fallout. That said, there is fallout from being identified with her. Her view is myopic. When I'm identified with her, all I see is the duality of good/bad and us/them. I'm quick to fight for justice and willing to punish. While the fight may lead to a temporary experience of "winning," it never leads to shared understanding. It never leads to the kind of justice I most deeply long for. It never leads to the resolution of the argument, the releasing of it, to peace. It only leads to a short-term win that is likely to be followed by a short-term loss. And the fight has an expensive price: my connection to others, my connection to the world, my connection to myself.

FROM THE PERSONAL TO THE COLLECTIVE

Consider for a moment how these different aspects of the personality that we all have are bouncing off one another in a global context. How would town hall look if the meetings led with creating an environment of CARE and privileged presence prior to punditry? Congress?

While I have no direct experience working in government, I can report about the transformational power of disidentification in the classroom. When students can rest in an environment of CARE (confidentiality, acceptance, reverence, and empathy) they naturally disarm. Since being identified with various aspects of the personality is often simply a way of being armored, this disidentification allows for vulnerability, openness, connection, and belonging.

To be clear, disidentifying with a particular aspect of our personality doesn't make us helpless or useless. Just because I choose to disidentify with the "Justice Judy" part of myself doesn't mean I'm rendered limp when it comes to my deep care for living in a just world. That false belief is simply the other side of the duality. When we step beyond the duality of vigilante/passive witness, we can manifest our care on behalf of the recognition of our shared being rather than as the felt sense that we're separate, victimized. What this ends up looking like can take infinite forms. It's freeing to realize that we can be involved in politics or grassroots movements, for example, without the habitual tendency to maintain the distortions, the recurrent identification with limited views of ourselves that is the source of so much harm—harm to self, harm to other.

Disidentifying with a particular aspect of our personality allows for the truth of our being to surface through our actions. Identifying and charging ahead with the aspect of myself who is "The Politician," exclusively, for example, veils shared being. However, recognizing that I am this shared being first, one that in this moment is using politics as a vessel for change, allows for change that is wholistic, universal, and nips off the story and complications of separation before it can even start. Again, *it's not what but how.*

If I want the world to be free, I must engage with it from the experience of my inherent freedom.

Through practice it becomes possible for the various aspects of the personality to live in service of Love and truth rather than act out the ego's survival strategies and coping mechanisms. Through practice, the seeming fragments of ourselves have the opportunity to realign with Love and truth, to return home, to act from being. In the alignment, we experience harmony. As we return to presence, the various parts of ourselves are given permission to coexist and we experience the peace that is sometimes eclipsed by our identification. Awareness, or pure consciousness, has infinite room for all parts of ourselves, for all experience. And it resists nothing. Why?

Because we are this awareness and it is our very nature to do so.

Can you relate to there being one part of you that feels one way and another part of you that feels another? If so, how do these parts of you interact with each other? And how do these parts of you interact with others? And the world?

In the same way that seeing how all the different aspects of the personality interact internally supports our personal liberation, the possibility for collective liberation opens as we see how our *collective identities* interact externally. Consider the interface between various groups working toward collective change, just as an example. Two groups may reach different conclusions about the significance of the same facts. When is there so much identification with belief on either side that the only result is fighting with each other, furthering the arguments and conflicts that encourage separation?

For us to have true and lasting change within our movements for ecological and social justice, it's paramount that we have the opportunity to see our own conditioning clearly. It's paramount that we know what we're bringing to the table—the part of me who feels entitled, the part of me who feels powerless; the one who is hopeful, the one who is angry.

What shifts in your interaction with another when, for example, you meet them from a deep recognition of who you truly are rather than being identified with the part of you who is righteous? What shifts when, even though the person you might be interacting with is identified with a particular aspect of their personality, you keep your eye on who *they* truly are? What shifts when you don't let this knowing drift away?

COLLECTIVE ASPECTS OF THE PERSONALITY

Remember "not one, not two"? The individual aspects of the personality are not relegated to a faulty definition of "the individual." Our so-called individual aspects of the personality cannot be teased apart from the collective.

Not only is your true nature awareness but this awareness is shared. Awareness is all of our true nature. And it is undivided.

The collective unconscious is often experienced as deeper than the personal unconscious. And this experience is, of course, shared. It exists in the shared region of the mind, rises up, and takes shape in the individual mind. So we aren't always simply unhooking and healing from our *personal* conditioning as we disidentify. Through disidentification, the collective is tended to as well.

Have you ever experienced a sadness you simply can't explain? That has seemingly nothing to do with a personal experience? Sometimes such sadness arises on behalf of all humanity, as an expression of the residual trauma that is shared across families, communities, species. Feeling sad on behalf of humanity is not the same thing as personal suffering. It's a sacred sadness—a sadness that arises to be seen and embraced. In the same way that disidentification with a particular aspect of the personality happens through Love, our collective unconscious cannot fester when it is brought into the light, when it is not only welcomed but also embraced.

In the embrace of Love, what isn't born of truth dissolves.

On the level of personal practice, it can be invaluable to recognize, when it occurs, that you're identified with a strong emotion. That you're angry, for example. To see that you're identified with a part of you—perhaps a resentful inner teen. It can be incredibly liberating, through awareness practice, to recognize that underneath this inner teen is a much younger aspect of the personality who is merely afraid. When seeing this clearly, from presence, you can respond to this part of you who is simply caught in the whirl of a survival strategy. You can consciously choose to step into the shoes of the unconditionally loving mentor (which, remember, is simply a form created in the imaginal realm for the unconditionally loving, aware presence that is—in every moment, beyond time).

On the level of collective practice, it can be invaluable to recognize various aspects of being as *not* the totality of who we are. I was born into a particular body, with a particular location in society, and that is one wave. My neighbor is another wave. We are arising in the same sea, made of the same sea. Our differences are beautiful expressions of the complexity of existence. They are here to be honored. And they cannot exist outside the sea that we share, the being that we share.

A Practice: Being With, Writing From

This practice is an adapted version of what's in our Peace in Schools curriculum for teens. I invite you to have a direct experience of this exercise. To really give it a go, to engage.

Find a way to spend some time outside being fully present to your surroundings, noticing when the attention gets absorbed in thought or time, then returning to now. From this place of presence, find an object you feel drawn to.

Sit down with the object. Spend intimate time with it. Let nothing distract you. Spend more time simply being with the object than the conditioned mind suggests you should. Linger with it freely.

Allow yourself to fully see the object, feel its texture, its weight. Engage all your senses. Notice how the light touches it. If this object had a particular energy, what would you say its energy is like?

Allow yourself to see things that you wouldn't notice if you just were walking by, texting, or not being present. Mindfully notice everything you can about it now that it's here with you and you are here with it.

Now write about this object. Please note, though: this practice isn't about perfect English grammar or about being a "good" writer but rather a way for you to explore, to inquire. In fact, I encourage you to let this writing be a stream of consciousness—once you start writing, try to not lift the pen from the paper, just see what comes out. Don't edit at all, if you can. In other words, watch for negative self-talk; watch for the voice that says, "Oh, you're not a good writer, you don't know what you are doing, this doesn't sound good." Notice this voice, practice letting it go, keep writing.

So, what should you write about? I encourage you to move beyond simply journaling about your observations of this object to imagining that you *are* this object.

Move *inside* the object. Move beyond the notion of interconnection with this thing. This object is you. Write from here.

For example, if my object is a piece of cardboard, rather than just say "This cardboard is four inches long, it looks like crumpled . . ." I'm going to write from the first person, using the words "I am . . .": "I am natural, I am not synthetic. I used to be part of a box that shipped things from one side of the country to the other. So you can imagine I am very, very strong. After being walked on by countless people, even though I may not look strong, there is still strength here, because—here I am. I still exist though I've changed form."

There is no right or wrong way to do this; you are letting yourself be creative, freeform, playful. You're not merely describing: "I am somewhat smooth. I am beige." As much as possible, you're imagining how this object might **feel**. What's its relationship to the world? What's its relationship to itself? Make sure to include at least one sentence that starts with "I feel . . ." And begin your writing with "I am . . ."

Allow yourself to write for ten minutes or so.

Pause.

I invite you to stop reading until you have done this exercise. I know firsthand how tempting it can be to read along without directly engaging. If that's a tendency of yours as well, no judgment. Give yourself the opportunity to break that habit in this case, though. The rest of this section will be much more impactful if you do.

After writing, ask yourself, what contemplative technology might we be exploring here?

PROJECTION

Projection is the idea that you can't see something "out there" that isn't "in here"; you can't project outward unless it's something you experience inward. What gets projected depends on what aspect of the personality you're identified with. Consider an actual projector: a projector has an image inside itself that is literally projecting outside onto a wall or screen.

A metaphor: Let's say that it's going to rain all day tomorrow. One person, or one aspect of the personality, might project onto the rain, "This rain is the worst! We're going to have to cancel our family cookout tomorrow. What a drag!"

Another person might project onto the rain, "This rain is such a gift! We're so lucky to have so much water. How nourishing after such a big drought!"

The rain is just the rain. Different people project different things onto it based on their experience. In general, our projections are also different based on our social location. Race, class, gender all play a part.

Within one cultural/familial context, a person might project one thing. From a different location, another. An example: In my Southern family, if you finish the sentence of the person who is speaking, it's a way to show that you're really engaged in the conversation. When someone does this with me, I project that they're "with me." (Providing they aren't blatantly interrupting to take the conversation in an entirely different direction. There's nuance here.) Do this very same thing with my husband and he might feel shut down. He might project that he's being disrespected, that perhaps you think what he's saying doesn't matter. He might take offense. The very thing that is *connecting* for me is *dividing* for him. (Thank goodness for awareness practice, since being able to be conscious of this conditioning and respond accordingly has been a game changer for our partnership, as you might imagine!)

Now an example that reflects larger conditioning within society: I've never been known for my sense of direction. When I got my driver's license and was out and about on my own for the first time, I remember getting lost a lot. (For my young readers, I know it's a stretch, but there were no apps to rely on for help.) If I was lost and came upon a police car, I felt relieved and happy. I projected that help was available. Help *was* available for me. The police officers I encountered likely projected that I could be trusted, that I was a "good, law-abiding citizen."

Now run through this same scenario but this time it's a sixteen-year-old Black girl who needs directions. She might not project that help is as available to her because that's likely not her lived experience. She might understandably project that the interaction with the police holds the potential of being dangerous or harmful, even life-threatening.

When a sixteen-year-old Black girl encounters a white police officer, she cannot simply disidentify with being Black. She cannot say to this officer, "But I am not this body and neither are you." She is likely to be met with projections—personal and collective all rolled up into one—existing within the conditioned mind of the officer. And there are serious, possibly fatal consequences.

Projection is a process of the conditioned mind. It's something the brain evolved to do. Within seconds, the brain tries to sum up new things and people it encounters to assess whether they are a threat. The brain does this by referencing our past experience, our memories, and the conditioned beliefs that have stemmed from these things.

We project our experiences, thoughts, feelings, and emotions onto other people and other things. This colors and shapes our experience of reality. And here's the thing—sometimes our projections reflect truth. Sometimes they don't. Just because we are projecting something doesn't mean it's not providing some accurate information. It's just that it's important to notice the lens through which we're filtering experience.

Learning how to notice projection can help remind us to come back to presence and ask: *What's really going on here? Am I identified with an aspect of the personality in this moment? If so, with whom?*

Seeing through our projections is yet another tool we can use to respond from presence and openness, instead of reacting from the small mindset of a fixed, illusory, identity.

A Practice: Owning Our Projections

Now let's go back and complete our exercise.

When we do this activity with teens, after defining projection, we go around the room and read what we've written, recognizing that what we've written is a projection of ourselves. (Whether students choose to read what they wrote is entirely up to them.)

Try this for yourself now. Share, or at minimum *imagine* sharing, what you wrote with someone else you trust, or with your group. If you are moving through this book on your own read it out loud to yourself. Watch for the voice of "Oh gosh, I don't want to read this out loud!" Any negative self-talk arise?

The reason I didn't tell you the theme of this practice before is because you'd likely be more self-conscious about what you were writing down, and you might be saying in your head as you write, *Is this really true about me?* I presented it this way so you wouldn't edit yourself, which can help reveal what aspect of your personality might be up right now. It's likely that a specific aspect of your personality was projecting their experience onto this object.

Here's an example: Imagine a key chain that has a bunch of keys on it—way more than normal. One day I might look at these keys and think, *Whoever owns these keys has way too many responsibilities; nobody should own keys to this many different things. How overwhelming!* On another day I might look and see, *Wow, whoever owns these is really engaged with the world; they have a lot of places to be. How exciting!*

See my point? What we project can really depend on the day and what aspect of the personality is present. As you read what you wrote out loud, whether by yourself or in your group, practice *owning* these projections. And keep in mind that it's likely simply a reflection of how you are feeling in this moment. Don't make too much meaning out of it and just see what you notice as you read yours aloud.

Do any parts feel really familiar? Are there some surprises in this? If you are doing this with someone you trust and/or in your group, and others read theirs aloud, notice, without judgment, whether any of what you hear feels true about what you know of this person.

Noticing projection is a useful tool because it can help us recognize, "Wait a minute, that's actually not true about me, so-and-so is just projecting that experience onto me." It's really helpful to remember that not only are you projecting much of the time but other people are as well.

I'll never forget the day I was leaving the Mindful Studies classroom and overheard Moses comforting another student. They were huddled together under the stairwell. As I locked up the classroom, I overheard the girl crying about some mean things her boyfriend had said about her. Had it been a different friend, I wouldn't have been shocked to hear a response along the lines of "What?! Where is he now? I'll kick his ass!"

Moses, who had taken our Mindful Studies class for several semesters by that point, paused and responded in a quiet, soothing tone, "Well, have you considered that perhaps he was projecting his stuff onto you?"

The girl fell silent, and she seemed to be deeply reflecting, noticing something new.

What do you notice?

What do you see about yourself based on what you wrote?

Can you see whatever is arising without judgment?

If doing this with others, what's it like to hear what other people in your group wrote?

What do you notice about other people's experiences?

Having facilitated this projection exercise with teens and adults for years, I've seen that one of the most beautiful outcomes can be when someone ends up recognizing and naming qualities about themselves—about who they authentically are—that would never arise if they were simply asked to describe themselves directly. Often participants get in touch with an aspect of their being they never thought of as "themselves," something beyond an aspect of the personality. Yet they can recognize in hindsight how it fits, how it resonates as truth.

I remember working with a retreat participant who had been struggling with depression for years and was practicing with the residue of a lot of serious trauma. The object she chose was a broken piece of glass. One would have thought that perhaps her writing would reflect a sense of brokenness. Perhaps words about being shattered, abandoned, discarded.

Instead, her writing reflected being full of light. It reflected being inherently beautiful and ultimately, unbreakable. It reflected being whole, despite the external experience of feeling fragmented.

Pause now.

Remember:

Your true nature is empty, open, shining with the luminosity of being.

Your true nature is ever-present. It cannot be divided.

It cannot be fragmented. It cannot be broken.

FROM THE ABSOLUTE TO THE RELATIVE

Can you imagine if every police officer was required to have training that included knowing how to direct the attention, recognizing when identified with the conditioned mind, seeing implicit bias, naming unmet needs and knowing how to meet them? Knowing how to disidentify and return to an experience of their own true nature? Can you imagine how different the police force would look?

What a gift that we can pause, disidentify from our thoughts and emotions, and return to presence. Touching on the absolute truth of our being benefits any moment. But if we are going to extend such helpful tools collectively, we must do so while recognizing what's true in relative terms. While I might recognize "I am more than the expression of this body in form, which I name as female," that might not change the fact that when I'm teaching in certain culturally conditioned contexts, men are more likely to be seen as the voices of truth, more likely to be respected than female teachers, and thus more likely to be paid a higher rate.

Recognizing projections in this circumstance supports me in not questioning my own worth. It helps me to see the collective and systemic issue, perhaps even go about trying to change it while not being confused that what's being projected onto me is true. It supports me in standing up in the face of injustice and disidentifying with negative self-talk, such as "Well, perhaps my teachings aren't as valuable as his." (Plug in any male counterpart.)

I was invited to teach at the Embodiment and Social Justice Summit. In my presentation, I referred to "the delusion of white supremacy." It felt important to do so as a way of not giving too much credit to white supremacy—to name upfront that it is delusional. To recognize that such a framework—such a way of seeing, thinking, believing, and therefore acting—can only arise out of the delusion that we are separate.

I appreciate that my friend Yolanda named that this designation could be quite triggering for some BIPOC. In her words, "There's nothing delusional about the impact of white supremacy on our bodies."

This points to the importance of being able to hold the reality of the absolute—that we are not separate—*along with* the reality of the relative—that much of the time in our conditioned world we do not act in ways that honor this truth, and that the manifestations of our delusion create real-world harm to each other, to ourselves, to our planet.

It does not serve our collective freedom to see the relative and the absolute as separate.
To fully realize our humanity requires being awake.

To fully realize our humanity, our potential to live in harmony, it is paramount to see, acknowledge, and name the ways we're not living up to this possibility; to come to grips with the manifestations of our individual and collective delusion.

It's all the same delusion, however it is manifesting.
We can address the delusion wherever it arises.
It's all the same delusion.

I believe that making true and lasting change depends on knowing ourselves in the most absolute sense. The true change we all seek is an awakened world, not merely shuffled policies. And let me be clear, shuffling policies is not a bad thing, but I believe it's not the deepest change we seek. It's not the ultimate resolution.

What is the ultimate resolution?
The ultimate resolution comes from knowing who we truly are,
directly experiencing our shared being,
and then acting in the world on behalf of that truth.

A Practice: Resting as Ourselves—R.E.S.T.

My friend, colleague, and Presence Collective teacher and board member Rashid Hughes came up with a brilliant and simple way to offer a map for folks, an invitation for all people to rediscover belonging in just being. He created R.E.S.T., a practice for realizing freedom through resting and being aware.

R=Relax your attention. **Release**

E=Exhale all striving. **Empty**

S=Sense the silence. **Surrender**

T=Tune in to awareness. **Trust**

About this practice he said:

> Sitting down and focusing on the breath can feel very confining and even traumatic for many folks, especially BIPOC, trauma survivors, and people from marginalized communities. When meditation instructions require a concentrated focus on a particular object or reference point for a long period, many of us often walk away feeling depleted and more exhausted than when we started the practice. R.E.S.T. is an invitation to recognize the natural perfection of our being without any method of control or manipulation. These pointers encourage us to reimagine ourselves liberated through being aware and resting.

And what a gift that we do not have to reimagine ourselves into something we are not! Our reimagining is actually an undoing, a letting go of what we are not, a releasing of who we've confused ourselves to be.

Meditation allows us to rest into ourselves—as ourselves.

A Contemplation: Resting in Being, as Being

Up until this point in this book, we've been practicing with object-based meditations. Such meditations use various objects—sound, sensation, the breath—as anchors, as supports for training the attention to return to the present moment when it wanders, to consistently guide the attention to the refuge of presence. Let's shift our approach now. If we were in a room together, I might share the following in a guided meditation format, leaving lots of space between each statement, between each question. I offer this here as more of a contemplation, an invitation to slow down and explore your direct experience within the open field of spaciousness. I'm not inviting noodling but rather inquiry and resting.

A reminder that you can check out the audio book if you'd enjoy listening to this, or perhaps recording it in your own voice and playing it back will appeal to you?

Come into a comfortable seat.

Rather than focusing the attention, rather than directing it or training it, soften it.

Remember the flashlight analogy in chapter one?

Rather than simply noticing what happens as the flashlight (attention) lands on various objects (like thoughts and emotions), rather than redirecting it to something else that is arising in the present moment (like the breath, which is also another object, albeit a subtle one), now visualize that its light is gently relaxing back into the source.

The light is slowly releasing back into the flashlight itself.

The light, your attention, is releasing. Releasing objects. It is free now to rest.

To rest in awareness itself.

Allow the attention to rest in its source.

As you rest in your direct experience of being aware, from this experience, how might you describe what's inherently and fundamentally true?

What is true about your true nature?
About your very being?
What qualities are present?

If you were to give words to what, in truth, has none,
how would you describe your true nature?

It's very different to touch the experience of true
nature—to know it, to rest in it, to move through the
world from the recognition of this true nature, versus
identifying with an illusion of a self that is separate
from life—and try to attain those very same qualities,
to try to be peaceful, to try to be accepting, to try to
be more liberated.

**Awakening is the recognition that we are that
which is already liberated.**

We've been confused about who we are.

We've been confused about what we are.

Awareness is inherently awake.

Awareness is inherently peaceful, unlimited, vast.

Awareness is fundamentally open and
unconditionally accepting.

Infinite consciousness (which I'm using interchangeably with awareness) is inherently free.

When we say our true nature is awareness, it's simply
one way to point to who we truly are versus who
we've been conditioned to see ourselves to be. We're
conditioned to perceive ourselves as separate body-
minds, separate selves with separate experiences.

From this conditioned perception of who we are, we
see ourselves as the subject of the story. We're in relationship with "other" as if other weren't the same as us,
as if we didn't share the same being.

There are many ways we could talk about our true
nature (while remembering that language fails us).
The true nature that is undivided, not separate. That is
infinitely whole, innately aware.

Our true nature, our actual identity, is identity-less,
unbound by the perception of separation. It is not
defined by I, me, mine, from an egoic sense. It is not
separate from others. It is not separate from anything.
It is not bound by time.

Free yourself from the stale and outdated idea of "my"
body and "my" mind.

In the same way that we grip, in the mind, onto our
conditioned thoughts and beliefs, we grip in the body.
These constrictions in the body are like flags planted
in the ground claiming "This is me." This constriction
is the ego, the activity of mind that views itself to be
separate from life, taking a stand.

Rather than identifying with this small, separate
self that takes a stand in a specific place, that's in
relationship with objects, thoughts, feelings in a
specific way; rather than taking a stand as ego; rather
than enhancing the activity of the conditioned mind
(which is all the ego is), take a stand as presence.

Take a stand as awareness.

It's an open stance.

A stanceless stance.

Conditioned activity—resisting, approval seeking, comparing, efforting—doesn't belong to you; it arises in you.

You, this open luminous awareness.

Rest in aware knowing.

Rest in aware being.

All things arise, pass, and dissolve. Take this stanceless stance as presence. Notice that it's not a hard, fixed stand at all but rather the intimate knowing of your own being. Simply go straight to the refuge of your very being.

Are there any conditioned voices arising?

"But how?"

"I can't do this."

It's okay. No worries if it feels difficult to access this today.

Simply let the imagination play for a moment.

Just consider a moment in your past when you had the direct experience of just being.

Perhaps you were resting in nature somewhere, by a creek or by the beach listening to the waves. Perhaps you were in bed at the end of a full day, feeling easeful.

This sense of okayness, this fineness, this ease—this is your very being.

Simply sink the attention, now, into the refuge of your being. Your being has nothing to do with the content of your life. Perhaps it's not a specific place that ignites this—maybe you were just washing the dishes but resting in yourself, feeling easeful, simply being.

Let it be simple. We can get so lost in the world of objects that we think of this refuge as something far away or even esoteric. There is nothing esoteric about your own being.

Allow yourself, now, to be freed from this world of objects.

Dropping, sinking, releasing into being.

We all know this place because it's the most intimate experience we have.

It is ever-present. A placeless place.

Meditation gives us the opportunity to establish this being as our refuge.

Remembering the refuge of your very being is a deep expression of Love emerging from the very thing we long for.

We long to know the refuge of our very being. Happiness without cause.

We all long for the very thing that we are.

Rest as this. We're always welcome here.

We are here. Always. We simply sometimes forget.

Allow yourself to stabilize in the experience of knowing this aware luminous being as you.

You are the brilliance of awareness. The luminosity of being.

That we fall for the distortion that being human means we are separate can be problematic. That's when great troubles arise.

Awareness is shared awareness. There may be many thoughts and perceptions, just as there are many body-minds, but there is only one awareness.

Unlimited awareness shines in each body, in each mind.
Take this stanceless stand as awareness,
welcoming everything in you,
embracing everything in you,
loving everything in you.

Simply being. You, awareness.

Collective Practice: Seeing What's True

- I invite you to follow up the projection practice in this chapter with further exploration.

- Go back to the lists you made in chapters two (page 40) and four (page 77). Make a list of what you believe about *the other* and a list of what you believe about *these groups* of people.

- As you return to these lists, everywhere you wrote the words *he/she/they*, replace it with *I*. Gently explore what it's like to *own* your projections.

- Practice owning what you think of as both positive and negative projections.

- While doing this, also consider what aspects of the personality are doing the projecting. What do you notice?

- Journal about your observations. If you are in a group, move into a discussion about your observations. As the twentieth-century psychotherapist Carl Jung was reported to have said, "The best political, social, and spiritual work we can do is to withdraw the projection of our shadow onto others."

- Then, move into a shared period of meditation in which you are, together, resting the attention in awareness.

- If you are alone, you could record the contemplation above for a guided experience or listen to the audiobook. If you are with a group, you might wish to have one person read the above for others.

- After the meditation, explore further, this time responding to the question:

Who am I truly?

If I am not the various aspects of the personality, if I am not what gets projected onto others, who am I?

Respond from your deepest knowing, not with "I am married," "I don't enjoy camping in the winter," "I have two dogs." Really listen for and give language to something beyond objects.

Conditioned perspectives don't reflect the totality of truth in the absolute sense. Can you allow yourself to enjoy releasing the grip of defining yourself through these smaller perspectives? What allows you to rest into the unknown?

- If you're in a group, allow each person to share their experience. If you are on your own, journal:

How do you describe your deepest and most intimate experience of yourself? How do you describe who you truly are?

A Practice: Recognizing Our Divinity

How is it to know others as awareness itself? To free them from your conditioned projections? To consciously return to "I don't know" mind? Does it feel relatively simple to do? Does it feel complicated? Where do you get stuck?

Move through the world practicing this "I don't know" mind—in the grocery store, at the bank. Practice it with people you're close to as well as strangers. What shifts when you interact with others from this open, aware mind?

What shifts when you interact from the recognition of who you truly are? What shifts when you practice seeing who *they* truly are? How are interactions affected?

As you practice this, hold this saying from Rupert Spira at the forefront: "In order to fully realize our humanity, it is necessary to recognize our divinity."

What, if anything, gets in the way of you recognizing your own divinity? And the divinity of others?

Chapter Nine

Return to Oneness

Resting in Luminous Being

God—infinite, self-aware Consciousness—is the
unlimited, open, empty field in which all experience
appears, with which all experience is known and
out of which all experience is made.

—Rupert Spira

I don't remember much about what led up to the insight. Over twenty years
later, all I remember is the insight—and the exact moment it arose.

Over time it's become clear to me that "I" doesn't ever have insights. In
other words, insights don't belong to the ego. I have heard that Jean Klein, the
French teacher of the great Indian tradition Advaita Vedanta, used to say that
the ego is the clown that comes in after the show to claim the applause. It says, "I
did that!" and takes a colorful cross-legged bow.

The ego, the activity of an illusory self, is the noisemaker, not the insight
generator. Insights arise out of the mind of spaciousness.

We view possibility when the sky is clear.

We taste possibility when the palate is cleansed.
In the space between the thoughts, insights appear.

But alas, I digress . . .

I was sitting on the right side of the meditation hall, other monks on my left, my teacher at the front of the room. I had been a monk for many years at this point and thought disappeared into silence often—much more often than when my training began. A subtle sense of being always remained.

When it came to practice, my teacher almost always focused on what we are *not*. I later came to understand this as the *neti neti* approach. *Neti neti* is Sanskrit for "not this, not that" or "neither this nor that." You are not these thoughts. You are not these emotions. You are not these objects of experience. If you keep negating, you will end up with nothing but your true nature, which cannot be negated. You will end up with yourself. When everything I'm not has been negated, that which I am, remains.

Imagine the sun as your true nature. As monks, we focused intensely on the clouds. What is it that blocks the sun? When do the clouds appear? How do the clouds form? What is the result of being in the shade? What part of you ends up in the shade?

I'm not suggesting that this was an intellectual process, by no means. Rather, I'm pointing to a metaphor that conveys where our focus was as we trained. It's not that there was no acknowledgment of the sun; it's that we didn't spend time focusing on it directly. And certainly we didn't give many words to it. In group discussions, we rarely focused on what we *are*.

Another monk had just finished speaking during a group discussion. I don't recall any of the content of what they shared. They were bringing attention, as we were trained to do, as we recited in meditation every day, to "see how we cause ourselves to suffer, so we can drop that and end suffering."

After they spoke, there was a pause. Out of the silence I blurted, "But we aren't what suffers!"

All this focus on how we cause ourselves to suffer. All this focus on how we need to end our suffering. I got that *we* don't cause ourselves to suffer. And *we* aren't what's going to end it. *We* aren't even what's experiencing it! The conditioned mind is the only place suffering lives.

We are not that!

"It's true; we aren't what suffers," my teacher responded. After pausing she continued, "But what kind of workshop title would that be: 'You Aren't Suffering.' No one would come!" The room erupted in laughter and she moved on.

I remember getting that she was joking, being tongue in cheek. But as she called on the next person, a deep disappointment welled. Why *aren't* we underlining this? If we keep focusing intensively on our suffering, doesn't that simply give a certain reality to it? And more importantly, to the "I" that experiences itself as separate? What are we doing here?

Now keep in mind that I came to practice without having any background in other spiritual approaches. I hadn't read books about pathways that focused on what we are. I knew one approach and that approach served me—deeply.

Until it didn't.

To be clear, I have absolutely no doubt that it is valuable to focus on how suffering gets created. All of the contemplative technologies offered in this book and in our curriculum for youth were created/learned/adapted/shared with adults and teens because they transform people's lives. I'm also clear that if we found a way to apply these tools collectively, we would transform society.

Many people have the good fortune to know themselves as awareness—that they are the sun and not the clouds—yet they still get trapped in suffering because they haven't had support in recognizing the various aspects of the personality they've become identified with. Or they struggle to own their projections. Or they have no tools for recognizing deep habits of mind such as implicit bias and/or other ways they uphold dominant culture and therefore suffer. Although they have glimpsed the truth of being, they don't have practices to assist in dis-identifying with the conditioned mind, supporting the return to being; to not have a distant memory or egoic belief in being but to truly rest in awareness.

All of these technologies can be learned—and they work. They help to end suffering. When fully engaged with, they transform lives. No one can convince me otherwise. It's been my direct experience for over twenty-five years.

However, it's also clear to me that at some point—and not necessarily after years of monastic training—it is invaluable to focus on *who you are* rather than giving your attention only to *what you are not*. It's invaluable to focus directly on the sun, although that's not an entirely accurate way to describe it, for here's the fun part:

You cannot actually *focus* on who you are.

You, infinite consciousness, can only *focus* on an object. Just as the eye cannot focus on itself, you cannot *focus* on who you are. The sun's rays cannot shine back onto itself. Its rays can only shine on objects, yet the sun illuminates itself. You are like that.

You illuminate yourself.

You can only *be* yourself.

Your aware, luminous being shines.

It shines on things. *You* don't get shined *on*.

You, pure consciousness, illuminate yourself and all that is.

WHO IS YOURSELF?

We've been talking about "yourself" in a specific way. For most of the book we've been referring to "I" as shorthand for the ego, which is how it was defined in my monastic training. "I" as in "the mind of *I, me, mine*"—the clown who always seeks center stage. "I" can also be one way we can refer to our self-aware being. In some traditions, they capitalize the *S* in *Self* to make this distinction. Lowercased *self* is a way to name the activity of the conditioned mind—the ego. Uppercased *Self* is a way of referring to knowing yourself as pure consciousness.

One approach I'm describing, the approach I was steeped in at the monastery, could be described as a progressive, or gradual, approach. This approach includes contemplative technologies, and it gives attention to what we are not. It can have a step-by-step feel to it. A direct approach goes straight to the experience of the sun, of who we truly are. When we know the heart of who we are, these approaches need not be viewed dualistically. Remember:

When we are free, when we know who we truly are,
we are free to move in any direction.

Call me impatient, but when I look at our relative world, it seems to me we desperately need all the tools, all the approaches, all the pathways we can get. To paraphrase the Buddha, we have no shortage of examples for how hatred, greed, and delusion manifest in our world. What a wondrous and miraculous gift that we have just as many ways home! I'm a huge fan of the question "Where's my entry point?"

What door are you called to walk through?

Any door that opens and invites you home is a valuable one,

one to be cherished, a portal to be honored.

What offers freedom, more ease, more joy?

What serves the remembrance of your very being?

Listen to that.

Just as speaking about the relative and the absolute requires nuanced balance, holding both progressive and direct approaches is a balancing act. For example, if someone came to me after experiencing serious trauma, I wouldn't say, "You aren't suffering." Even though I may never take my eye off the deepest knowing of who they truly are—that they are unbreakable, untarnishable, infinite—it might be more fitting to remind them of the value of reassurances, to shine light on the tool that has the potential to gently remind them, gently guide them, to the remembrance of who they truly are.

Life is not either/or. Why should our practices be?

You'll find this "whatever works" approach modeled in this book. It's not a secret. If a portal to the remembrance of your own being is through a story, seek stories that remind you. If it's through poems, find poetry that ignites truth. If it's through descriptions about what actually has no language, turn there. Perhaps it's in practices you can engage in, practices that prompt direct experience, or igniting the imaginal realm. It's all good. Let your mantra be:

Trust what works. Trust your Self.

What you long for is whispering in your ear.
If you are quiet, you will hear it.
You don't need someone else's formula
to know the brilliance of your own being.
You don't need a holy book
to be intimate with all things.

(And if you enjoy reading holy books,
by all means read them!)

I AM [FILL IN THE BLANK]

Remember the I am [*fill in the blank*] conversation from chapter seven? Filling in the blank can be a helpful way to see how duality takes shape. It can also be incredibly helpful to name what you are conditioned to believe you are, as support for revealing what, in truth, you are not.

I remember the first time that Maddi, a teen from one of our classes, got it.

"Wait a minute. I am not angry! Anger is arising in me. I don't have to call it mine, and I certainly don't have to call it *me*!"

I recently had an exchange with Maddi. She's long graduated high school and hasn't had the same relationship with her emotions since. It's such a blessing to learn these lessons early in life, but anytime is the best time.

We can take this a step further. We can simply drop all the blanks and surrender the attention to

I am.

Who is that?

Where is that?

What is that?

THE IMPORTANCE OF KNOWING YOURSELF
AS THE WITNESS AND BEYOND . . .

There is a profound shift that happens when we realize we are not our thoughts, that we are *aware* of our thoughts. Through practice we ground in the experience of recognizing ourselves as the conscious witness. (I'm using the words *conscious* and *aware* interchangeably here.)

I am aware of these thoughts. I am aware of these emotions. I am aware of these sights, sounds, objects of experience. Here, too, we could drop what we are aware of—drop the blanks, if you will—and simply rest into *I am aware*.

This kind of disidentification in practice is imperative.

Our liberation depends on it.

Recently I was guiding a meditation practice in one of the weekly groups I offer. In the meditation we moved through these prompts:

Look for space between the thoughts.

Know the space between the thoughts

(the way you *know* love; this is not an intellectual knowing).

Feel the space between the thoughts.

Be the space between the thoughts.

After the meditation, Sharon exclaimed, "For a moment there I really felt like that open space!"

I responded, "It *felt* like that, Sharon, because you *are* this open space. This isn't some kind of sweet metaphor. This is the experience of your very being."

Tears of recognition streamed down her face.

THE LIMITATION OF THE WITNESS

For many of us on a journey of liberation, we get stuck at the point in practice where we feel ourselves to be a witness *observing* objects, separate from them. When stuck in such a place, it can be easy to fall for negative self-talk, like "I am seeing all these thoughts arise in meditation. If only I could clear my mind,

I would be at peace. I *must* keep practicing." We become identified with seeing ourselves as the witness, the subject, with thoughts as the object, and in this process we become the "I" who strives in practice.

Most of us spend our whole day moving through the world experiencing life through the lens of *I, me, mine* in relation to what is "out there." Subject-object. In spiritual practice, this process of othering internally often simply becomes a more subtle subject-object relationship. (*How you do anything is how you do everything.*) "I" notice these thoughts. "I" try to clear the mind. "I" had a bad meditation today because the mind was busy. "I" long for enlightenment.

Within this phase of practice, we are not truly free. We might be better at responding versus reacting, we might have less suffering in our lives than we used to, we might have increased our concentration skills, but we are not truly free.

It is ego's ultimate disappointment
that there is no such thing as enlightened ego.

In this created story of separation, we also are prone to hover above our experience, witnessing it rather than fully embodying it. We step outside experience, albeit in a subtle way. (More on the problematic nature of this kind of disembodiment in the next chapter.)

From this perspective, even focusing on the breath can create a subtle subject-object relationship. The witness, the subject, "I" am focusing on the breath, or sounds, or sensation (objects). This lens maintains relationship.

Truth is revealed in the collapse of all relationship.
It is the shining of the unity of oneness.
Liberation is not only the recognition of this oneness—
it is the realization that we are this.

Remember "not one, not two"? Language fails us. The oneness we're referring to in this chapter is prior to the singularity of *one* and the multiplicity of *two*. It is prior to emptiness and fullness. As taught by Rupert Spira, it is the luminous infinite consciousness in which all experience appears, that with which all experience is known, and that out of which all experience is made.

At some point, we must retire the mythology that suggests that you, awareness, are separate from what you are aware of. I say "at some point" because it's a very important teaching tool until it's not.

A new level of disidentification with the illusory self is available to us when we collapse this distinction. When we realize

> **We, this body-mind, are not conscious *of* something.**
> **Consciousness is not separate**
> **from what we are conscious of.**
> **Consciousness is always conscious of itself**
> **and forms arise in it.**
> **Forms arise in us.**
> **How do we know these forms?**
> **Through consciousness.**
> **Through ourselves.**

You cannot identify with awareness the way you identify with the conditioned mind. Why? Because you *are* awareness.

> **Anything that exists vanishes.**
> **It appears in a medium and vanishes back into a medium.**
> **A cloud appears in the sky and vanishes back into the sky.**
> **The wave does not exist outside the ocean.**
> **Everything we experience arises, exists, and then vanishes.**
> **In what does the entire content of experience arise and exist?**
> **And how do we know this experience?**

GOING AGAINST THE GRAIN OF MATERIALISM

In one of Mindful Studies' first semesters, a particularly astute teen, at the end of the lesson about duality, piped up: "Well, we've focused on the conditioned mind, and we've focused on awareness, but I'm really gettin' this whole duality thing. I get that it's made up in the mind. So I can see that it can sound like awareness and the conditioned mind are two sides of a duality. But I'm betting they aren't, huh?"

It was striking to me that this student, unprompted, recognized that the conditioned mind is not the opposite of consciousness itself. Though we don't speak of this in our high school curriculum, he realized that even the conditioned mind is made of consciousness.

Why don't we speak to this directly in our curriculum? It's always been very important to me that the tools we offer are equally accessible to a Muslim student, a Christian student, an atheist—anyone. We don't tell teens who they are; we invite them to explore their experience.

In the same way that Love and presence cannot be relegated to any specific religion, returning to your own being and recognizing this being as home is an opportunity we can all partake in, an invitation we can all respond to regardless of religious beliefs. I've always appreciated that students from various religious backgrounds and nonreligious backgrounds, in my experience and according to our research, are able to connect with and benefit from the class equally.

Much has been written about McMindfulness, the way modern mindfulness in many contexts has been whitewashed and co-opted by an individualistic, capitalist culture. Mindfulness often ends up being employed in a fashion that maintains the separate self rather than undoes it. Such an approach tends to strip the practice of spirit, as often happens as any practice is colonized. Such an approach maintains dominant culture.

Within dominant culture we are habituated to worship the conditioned mind.

It is an unnamed religion of separation to which most of us are devout.

I have found it very helpful that Peace in Schools, operating within the realm of public education, is proscribed from offering religious instruction. In the best of circumstances, this "secular" realm allows everyone to bring all their values, aspirations, backgrounds, beliefs, and so on into a safe, public space where no particular religion or ideology is privileged over any other. Although, ironically, it seems to me that modern society resists anything that recognizes God in any form because it conflicts with the dominant "religion," which is materialism.

Materialism is the belief that everything is either made only of matter or is ultimately dependent upon matter for its existence and nature. A philosophy can be materialistic and still have some room for spirit, but it's often only in a secondary way, if at all. Most forms of materialism tend to reject the existence of spirit and/or anything nonphysical.

At Peace in Schools, we offer a practice of inquiry. We offer a practice that honors the role of reverence, which we define as "respect tinged with awe." We acknowledge and honor the roots of practices offered. We give teens a way to contemplate their inner landscape in a setting (high school) where the attention is otherwise almost entirely directed to external things. We teach the value of presence.

When our semester-long curriculum was birthed, I envisioned it as a layout of reminders. Exercise after exercise: "Here's one way we forget who we are, here's another way we forget, here's another. And here are just as many ways to remember."

We offer an inner curriculum, a way home to yourself. No one is excluded from their own being. It's not humanly possible.

To experience being you don't need to believe anything.

To experience yourself as separate, belief is required.

So I offer this to you too—the invitation to know the peace we all long for, the contentment of being, the truth that is there prior to the perception of dualistic thinking (yet includes dualistic thinking), without believing that this requires religion, without adopting belief systems or dogma, without having to exclude anyone or anything.

CROSSING THE STREAMS

It was May of 2012 when I drove over to a little center in Portland, Oregon, called Opening to Life. Lynn, a friend from North Carolina who had attended some of my workshops, had called to say that I needed to go check out this visiting teacher.

"You are cut from the same cloth. The way he works directly with students, meeting them in the moment with no agenda . . . there's something you two share. Just go."

I looked up the event online. I had never heard of the teacher presenting in Portland that night. I had never heard of the school of Hindu philosophy he worked with: Advaita Vedanta. I had never heard of the direct path, and I knew nothing of the sages who shared this path, such as Ramana Maharshi or Sri Nisargadatta Maharaj. I saw that the cost of the workshop was twelve bucks; I had nothing else going on so I hopped in my car and went.

Among the list of things I didn't know was that I would meet not one but two people integral to the formation and running of Peace in Schools. And I certainly didn't know that in that hot and stuffy room I'd end up hanging on every word Rupert Spira said.

Not long after the workshop, I began attending Rupert's retreats. At this point I had only been on traditional Zen retreats, and this first step out of that structure shook me in a delightful way. Number one: everyone was talking—scandalous. Number two: people were engaging as personalities—scandalous. Number three: people were hootin' and hollerin' and even playing music together after groups let out—scandalous. They were having a ball of a time the whole week. Scandalous, scandalous, scandalous.

My head spun. If I hadn't recognized the depth of teaching, I might have written off the whole thing as insincere. But I felt him, I saw him. I knew where he was speaking from and recognized him as my next teacher.

Little did I know at the time that Rupert has guru Teflon and that he'd be diligent about not allowing me to put him on a pedestal. He didn't need me to be on the floor. He saw that I had engaged in plenty of that kind of student-teacher dynamic at the monastery. He wanted nothing of it.

I now understand the true value of breaking down the power dynamic of the student-teacher relationship; the value of true spiritual friendship, of mentorship that is a reflection of power *with* versus power *over*. This couldn't be more different from the intensive context I was trained in, yet it is the context that has been most fruitful for my growth.

When we approach another person free of dualistic and hierarchical relationships, we give them permission to do the same. And that spills out in the world. Why? Because this type of freedom is a manifestation of Love—the very Love we all long for.

When one of us touches freedom, it gives others permission to do the same.

On a deep level, we all long to return to the experience of what is the same in all of us—the experience of peace, our very being.

In one of the first retreats I attended with Rupert, I recall sitting up front. Most participants sat in chairs—scandalous! I, of course, sat motionless on my traditional Japanese zafu through his two-hour-long meditations, thank you very much. *Cue proud uprightness and a straightening of my imaginary robe.*

One particular meditation he guided invited the release of discipline. It was music to the part of me who had been so focused—in fact, prided herself—on discipline. To the one who was forever willing, forever committed, forever focused, this meditation was like being held by someone who loved me. So loving, so soft, so gentle to be guided to recognize:

"Meditation is not what we do, it is what we are."

And then later:

"Simply be aware of being aware."

I will remember these words forever. These sentences resonated so deeply and so thoroughly with my experience, yet I had never given myself full permission to let go into such an approach to meditation. The conditioning to effort, though it was a very subtle efforting at that point, was simply too strong. In meditation, I knew the experience of the witness falling away. Rupert gave it language.

Now when I attend retreats it's simply to be in the company of friends who share a deep love of truth. And to rest. Not to strive. Not to effort. Not to gain. Sometimes I even find myself lying down in the back of the room for the meditations—scandalous.

One of my favorite things about this falling away of efforting is that it's a replicable experience. It can be practiced—although the irony is, of course, that it's a nonpractice given that it doesn't require *doing*. It is an experience that can be accessed at will. For some, the falling away of the witness may happen seemingly randomly during periods of meditation, yet not be the direct result of a specific approach to meditation. Here, now, you too can be freed from efforting, even the subtlest efforting.

How? By allowing your attention to rest in awareness itself rather than focusing on an object during meditation, even a subtle object such as the breath. By allowing the attention to come home to its source, to being. In being, there is no separate witness of any object.

There is

only This.

A Contemplation: Resting in Love, as Love

Find a restful place where you can read through this contemplation, treating it like a poem of sorts, something that invites pause and awareness of the stillness out of which the words arise. The point is for this to be experiential, not simply something you think about. Allow yourself to sit with it for a bit afterward too. Allow yourself to rest.

Come into a comfortable seat. In this contemplation, we're going to explore two approaches.

Begin by simply being aware of being aware.

APPROACH 1

Notice for a moment what it's like to *try* to clear the mind.

Don't have thoughts.

Try that now.

Obviously you cannot really do this. You know that.
But just let this be play. Really lean into what it feels
like to try.

While you're at it, don't have emotions.

Put fear, anger—whatever emotions might be
present—somewhere else. Just get rid of them.

Don't let worry in. Keep the mind clear. Try to get rid
of all emotion so nothing is in the way.

While we're at it, we should probably not let strong
sensations in. That might disturb our clear peace.

Don't let strong emotions enter.

Keep thought out, intense sensation out.

Again, simply allow this to be a playful experiment
and notice, what is your experience of this?

What's the felt experience of *trying* to keep the
mind clear?

Of holding experience at bay?

I'm being playfully dramatic to underline the impact
of our habit to fall for the story that we need to "clear
the mind," that a "good" meditation is one in which
things don't disturb us. This is a distortion.

If you trace this distortion back, you will find truth.

**The truth that consciousness itself is not disturbed
by a busy mind.**

**Consciousness itself is not disrupted by strong
emotions.**

Consciousness is not tarnished by pain or intense sensation.

In practice, the ego takes this truth and says, "I will get rid of these things." If you've been practicing awhile, you may have an "evolved ego." There really is no such thing, however. The ego just adapts new language to describe things while keeping itself center stage. It may say, "I will transcend these things" or "I will let go." It can sound like a helpful spiritual coach. It can be sneaky that way.

The "I" that experiences itself as separate from life

cannot and will not ever know liberation.

There is no such thing as an enlightened ego.

APPROACH 2

Notice what's arising. For example, are there any emotions present?

Let's say you notice something you label as "anxiety." Rather than hovering above this experience—naming, seeing, evaluating, getting space from it, trying to accept it (this all can maintain the ego); rather than identifying with the subject—"I am aware of . . ."—in this approach, simply notice, what is whatever's arising, arising in?

In this body-mind?

In the separate self that claims observation?

What if that was just a habit of perception?

What if what gets labeled "anxiety" is simply sensation arising in vast, unborn, undying consciousness?

Notice how all emotions are simply a flicker, something coming and going, within something that doesn't change. These fleeting experiences are known by something that doesn't change.

Rest into this now.

So in approach 1, we consciously identify with a separate self that's trying to **do** something to or with what's arising—name it, let it go, reject it. We move into relationship with what's arising: Subject. Object.

In approach 2, we recognize ourselves. We turn attention to who we truly are rather than to the object. In approach 2, we recognize ourselves as awareness itself. We recognize that we are the open, inherently aware space in which things arise and that we know what arises through ourselves—through being consciousness.

Is infinite consciousness in relationship with what arises?

Does it like it/not like it?

Want it/not want it?

Push it away/cling to it?

Only the illusion of a self that is separate engages in this way.

Trying to do something, practice something, to **achieve** this state of infinite consciousness is like the sky trying to get rid of clouds, planes, birds so it can have an experience of openness.

Now we are exploring practice as a nonpractice. It is like the releasing of a clenched fist. It takes more effort to keep the fist tight than it does to allow it to relax, to let the hand return to openness.

This inherent quality of aware openness is what gives rise to all that appears, to all form.

Where else could anything appear?

Rather than trying to achieve this state of openness, simply allow yourself to enjoy what is—the way you might imagine the open, aware sky finds delight in the various weather patterns that arise and pass through and dissolve back into it. It's a stretch of the imagination because the open expanse of the sky isn't disliking or liking, wanting, or clinging. But play with it.

The open sky is naturally allowing, naturally accepting. It doesn't try.

Acceptance is a quality of awareness. It belongs to awareness.

We don't have to try to accept or try to achieve equanimity.

Equanimity is present when we are not identified with the conditioned mind.

Our experience of equanimity is stabilized by the repetition of recognizing and knowing ourselves as awareness.

Of you being yourself, knowingly.

Most people report that as we let ourselves rest in and as who we authentically are, if we were to describe that innate experience, we might use the word *happiness*. Not the happiness that's the opposite of sadness.

Some might use the words *deep well-being* or *contentment*. It's what we all long for—this kind of happiness.

What we long for is our very being.

We are what we've been striving after.

Who we truly are, what we truly are,

has been calling us home.

Rest in who you are rather than trying to become who
you think you should be.

If you meditate

to be a better person,

you'll always be busy

trying to be a better person.

If you meditate

because you are in love

with resting in your own

luminous infinite being,

you'll always be in Love.

FROM THE PERSONAL TO THE COLLECTIVE

When you consciously immerse yourself in what is real, in what is unchanging, how you relate to yourself, others, and the world shifts. Through the practice (although, again, perhaps better described as a nonpractice) of resting in ourselves as ourselves, our recognition stabilizes.

The constantly changing relative experience of life can be a welcome and endlessly fascinating field of human experience, but it's not real. The relative, simply put, could be described as what is temporary, in flux, changing, impermanent. We can describe the physical body this way, the emotions this way, all material things this way.

Nothing that comes and goes can be defined as real on the deepest level. Of course there is a particular reality to a temporary experience; the emotion you're experiencing is not entirely unreal in that it does have a particular existence, but it is not real in the same way reality is real. The reality that doesn't change. The infiniteness of aware being.

Emotions come and go, the personality expands and contracts, the body is born and dies. Those relative things borrow their reality from absolute reality. Those things have a *particular* reality, but they are not *real* in the absolute. They are dreams in the absolute. It is possible to stabilize in our direct experience of knowing reality. In this way, we access inner certainty, no matter the weather.

Through practice it is possible for us, collectively, to approach our longing for change on the relative plane, seeped in the knowledge of what is true in the absolute sense. What is undisturbed. What is unchanging. The collective field of human consciousness is deeply affected by shared awakeness, just as it is affected by shared distortion. Approaching relative change in this way is born of Love and guides us back to Love.

By looking through our conditioned dualistic lenses, we create and maintain limited and distorted systems that revolve around imbalance. In fact, unjust societal systems cannot exist without such an imbalance. The fallout from clinging to our dualistic lenses is *collective suffering.*

Through practice we have the opportunity to free ourselves from such systems. Remembering the truth of who we are in our daily lives, recognizing that we are not these systems but something that participates in their creation—particularly when we are blind to them—allows us to see through the distortion, to burn the systems that are broken and allow the phoenix of truth to rise.

In stating the above, I want to be clear: it is not my intention to reinforce the popular narrative that the world is broken.

In an online dharma session I led in May 2020, during the pandemic and the height of the fallout from George Floyd's murder, some words arose in me about what's broken and what isn't. I offer them here, in the name of not losing sight of the essential beauty we share as we acknowledge things that, within dominant culture, have long been ignored.

IS THE WORLD BROKEN?

Something that's arising in me to name is that I've been seeing this phrase float around the internet: "The world is broken." Maybe it's prevalent in my circles because I do follow a lot of voices who are illuminating the inequities of this time, illuminating the ways the pandemic has highlighted massive disparity. Of course, the disparity has been here, and we're seeing this disparity more clearly, collectively, during this time.

We can't let go of what we don't see. What we're unconscious to silently governs us. So it's an important seeing, and it's also worth acknowledging that this is an important seeing from the seat of a person who holds proximity to power and white "privilege." So that ought to be named. For some, it's survival, not simply "seeing." For some, there is nothing new to be seen here. White folks are waking up to what BIPOC have known, experienced, and been harmed by for years—hundreds of years.

What I want to point to today is this notion of "the world is broken." Be mindful of falling for this narrative. Our conditioned systems are broken. Our habitual ways of relating to each other, as though we were separate from each other—that is inherently broken. That's being revealed as broken now.

But reality isn't broken. The truth of the open sky, the infinite vastness of your own being is not broken. So we must know this unbrokenness too. This deep recognition of wholeness must be illuminated. Should we have an intention to create systems that are not broken, this deep recognition of wholeness must come to the forefront.

That is the creation of an enlightened society—one that reflects our deepest love and understanding; one that reflects the unbrokenness, the wholeness of reality; and one that reflects our shared being.

That is a tremendous opportunity in this time—to create from this recognition rather than maintain narratives that imply separation. Narratives that imply brokenness call us into the action of becoming that which is always fighting, that which is always trying to fix, that which is always in an adversarial relationship with others and with life.

That's not the same thing as saying "Racism doesn't affect me" or "Injustice is completely permissible to me." It is true that the infinite nature of consciousness is undisturbed by our conditioned activity. But as we know this wholeness, as we know this awareness, this consciousness, we see that to cause harm, to create broken systems, to leave anyone out is out of alignment with our deepest understanding.

We extend our arms and our hearts to each other from our deepest knowing that we are one, that we are together in this. So, yes, there is great disparity. Please, let's all be clear about this disparity so that we can see through it and create something new.

But let's move from the recognition, from the deepest knowing of who we really are, of what we truly are. Let's surrender this narrative that we are broken, that the world is broken, that we must be at war. Let's instead live the truth of what is.

Living this truth, what then do we create?

What do we build, together, when living this truth?

Just imagine for a moment if the hundred-plus people on this call, in this moment, all set the intention to live this truth, even just for one day, just for today. Allowing your actions to be on behalf of your understanding, your knowing, of oneness. Allowing your speech to be on behalf of your deepest knowing.

How does your day appear differently if your actions and your speech aren't on behalf of the belief that "I am broken," that "we are broken," that "the world is broken," that "truth is lost?"

So, friends, become the sky. From this becoming, simply allow your overflowing love to touch all that you encounter. It's from overflowing love you will care for others, build systems that are just, share truth, uplift those who've been marginalized, and own the ways you participate in marginalizing others within this conditioned story. From Love, we will own the ways we participate in and maintain the conditioned narrative that we are *other than*, that we are broken.

It's the narrative that we are broken that creates the conditioned impulse for us to attempt to have power *over*. We must see those conditioned habits and narratives and be willing to surrender them. We cannot cling to those narratives and create an enlightened society at the same time.

Collective Practice: Exploring *There Is Only This*

Enlightenment is intimacy with all things.

—Zen Master Dōgen

Continue with the collective practice from the previous chapter, Seeing What's True, with your group. You might choose to simply discuss your observations with each other. You might also choose to engage in dyads, with one person sharing about a place they feel stuck in their life or practice while the other consciously practices with the questions below. (If you do this, be sure to switch so that both people have an opportunity to be in each seat.) Allow yourselves, as a group, to lean into creativity. Please feel free to create your own collective way to explore this. The only instruction is to pay attention and notice what you see.

How is it to know others as awareness itself? What shifts when you interact from the recognition of who you really are? What shifts when you practice seeing who they truly are? How are interactions affected?

Now:
Practice seeing what's arising—whatever that is—as arising in you, awareness. What shifts when you view *everything* that arises in this same way? What is it like to experience others as different forms all arising in the same vast, infinite consciousness? And not just others, but all things!

Now:
What's it like to experience others as *made* of the same consciousness? We're practicing in this way so that we're not only deconstructing the notion of separation in an intellectual sense. We want to experience it. To be truly free, it's not enough to understand that we are all made of the same thing, that we *are* the same thing. It's important that we *feel* it.

Explore, experientially, what it's like to rest in this open, aware, infinite vastness—the open, inherently aware space in which things arise—in various group contexts. For example, if you are on a bus, focus on the aware, empty space your body-mind is arising in, that others are arising in, that the bus is arising in! Or if you attend a dance party or a yoga class, what's it like to give your attention to yourself as the aware openness in which everything and everyone appears and out of which all is made? How does it shift your interactions to practice this? Move beyond the boundary of skin. Feel into the world beyond thought.

Sense into the collective on an energetic level. Allow yourself to be freed from beliefs, assumptions, judgments. Feel into collective movement. Collective intelligence. Collective knowing. Collective being.

What do you notice?

Take the stanceless stand as presence,
welcoming everything in you.

Embracing everything in you.

Loving everything in you.

Feeling everything as you.

Chapter Ten

Return to Embodiment

Releasing the Mind into the Heart

The mind creates the abyss, the heart crosses it.

—Sri Nisargadatta Maharaj

The gun was not what scared me. What got the adrenaline going was how in the moment he felt my resistance to his unwanted, uninvited touch, he calmly pulled back his plaid overshirt to reveal to me a .45 that happened to be on his belt. A moment when we both knew he was the owner of the store. A moment when no one else was around. A moment when he had me cornered in a dressing room that he entered, unannounced, uninvited. I was trying on a pair of tan Carhartt work pants, which in those parts were best found in feedstores. It was rural North Carolina. It's not like I hadn't seen a gun before. The gun is not what scared me. It was the quiet way he was sure to show me the power he had. No need to raise a voice. No need to lose control. Just a cold, silent assertion of dominance.

By this point in my life I knew the game. In college I had worked as a waitress serving frat boys two-dollar pitchers of beer and souvlakis. The restaurant owner was accustomed to flirting with the waitstaff. We all made great money in tips, so we put up with him. That is, until the night he grabbed my hand and forced me to feel his "excitement for me." Until he tried to pull me into the darkness upstairs. Tried and ultimately failed. I had become skilled in slipping out of such things. I knew how to sweet-talk my way out the back door.

And then there was the time in Sacramento when, after walking my dog, I returned home to find someone who had been stalking me standing in my kitchen. Getting completely free of that situation required a restraining order.

I don't know many women who haven't been sexually harassed or assaulted. Before I even had language for it, I saw through the power dynamic men are conditioned to enact, and in particular circumstances, I knew how to sidestep it by tapping into something I didn't even have words for.

I offer these stories as commentary about conditioned patriarchal power; about the survival strategies that women as a whole are conditioned to employ and are sometimes required for survival. I also want to open a conversation about trauma.

I am no trauma expert. Thankfully, many professionals have made tremendous contributions to our collective learnings about the formation, impact, and healing of trauma. (I've been especially influenced by the teachings of Resmaa Menakem, the author of *My Grandmother's Hands* and a somatic psychotherapist who brings the work of healing collective trauma into our bodies.) I speak from direct experience. I offer my personal learnings in the hope that they provide some benefit.

One could easily assume the experiences I described above would be high on my list of personal traumas. What's fascinating to me is that they barely make the cut. I rarely think about these events. I've seen that trauma isn't always about the specific external experience; it's often about what we do with the experience internally. It's about how the experience imprints and what the conditioned mind makes it mean.

The conditioned mind is a meaning-making machine.

And whatever the meaning is, it dramatically shapes our sense of self, our sense of belonging, and therefore the choices we make in our lives.

There was very little internal residue for me after the above experiences and others like them. In fact, it's as though some part of me felt powerful rather than powerless in these circumstances. Even accounting for moments of heightened adrenaline, I saw these men's actions as fundamentally weak, not powerful. Imagine the place one would need to be in—mentally, psychologically, spiritually—to resort to forcing physical touch, to violently uphold domination.

To try to satisfy an internal unmet need through violence, a person must become disembodied.

I can only imagine that an unmet need of attention, affection, love, belonging does not manifest through force unless there has been trauma. The trauma that results from believing that *power over* is the only means to have those needs met. The trauma of having been on the other end of that duality yourself. The experience of having been indoctrinated into the language of dehumanization—a language in which bodies become objects.

While it can still be triggering for a part of me if I feel trapped physically with men who are larger than me, I've never had recurring nightmares about such incidents. The events of my life that have created the greatest opportunity for practice, the ones that haunt me in the middle of the night, are all more psychological in nature—circumstances that the conditioned mind has twisted into the threat of no longer belonging, of being cast from community, being cut off from Love, outside presence.

For me, this type of quiet trauma activates the survival strategy of trying to appease in order to "keep love intact" even at the cost of self-abandonment: the abandonment of who we truly are, the abandonment of knowing ourselves as presence. And in my experience, that is the root underlying all trauma.

Trauma creates the illusion that there is something outside presence. Knowing yourself as presence is the ultimate source of resilience, of strength, of *true* power.

In working with others, I've noticed that it's often the case that the more trauma someone has experienced, the more cut off from being they might feel. Of course, not the more cut off they *are,* rather the more cut off they might *feel*. Certainly not in all cases, but in many.

Supporting someone in returning to being is a tremendous expression of Love.

Recognizing that well-being is a human right is transformative.

Well-being is a by-product of being able to rest in presence.

Trauma often veils being and results in disembodiment from the physical body or a direct experience of presence or connection. Often both. I've witnessed plenty of people connect even more directly to presence through their hardship. This seems to come when they know themselves as more than their trauma and that this knowing is their greatest resource.

From knowing ourselves as presence we access authentic power. While we know the shifting and changing landscape of our immediate experience, we also know on a deep level that we *are* what is infinite, unchanging, and untarnished by experience and that transcends anything and everything on the relative plane. This is not to diminish the reality of harm that happens on the relative plane, or the by-product of this harm, but rather to offer a pathway to return to freedom—the freedom that comes, in this example, when we remember that we are not simply what has happened to us. We are not our trauma.

STABILIZING THROUGH PRACTICE

In personal meditation practice we learn to stabilize in an experience that is not swayed by the content of our lives. Even in the most basic mindfulness practice we are learning to respond rather than react. Through practice we have the opportunity to be reminded of the inherent equanimity of our being. We learn to stabilize in presence *no matter what the conditioned mind is doing*.

Collectively we have the opportunity to stabilize in the same way. If you've been on a long meditation retreat, perhaps you've felt the collective shift that happens when the entire group, together, drops into stillness. When the group as a whole sinks into presence. Retreat is just one environment where this can happen with ease. We can create others—for example, spaces that prioritize CARE. When we collectively recognize opportunities to stabilize in presence, together, no matter what is happening "on the outside," we have moved into the heart of who we are as a community. Here we take the stanceless stance in presence, as presence.

Together.

Collective empowerment arises in such a stanceless stance—and becomes a crucible for transformation.

Empowerment is an embodied experience. When we are grounded in the body, we often feel a power that cannot be easily shaken. Grounding in presence, too, is empowering. Equanimity is the by-product of standing on our own two feet, literally and figuratively. And standing on our own feet, staying in the body, grounding in awareness itself can be done as a collective. If we can create systems of inequity together, certainly we can stand together in collective presence to create systems of equity instead.

WE ALL SUFFER IN A SYSTEM OF INEQUITY

Rev. angel Kyodo williams was standing at the front of the room with Dr. Jasmine Syedullah, one of the coauthors of *Radical Dharma*, to her right. Over ninety of us filled the space, yet the captivated stillness of the crowd at the Shambhala Mountain Center made it feel less like a crowd and more like a group meditation in the middle of a silent retreat. This was no silent retreat, however. Far from it. Collective transformation was simmering. Rev. angel was speaking about disembodiment, and I'll never forget how she used her hands: outstretched arms, as if to hold a precious object, her palms filled with space.

In a particularly gut-wrenching example, Rev. angel asked us to consider how disembodied we'd have to be to tear a Black baby from their mother, turn them over in our hands, inspect them like a potato before purchase, and then sell them into a life of bondage. How deeply cut off from our humanity would we have to be? How removed from the knowing of our shared being would we have to be to sell, purchase, own another human? How cut off from feeling would anyone in the crowd need to be to witness the transaction as though about to get a new car? How disembodied?

Pause.

Take a moment now to check in with your body. What happens within as you absorb the above? Stay here. To the best of your ability, stay here. Notice if there is a temptation to check out. It's not bad or wrong if there is. Simply notice. Leave if you need to, come back when you can.

While on one hand, in truth, it's not possible to be outside presence, on another:

Leaving the body, leaving presence, results in suffering. For everyone.

Our greatest wound, personally and collectively, is the abandonment of Self.

And that is a wound that can be healed.

Awareness practice is a process of more and more fully recognizing the truth of who you are—Love, pure consciousness, being—and allowing this recognition to inform all experience. Every human being, by design, has equal access to who we truly are. What a tragedy of the heart that, in our delusion, we've created systems that can make it seem otherwise. That can make it feel otherwise.

It seems to me that all crimes begin with a root crime—a crime of the heart. The greatest crimes are manifestations of the greatest breaches in the recognition of our shared being. They start with one fundamental delusion of separation, and everyone involved is harmed in this delusion.

To be clear, I am not suggesting that the harm borne by the perpetrator and victim are the same—rather that in our conditioned society, especially in circles of "privilege," of unearned benefit, there is little focus on the harm experienced by the one committing the crime. There is little focus on their delusion and the fallout of their delusion, and sometimes little attention brought to the systemic causes and conditions behind their motivations. Imagine the suffering one would have to be in to go into a school and begin shooting people at random. In such cases I often wonder, what if some of those hurting individuals had experienced the Peace in Schools curriculum? Or had some other support for remembering truth, presence, wholeness, belonging?

The systems we've created affect the whole. For true healing to occur, we must address them holistically. We cannot simply punish the wrongdoers and expect our society to transform. For true transformation, it is critical to begin by recognizing that the harm experienced in the conditioned systems we've created is not dualistic. We all suffer in these systems.

I am reminded of bell hooks:

> "The first act of violence that patriarchy demands of males is not violence toward women. Instead patriarchy demands of all males that they engage in acts of psychic self-mutilation, that they kill off

the emotional parts of themselves. If an individual is not successful in emotionally crippling himself, he can count on patriarchal men to enact rituals of power that will assault his self-esteem."

One of our Peace in Schools teachers described to me how moved she was by working with a handful of male teens in her Mindful Studies class, a group of guys who many would label "jocks." They were white. They came from families that had deeply conservative political views very different from her own. The teacher, a woman, was married to another woman. She and her wife identify as quite liberal.

She did something important when starting the class, which was to internally own that the conditioned machismo of these young men—their political views, how they treated each other and fellow teens—triggered a reaction in her. Owning this supported her in not allowing this internal bias to dominate how she interacted with these students.

As the class progressed, through her skillful teaching and the contemplative technologies of the curriculum, I heard more and more stories about the softening of the armor these young men came into the class with. In fact, the more the class unfolded, the more disarmed they became. In their own time, at their own pace, they integrated in the class and fell into the environment of CARE that formed. They began to rest in the heart of who we are: presence, Love, being.

This was a big deal not only for this group of young men but also for the many immigrants who happened to be in the same class. Though it wasn't just immigrant students who felt uncomfortable with these boys at the start. Many girls, especially those who were survivors of sexual assault, and trans and queer students felt uncomfortable as well.

About this particular class the teacher now says,
"By the end, CARE really felt in place for all. Safer. Humanity acknowledged all around. Compassion abounded. That year of teaching really changed me forever in so many ways. I feel like I lived unconditional love in an entirely new way. And it felt so freeing and liberating to do so in the context of national hate and relational upheaval."

This particular class was an incredible case study of the importance of an entire context shifting, all together. Teacher included. The students who were not US-born felt safer, girls felt safer. All felt safer, including the boys. All could naturally disarm, together. The class became beloved community, no one left out. Lines of difference were loved across—a chasm that would most likely never have been crossed in the locker rooms, school cafeteria, courtyards.

This process cannot be forced, and it takes time. The outcome, however, is a more lasting and significant transformation than our conditioned focus, a dualistic focus, could ever allow. Any view that keeps the labels of *us* and *them* intact has little room for true healing.

Most importantly, this kind of learning, this kind of evolution, can happen collectively. Aware, enlivened community gets created together, the next generation supported. Acts of being are freed to arise organically as we create collective environments of CARE, presence, Love.

Our support for our children must go deeper than simply teaching them to stop harming—themselves and others. The deepest support we can provide is in fostering their remembrance of who they truly are.

When we know who we truly are, we don't have to restrain ourselves from causing harm. We lose the taste for it.

And through collective focus, we can lose our taste for it, together.

Significant transformation comes through a collective focus on the whole. As we collectively focus on who we truly are, loving across lines of difference is not an assignment, rather the by-product of our understanding. It is the outcome of our realization. We become less and less capable of anything else.

A PRAYER FOR THIS BELOVED COMMUNITY

If we fully take *this* on as ours,
whatever arrives on our doorstep,
the messiness, the discomfort, all of it,
if we say yes, this too is us,
if we move toward rather than away,
if we embrace, all of it, leaving nothing out,
may we be freed to ask,
free to listen:

Now, in this moment, how are we called to respond?

How, with our shared, disarmed, open heart, are we moved?

How will our lives be a loving response to what is?

How will we serve the vision of healing and remembrance for all?

As we realize that everything is us, and none of it is personal,
may we be freed to touch the possibility of choice.
Free to make decisions informed by the qualities
inherent in us, in true nature—

Love, peace, justice.

How will this manifest?

In this moment.

Here. Now.

May we be a conduit
for *this*.

CHEAP MEMBERSHIPS IN BELONGING

The conditioned fear of being cast out, of not belonging, of being isolated, is a source of tremendous personal and collective problems. On the relative plane, we grasp to belong, though our longing for belonging has its roots in something much more existential. As conditioned humans, based on our capacity to experience ourselves as separate, we are habituated to long for belonging, connection, wholeness, as if it were "out there" rather than, on the deepest level, inherent. Ultimately, we long for the beloved, for union.

It's no accident that one of the greatest punishments we can think of is solitary confinement. When lost in the perception of separation, we feel disconnected and isolated, and it is no wonder that the French philosopher Blaise Pascal once wrote, "All of humanity's problems stem from man's inability to sit quietly in a room alone."

Within dominant culture, in our confusion, we turn to cheap tricks to meet the shared need to return to our shared being. Collective survival strategies are crude attempts to know ourselves as belonging, connected, whole, and beloved.

We know union in the marrow of our bones

because it is the heart of who we are,

our very being, yet in our confusion

we long for what we already have,

for what we already are.

Examples of cheap tricks, conditioned attempts to meet our shared need for belonging? Joining any group that creates a false and superficial sense of belonging through fear. One where I know I'm on the "inside" because there is an "other," someone on the "outside." (Cheap memberships thrive in duality.) Hate groups or having membership in the club of "privilege," or unearned benefit.

Within dominant culture, these memberships can be taken away just as quickly as they're handed out. "The club" is often shifting and changing, keeping everyone on their toes. Like mice on spinning wheels, we try to keep up. We try to keep up in a system that can never and will never deliver the results we long for. All of this is the by-product of individually and collectively forgetting who we truly are.

Our deepest unmet needs will never be collectively met in a system that arises out of and is informed by the distortion of our separation from each other.

Think of the conditioned system as the third person in the room. On the relative plane, there's an idea of you, then there's an idea of me, then there's the system we are operating in. *Are you in **my** club? Are you not in **the** club? Do you belong? Do I belong? I'm going to shut you out. Oh no, you are going to shut me out!* We run, jump, run again. We go around and around. We're in relationship with this third person, yet we are conditioned not to recognize them.

The system, this created third person, has been designed. We imagined it into being out of a limited view.

What has been designed can be resigned.

Redesigned.

What has been imagined can be reimagined.

When I started Peace in Schools, I did a lot of listening. What did the principal have to say about the issues in the school where I was working? What were the parents noticing? The counselors? What collective fears were present?

It was noteworthy how many people complained to me about technology—teens on their phones, teens playing video games, teens with screens. So many pointed to it as the root of all issues. What I soon saw, however, was that something deeper was going on. I saw that most of the teens I was working with felt disconnected and that through the phone they had *some* sense of connection. I learned that even with something like video games, the teens were often playing with other people and there was some sense of community around it.

Many adults were keen to attempt to take away the technology, but few were offering an alternative—a healthy way to feel connected; a holistic portal into authentic community, truthful belonging.

It seemed critical to me that rather than strip away the technology, it would be more helpful to have healthy inquiry around it:

What need am I trying to have met through my phone?

Is it running my life, or is it a tool that I make conscious choices about?

Are there other ways to have this need met?

Does the phone really cut it?

This kind of inquiry frees teens from being in a love/hate duality with their phones. From labeling it bad, then feeling guilty for wanting it. Or labeling it good, then not being able to let it go, even for a few hours. It frees them from assuming that the phone can actually meet the deepest need at all.

We can all inquire into our experience of all the devices—technological and otherwise—that falsely promise membership in belonging. We can see through them in the same way. Rather than grasping for cheap membership—grasping that lives in the conditioned mind—we can rest the attention in the heart. We can remember the inherent membership of being, a membership that, in truth, can never actually be taken away.

GROUNDING IN THE BODY

Embodiment is necessary to manifest in a physical world, to have acts of being on the relative plane. Through practice, we can learn to ground in the body. We can ground into presence.

Unfortunately, as we all know too well, the relative plane is full of dehumanization—any news feed can tell you this. The disembodiment required from all parties either engaged in these acts or sometimes just from reading about these acts has fallout. Feeling cut off from presence results in suffering.

I recognize that devices and social media can be a way to know community. At the same time, how many times have you walked into a meeting, into a waiting room, and everyone is staring at a screen of some kind? Collectively we are living in a time when humanity is ungrounded from even our relative existence. As a teacher I've noticed that inviting others to ground, to come into their bodies, to feel connected to the earth, can bring up fears they don't want to feel. Even to focus on grounding for a moment can reveal the degree to which you aren't grounded, and that can be frightening. As we bring attention into the body, as we feel our tailbone and our feet under us, our animal body can have anxiety about not being directly connected to the earth. Most of us, for example, don't think about how ungrounded we are when we fly on a plane. We treat being in a plane like being in a tube-like living room of sorts, since to focus on how ungrounded we really are might bring up anxiety.

Here is a favorite breath practice to help ground you in your body. This one can be particularly nice to listen to versus simply read. A reminder to check out the audiobook, to have someone in your group read it, or to record it for yourself and play it back, allowing you to rest and receive.

A Practice: Freeing the Head, Breathing Through the Heart

Begin by bringing all your attention to the head.

What self-talk is present?

Now reflect on your body for a moment.

What do you believe about your body? Consciously think about your body for a moment.
Do judgments arise?

Are your beliefs about your body true?

How do you know they are true? Where do you turn for verification?

If you weren't referencing the conditioned mind, what would be true about your body?

Free the head. Imagine the brain softening.
Like a stick of butter on a warm day, sitting on a sunlit plate in the windowsill, softening.

The brain, releasing.

Now, as if you were in a glass elevator, visualize traveling down.
Leaving the floor of the head.

Gently travel down to the top of the spine, then into the neck.

Allow this elevator to sink into the throat.

And then down to the top of the collarbones.

Continuing to sink, coming into the top of the chest.

Rest there for a moment. Breathing.

And now rest into the heart.

What does your body feel like from the seat of the heart?

Let go of any temptation to think about the body.
You're in the heart now.

Feel your body from the inside.
What sensations are here?

You're in a glass elevator. What does the world look like from the heart? How does it appear?

What do you see from inside this epicenter of presence?

Inhale as if air is coming in through the entire front of the heart, flowing through the heart, and with your exhalation, release out the back of the heart.

As you inhale again, pull the breath into the center of the heart; as you exhale, release out the front of the heart.

Then visualize that the breath is to the left of the heart.

As you inhale, draw the breath in the left side of the heart; as you exhale, release the breath out the right side of the heart.

As you inhale again, pull the breath into the center of the heart from the right side; as you exhale, release out the left side of the heart.

Lastly, visualize the breath above the crown of the head. Inhale and draw the breath in through the crown of the head and bring it into the heart.

Exhale and release the breath from the heart out the bottom of the feet and into the earth.

Inhale the breath from the earth into the center of the heart; as you exhale, release the breath up and out the top of the head.

Repeat this breathing pattern by visualizing the breath at the front of the heart and begin again. Repeat this pattern as long as you wish.

When I first offered a version of this breath practice to teens, it quickly landed on the top-ten list of meditations. I love that they titled it "The Dental Floss Meditation." It can be incredibly powerful to feel the attention come into the body, to ground there, to get out of the head, to rest in the heart. Then to feel the breath move through the body, cleansing it, revealing its inherent openness. The spaciousness of it. To allow our felt sense of the body to expand.

LOCATING THE EGO

At the monastery where I trained, there wasn't a tremendous emphasis on the body. We would practice yoga a few times a week, and I recall in those sessions appreciating the relief of feeling connected to my body, yet much of the time I still perceived my body as separate from everything else—separate from others, separate from consciousness. For me, my body was still an object I could be aware of rather than something I experienced as made of the same thing as *me*, which later I experienced as consciousness itself.

The ego is tricky. It can lodge in the body, hiding out there even when there is clear recognition in the mind that we're not separate. It parades around as a felt sense of "I" or "me" separate from everything else. It is the thing we are conditioned to point to when we say "me."

But if we were to look for this ego, where would we find it?

Do this now.

Find the ego.

Does it live in a certain part of the body? Some might say it lives in the brain, but can you actually find an entity there? Certainly you might find activity in the brain, the way that you find activity on the surface of a pond after a boat passes, but that is not the same thing as an entity.

Where does the entity of the ego actually live? Can you pinpoint it?

The ego is the illusion of an entity that comes into being when we believe that pure consciousness is limited to a body. But let's be clear: the ego isn't actually an entity at all. To call it an entity can give it a particular reality that it does not, in truth, have. In fact, the ego is a process; it's simply the *activity* of the finite mind. And even this activity is made of the same consciousness that is without limits, that is unborn, that is unbound by time and space.

Time and space appear in the finite mind. The activity of the ego, in the finite mind, creates the perception of lack—along with all the coping, grasping, grappling, striving, and suffering in response to this perception. When we are identified with this activity, as we've discussed, its narratives can be all too convincing.

Ultimately the ego asserts that you are separate, that you are bound by your physical body. You cannot perceive yourself as separate without the activity of the conditioned mind. But you are not your physical body. Your physical body arises in you, consciousness. Your physical body is made of you, consciousness. Your physical body is perceived by you, consciousness.

THE BODY AS ILLUSORY

I recall as a child being fascinated with this notion of "I" and "me." I recall wondering where the lines of this thing I called "me" were. As a kid, I remember asking myself, *If I cut off my hands, am I still me? Of course I am. What about if I cut off my arms and legs? What if I cut off part of my torso? How much of "me" (in terms of my body) has to be there for me to be me?* As a kid, something in me intuited that I am not limited to my body. Yet I didn't have a lot of words for what I *am*. Still, with the persistence of a rushing river, a deep knowing always welled.

Truth itself is the source of the call for truth.

What you are seeking is causing you to seek.

Presence knows presence.

Up until this point in the book, I haven't specifically defined presence because I believe there is value in your exploration. I've trusted that you would be intuiting, feeling into, and inquiring into your experience of what presence is, which allows for open experiential learning. The most important learning comes through direct experience. You can only learn of presence through presence.

Here's some food for thought: I invite you to play with this framing of reality as you move through the rest of this book:

Illusion—that which comes and goes

Reality—that which never disappears and therefore never appears

Consciousness—the reality that perceives, the reality out of which all forms arise and are made

Presence—being aware of being aware; in other words, consciousness being conscious of itself

Being—presence, sometimes temporarily clothed in human experience

**Our experience of existence cannot shift
if we keep perceiving reality through the same lens.
When we keep defining reality the same way,
when we only perceive what we've been conditioned to perceive,
our world is small, limited, constrained.
When we only perceive what we've been conditioned to perceive,
we suffer.**

What shifts when you consider that the ego is simply activity, a modulation or vibration arising in and made of consciousness? Now consider that the body, too, is simply another vibration in and made of consciousness. It's difficult to think of the body as illusory because it has density to it—we can see and touch it. It's obviously material, and material means *real*, right?

It can be easier to recognize the ego as illusory, as a hologram of sorts, because when you try to look for it, you come up empty. There is no physical ego, only a conglomeration of conditioned activity in the finite mind that we're conditioned to assume is a separate self. But if I suggest the body is also an activity of consciousness, that can be harder to grapple with. I'm suggesting that if you really look for it, you can't find the body either.

Yes, of course we have this thing we can tap with our hand and call "my body," but when we close our eyes, what do we know to be true about our body? Check out this meditation. Allow it to be a place of inquiry.

A Contemplation: Resting in Freedom, as Freedom

As with previous contemplations, find a restful place where you can read through or listen to this meditation at your own pace and rest with it a little bit afterward.

Begin by allowing your experience to be exactly as it is.

By allowing yourself to say yes to what is.

If you're in physical pain and there's a way you can adjust yourself that would be supportive, please do.

Otherwise simply allow your experience to be free to be however it is in this moment.

Allow your attention to rest in the body.

You call your body "your" body. What makes it yours?

What makes it belong to you?

If you drop the thoughts about the body—the judgments and beliefs; if you release the idea of ownership of the body, what's left?

With your eyes closed, what's your experience of the body?

Where does the attention go to answer this question? Simply notice without judgment.

What's it like to experience your body the way a newborn baby might experience themselves? Before a baby becomes a child that says, "This is my leg, this is my arm"? Before thoughts of ownership, what's there?

With your eyes closed, do you have an experience of the body that is other than the conscious awareness of sensation?

What's it like to stay with this conscious awareness of sensation?

To stay in presence, with sensation, in sensation, rather than hover above this thing you call "body," as if aware of it from the outside?

As if the body is separate from awareness.

As if it is separate from you, infinite consciousness.

From the perspective of the finite mind, the body is separate from awareness and separate from the world. From infinite consciousness, the body is like a wave in a vast sea.
Not separate from the ocean.

The wave cannot be parted from the sea.
The wave is made of the sea.

Allow yourself to experience the body like this.

Open.

Transparent.

Empty.

Part of . . .

Feel yourself as a wave while remembering that you are the ocean.

We've all experienced pain in the body. Can you find pain in the body now?

Without the label "pain," what do you know of this experience?

Without wanting it or not wanting it, liking or disliking it, what is this thing we call pain? Drop the temptation to think about it or try to understand it . . .

Feel . . .

What shape is it?

What texture?

Does it have a color?

Now explore, how do you *know* what shape it is or what texture? How do you know *anything* about it?

Is there anything going on other than the awareness of sensation?

The body is illusory. That doesn't mean it doesn't exist or that it isn't real.

It means that the body is not what we are conditioned to think it is.

We are conditioned to think of it as dense, solid, fixed in time.

With your eyes closed, simply aware of sensation, is there anything solid, dense, fixed about your experience of awareness? Or of the knowing of sensation?

If, and only if, it feels safe to lovingly inquire into an experience of trauma from your past you might gently explore the next section in gray. If this doesn't feel safe or supportive, or you wish to do this in the company of a therapist or a trusted loved one, simply skim past this next section. There's no harm in that. Trust yourself.

Perhaps this body has experienced pain or some sort
of trauma in the past. Without diving into memory in
the mind, where does this experience live now?

What do you find of this trauma, in this moment?
Again, without referencing thought. What is true *now*
about this trauma?

Explore this without referencing this conditioned
idea you call "the past."

What's here?

Thought comes and goes. The body comes and goes.
Sensation comes and goes.
What remains?

Allow the attention to come home to what remains.

Rest the attention in the boundaryless body of
consciousness.

The open, luminous, deathless consciousness that is.

All is welcome here.

Rest in being.

Unbounded by conditioned definitions and limited
views of the body.

Free.

Rest.

Freely.

In freedom.

As freedom.

THE BODY AS A PHYSICAL GATEWAY TO PEACE

Our experience of the body changes when we don't perceive it as "ours," as something we possess, or when we don't perceive it as solid and dense, simply made of matter. With these realizations, our experience of reality also changes. Why? Because we no longer identify with the perception of separation in the same way.

What does this have to do with collective transformation? We can only cause harm to each other's bodies from the experience of being disembodied and/or from a distorted view of "ownership." If I believe "I" own "my" body, then a leap can be made, albeit a big one, to the delusion that it is possible that I can own another body as well.

We have the capacity, through practice, to be embodied. Our relationships with one another transform and evolve as we drop our attention into the body, as we move from the head to the heart, as we are freed from distortion.

And the news gets even better: Dropping the attention from the conditioned mind into the physical body can be a gateway of sorts. We can allow the activity of the conditioned mind, including conditioned perceptions of the body, to drop into the heart of awareness. We can move into the reality of the body, the unborn nature of the body. Again, why?

This is where peace lives. This is where the wholeness we all long for lies. It lies in the heart of who we are. This is where we don't identify with this notion of separation, where we have a direct experience of our shared being. Here in the body, we experience oneness not as an airy-fairy belief but rather as a grounded reality we can test in our own direct experience.

And, like so much discussed in this book, there is a beautiful paradox here. We need our physical bodies to create acts of being. Grounding on this relative plane, grounding in our physical bodies, heals our habit of disembodiment and therefore cuts off the fallout of disembodiment at the pass. It cuts off harm. When we stand firmly on our own two feet, change on this relative plane can happen.

And even more becomes possible as we know the reality of the body, as we explore the notion that our bodies are known by and made of the same thing—consciousness itself. More is possible when we realize that we are not limited to physical form. When we know this as we act, we still are creating change, but we're doing so from an embodied experience that we are not separate, rather than an intellectual one. We can allow our change to be informed by the absolute truth that we are one. Here the door to transformation opens wide. Here acts of being are born.

The body can become a physical gateway

to the infinite body of consciousness.

Though given that the body is made of consciousness,

and not separate from consciousness, in truth

there is no gateway to consciousness.

While knowing the body is made of consciousness, we can still use the physical presence of it to help us when we feel ungrounded. As much as we like to believe we've "outsmarted" the inner critic or the content of our survival strategies, sometimes we get lost in these things—in fears of the future, in the weight of the past. In these moments it can be an invaluable tool to "come back to the body," even if that means returning to an experience that at first might feel separate or bound. This is useful because when we're identified, again, so much of this identification happens within the conditioned mind through the activity of thinking.

This is where the contemplative technology of Directing the Attention on page 38 comes in handy. We can notice that the attention is absorbed in thoughts and redirect it to the physical body. The body—always here, always now: a wonderful anchor in the present moment for this very reason. Especially when we're triggered, we might find it extremely grounding to direct the attention to the physical body; to get out of the head; to drop the attention to the sensation of our feet on the floor or to the belly, for example.

Even knowing the body can be a useful physical place of grounding, we can access deeper peace, a more lasting peace, if we rest in the truth that our physical body is not limited in the way we've assumed it to be. We access true peace when we ground into consciousness itself.

GROUNDING IN THE ABSOLUTE

We experience our inherent freedom when we ground into presence itself, when we ground into the experience of stabilizing in what never changes. Doing so can create profound engagement with this illusory thing that we call "the body."

(It's important to underline that by saying "illusory," we're not saying that the body has no reality but rather a reality beyond conditioned perception.)

We can tap into the reality of this illusory body, sparking deep love and gratitude for this human experience. Feeling our feet on the earth. Mud in between our toes. Relishing the knowing of sensation versus the felt sense of limitation that comes with identifying with the body as proof that we are separate.

Consider how, earlier in the book, we journeyed through not simply being aware of thoughts but becoming aware of what's aware of the thoughts; resting the attention in awareness itself, thereby changing our relationship with the mind. Now we do the same with the body. Rather than simply being aware *of* the body, of sensation, we allow awareness to come to the forefront. We sink the attention into the awareness in which sensation arises rather than simply directing the attention to and focusing on the sensation. Recognizing that the sensation is arising in awareness and made of awareness frees us from maintaining the limited view of a separate body. When we ground into being, we know ourselves as what's real, as what doesn't change.

We can know ourselves as what doesn't change while embodying what does.

The body is always changing. We more fully rest, our bodies more fully relax, when we know ourselves as pure consciousness. Unborn. Undying.

Our conditioning comes and goes. Collective power dynamics come and go. Our thoughts come and go. Our bodies come and go. All of these things flicker in and out. Yet the true flame of what's real remains.

We can only know our inherent freedom through knowing what is real.

As we ground into what is real, we experience contentment. We experience the well-being we all long for—the ease, the peace, the happiness.

Grounding into what never changes, aligning our experience of the body with this knowing, is freedom.

FREEING THE BODY, NOT TRANSCENDING THE BODY

The fleeting world is full of ideas, yet we hunger for the nutrients of the earth, groundedness, unity. Every time we return to this experience of unity, every time we ground in this way, we more fully experience our body as luminous, the substance that the light of consciousness shines through. Valuable and sacred. A vessel for life force. A servant of Love.

This animal body isn't secreting fight-or-flight hormones when we're grounded and there is no physical threat. When there is no physical threat, such chemicals only rush through in the presence of a conditioned story that we believe, that we identify with. A sound in the brush, for example, sparks such hormones the moment we believe that it is a bear. In this moment of belief, the bear becomes more real to us than the wind.

When we ground the physical body with the Self, we no longer fear the impermanence of the body in the same way—on a moment-by-moment basis and at large.

We can ground the relative body in the absolute.
It is made of the absolute.

There is
only This.

From the view of the separate self, "I am these thoughts" and "I am this body" feel real. From the view of the heart we drop into the reality of the body.

We can allow the physical body to guide us home.

Home to being.

For those who have experienced trauma and know the experience of dissociation from the body as a survival strategy, be gentle as you explore this. *We are not describing dissociation here.* We are not coming to the body so we can leave or forget the body or write it off as "not real." We are not abandoning or "transcending" the body.

We are moving *into* the body. As we do, we are releasing the distortion that the body is separate from consciousness. We are recognizing the body as inherently open, spacious, allowing, vast. Moving *into* the emptiness of the form, moving *into* the reality of the illusion. We are freeing the body from the outdated distortion that we are separate. We are moving *through* the hologram.

Our liberation depends on knowing the reality of all illusion.

The reality of all illusion is the same.

Explore the ways that constriction in the body is often a physical manifestation of conditioned thought. The ego, albeit illusory, like a hologram, takes shape in the physical body. It can seem to lodge and find its home there, taking the form of tension, and constriction.

Making the body seem dense. Solid.

Fixed in time.

This is why in the old tale about a Zen master on her deathbed, when her students asked about her experience, she spoke to them about how her mind was ready, at peace, empty, open, and yet her body, she reported, had some catching up to do!

SEPARATE BODIES DON'T PROVE WE'RE SEPARATE

We are often numb to watching violence on TV partly because we've been desensitized to it, but more importantly because we're conditioned to perceive separate bodies as proof that we are separate. When we recognize our shared being, we don't, on the deepest level, see physical form as something that makes us separate. So we lose our capacity to cause harm in the same way.

That isn't to say that bodies aren't treated differently based on physical traits, because of course they are. In fact, that's why it's all the more important to understand and reconcile the paradox of the absolute experience of oneness and the relative experience of a body. Otherwise we will continue to inflict harm on each other. If we continue to maintain the story that we aren't made of the same thing, if we continue to feed the distortion of "other," we will continue to inflict harm.

TRANSFORMATION THROUGH LOVE

One morning, during an online offering through Sangha Live, Beth, a participant in the session, came on screen to dialogue with me. She asked me if I'd speak about illness and consciousness. Beth shared that she had been bedridden for twelve years, that she'd been on an enormous journey and didn't want this to be the rest of her life. She'd lost caregivers and was completely on her own.

Other participants on the call began writing in the sidebar. Loving, support-ive comments flooded in; they flowed through the screen like water. I read them aloud, inviting her to take them in, to absorb them.

Here is a transcription of my response to her inquiry following the flood of collective compassion:

When you're identified with this body-mind, it's easy to become hyper-focused on what gets called the limitations of this body-mind. But your very being is shared.

Allow yourself to draw energetic resource from something that is actually unlim-ited, unbounded. The body-mind is experiencing limitation, constriction, illness. But your very being is unlimited, unbounded, unborn, and infinite.

That's a flame that can't be extinguished.

You can remember the body while knowing who you truly are. You can see the body as another beautiful modulation of consciousness that has the form that it does in the moment that it does.

You have breath, the capacity to think, understand, receive, have an exchange, hear, taste, and most importantly... Love.

No matter what happens to your body, Love cannot be taken from you.

Beth broke open while being held by beloved community. It was clear that she tasted the freedom of her being; that an old view of the body as limited, the sto-ries of what it means to be sick, were retired, even if just for that moment.

Once we've tasted freedom, we know freedom.
This knowing cannot be extinguished.
Perhaps temporarily forgotten
but never permanently extinguished.

Friends, I offer this as medicine for all of us. How might we remember this body as holy, just as consciousness itself is holy?

Remember, though our bodies, like holograms, have the appearance of sepa-ration, we are in truth one body, one being.

THE BODY AS BELOVED

To end war
we have to see through
the illusion of separation
that is the source of war.
To cease harming each other's body,
we must remember that, in reality,

there are no other bodies.
For collective healing to occur,

we must know and live the truth
that there is only one, beloved body.
And that this beloved body
is here to be cherished.
It is here to be loved.

This glorious, beautiful,
luminous expression of Love
is here to be loved.

There is nothing
outside *this*.

Collective Practice: Creating Acts of Being

PRACTICE 1: THE SHARED EYE OF AWARENESS

- Find a partner with whom you feel safe.
- Practice, in silence, gazing into their eyes for five minutes without interruption. Simply notice what happens.

- If you get uncomfortable, lean into the practice you have cultivated. You've practiced being with discomfort. You've practiced saying yes to what is. Allow identity to become secondary to the experience of connection and stay with whatever arises. Allow yourself to feel the embodiment of this connection.

What do you notice?

PRACTICE 2: ENGAGING FROM THE HEART OF AWARENESS

- As you move through your interactions with others in your day, pay particular attention to where you get caught in the conditioned mind—that is, moving through the world from the head.

- Sink the attention into the heart by lightly placing your hand or the tips of your fingers on the center of your chest as you engage with others. As you listen fully. As you receive and as you give. No one else has to even notice you're doing this. No fanfare required.

- As you sink the mind into the heart, rest into the way you aren't simply focusing on the organ at the center of your chest. Allow these places to be starting points, doorways. Ultimately, you are sinking the mind into the heart of awareness while engaging with others.

What do you notice?

PRACTICE 3 INQUIRY—MOVING FROM THE HEAD TO THE HEART

Explore these questions on your own and/or with your group:

- As a collective, where and when do we collectively become disembodied?

- Where and when do we, as a group, collude to remain in our heads, together?

- Where and when do we abandon feeling?

- Where and when do we leave the heart? And what are our collective "excuses" for doing so?

- How can our practices be a resource for moving into the world rather than avoiding it?

- How can our love of humanity be the ground from which we address racism, the climate crisis, injustice?

- What would a society look like that prioritized collective well-being? The collective remembrance of who we are?

PRACTICE 4: CREATING ACTS OF BEING

Take the questions from practice 3 out of inquiry mode and into an *act of being* mode. Create a project that reflects an act of being. You might enjoy thinking of it as a gift for the collective. I can't underline enough that there is no right or wrong way to do this. You could do something on your own, you could do something with a group. Honor your own still, small voice within.

You might be drawn to create a community event that uplifts everyone in a particular way. You might be called to create something that has a lot of splash or that has a quiet and subtle feel. *As always, it's not what, it's how.* What's important is that you are following a call on behalf of your deepest knowing, your deepest experience of truth. What a glorious thing it is that this emerging experience will look different for each of us. For some of us, it's doing what we already do but simply changing the approach. For some, it will involve political action. For some, it will involve art or education. For some of us, our acts of being will blend all these elements together—and perhaps more! This is yet another opportunity to trust yourself, to be in beloved community in any way that is authentic for you, to allow practice to be a catalyst for collective transformation.

Share what you create with others. Let joy thread through the creation as well as the expression. You don't need to get rid of "the head." Let it play a role. And let the heart guide.

Chapter Eleven

Return to Surrender

Turning Toward What Is

When we realize all existence, ourselves included,
as uncreated yet potent spaciousness, there is
no fear of being destroyed.

—Justin Forrest Miles

Many years into my training, when considering leaving the monastery, I recall speaking to a mentor who said, "You are the only one who can determine whether it is time for you to leave right now. The question you must ask yourself is whether you can hold the truth of the true nature of all things in a dog-eat-dog world." (And by this he meant the conditioned world.) Needless to say, at that time I felt I had not cultivated this skill.

At that time I believed that once I left my protected cloister of truth, I'd lose my capacity to stay with this truth once thrown back into the world of the relative. I feared that I could only know the intimacy of being if the content of the world had been simplified and reduced. Because I valued knowing truth more than anything, I felt I had little choice but to stay.

Years later, when I left the monastery, being "back in the world" proved to be the best training for being back in the world. As I look back, I don't believe that it was more time in a silent monastery that prepared me. I believe it was being thrown into everyday life coupled with my dedication to still know the truth of experience that illuminated the way.

Some years ago, I asked Rupert Spira for feedback about my facilitation. I was feeling unsure, unsteady about my teaching. In response to my queries he said something I'll never forget: "You learn to teach through teaching." In that vein, it's been my experience that you learn to find the true nature in experience through finding the true nature in experience!

What's required? A conscious turning toward experience rather than away from it.

As mentioned in chapter nine, a neti neti—not this, not that—approach in practice is an extremely useful one.

I am not these thoughts.

I am not this body.

I am not these conditioned systems.

I am not a separate self.

It is an approach that negates. My monastic training reflected this approach. Whatever was deemed a distraction was removed.

No emailing.

No speaking.

No eye contact with others.

No expressions of the personality.

Stripping distractions indeed supported, and perhaps allowed for, my first life-altering glimpse and direct experience of true nature. Turning away from relative experience allowed for the consciousness in the backdrop of experience to shine more fully at the forefront.

It wasn't until I came back into the world, however, that I was required to more fully practice recognizing what is normally in the backdrop of experience, in the forefront—no matter the circumstance.

TURNING TOWARD VERSUS TURNING AWAY

In your own life, have you ever found yourself identified with a self who is on a mission to annihilate the self? Have you found yourself believing you have to *get rid of* in order to experience truth? Believing that the conditioned mind can take charge and try to control and omit thoughts, experiences, people is a distortion of a negating approach. And we do it in the name of spiritual practice.

One way I see this take shape in those new to practice looks like this: "Oh, I tried having a meditation practice but I never could stick with it. I couldn't ever seem to clear my mind." As if that is the goal of practice and as if practice requires a sergeant to be in charge of the assigned perceived task.

As an illustration, Rupert uses the analogy of a self-aware screen and a movie playing on this screen. The screen stands in for the true nature of all things. It's pure consciousness. In a negating approach, the movie is considered to be a distraction from the screen. In the negating approach, we turn off the movie to see the screen. We turn away from the *content* of our relative experience.

Rupert expands the metaphor to describe what could be referred to as a *turning-toward* approach. In this approach, it is recognized that all movies are merely a coloring of the screen. To see the screen clearly, you don't have to turn off the movie. You can watch any movie you'd like on this screen. The content of the movie doesn't change the nature of the screen. In this approach, we turn *toward experience*, recognizing this experience isn't separate from what it's arising in, what it's observed by, or what it's made of. We move toward experience rather than away from it.

In this turning-toward approach, we look for true nature in *all* things. We see the inherent spaciousness in all things. We see the reality of all things. As we move into experience, we recognize ourselves as not separate from experience. Or to state it without negation, we know the unity of all things. We learn to see *through* the movie and we find the screen everywhere, in everything.

Turning-away and *turning-toward* approaches need not be viewed dualistically. Both approaches lead to the same heart—the heart of awareness, the heart of truth. Both approaches end up with the same recognition—the nature of the screen, the nature of the reality projected onto the screen. All realities share the same reality.

THE COSTUMES OF CONSCIOUSNESS

In activity

you hide behind things.

In the noise of the world

you appear clothed.

In silence

you emerge naked.

In stillness

you are everywhere.

In one approach, it could be said that true nature can be veiled by the activity of the conditioned mind. In the other approach, this activity is seen to be nothing more than a variation of consciousness, within consciousness. A coloring of reality.

One of my favorite Zen stories is from the Platform Sutra. Hóngrěn, the Fifth Patriarch of the Chinese Zen lineage, was recognized as an enlightened master in the 600s CE. Shénxiù, a senior monk who apparently prided himself on being very learned—and who had his eye on becoming the Sixth Patriarch—presented a verse to the master to exemplify his understanding (and to impress him):

The body is the bodhi tree,
The mind is like a clear mirror.
At all times we must strive to polish it,
And must not let the dust collect.

Then along comes Huìnéng, the illiterate woodcutter from the "barbarian South," as those from the North labeled such people. (Sound familiar? There is nothing new about the delusion of othering, friends.)

Huìnéng offered the following alternative verse:

There is no bodhi tree,
Nor stand of a mirror bright.

Since all is void,
Where can the dust alight?

Hóngrěn recognized the depth of Huìnéng's understanding, and Huìnéng became the Sixth Patriarch, the head of the Chan/Zen Buddhist order in China. A pretty big deal. (Huìnéng apparently had to be given the title in secret and was instructed by his teacher to flee the monastery lest the other envy-filled monks try to kill him, but that's another story—though it's also not unrelated to our themes about othering and *power over*, of course.)

While we can understand this story in the context of the progressive versus the direct path, as we discussed previously, it is also illuminating for understanding the practice of *turning toward*. This story illustrates the truth that all is void or empty, that all is consciousness. There is nothing outside this.

Given that, fundamentally, all is void,

there are no things.

This void is *within* all things.

All things cannot exist

without it.

Ultimately, thinking and perceiving is what creates the appearance of things being divided. What's created is form—on the subtlest level, the forms of time and space; on a more gross level, thoughts that center the illusion of a self separate from life.

These forms can be seen as veiling our true nature—the way that time veils the infinite nature of consciousness. These forms can also be seen as shining with true nature—the way that something you call beautiful shines with the reality of oneness.

Of course it can be more difficult to see how something that a part of us might label as "unacceptable" shines with true nature. Here *turning toward* really comes in handy. If we wish to not only know our true nature but also live on behalf of this knowing—move through the world in alignment with this knowing—we must become adept at recognizing the true nature of all things.

We must become skilled at keeping our eye on it at all times, in all circumstances. Not just in the places (internally and externally) where it is easy to do this but especially in the places where it is hard.

But enough thinking about this! Let's turn to an experience.

A Contemplation: Turning Toward

As before, find a restful place where you can read through this at your own pace and rest with it a little bit afterward.

Begin by asking, What's here now?

Begin by asking, Who, what part of you, is here now?

Whatever is, whoever is, let this be.

Allow whatever is to be exactly as it is.

And now consciously bring in the image of something you tend to believe you don't like.

Pick something you don't have a lot of charge around to start with.

We could play with . . . feeling lonely, for example.

Choose something that's relevant for you.

Allow yourself to be quiet and still. No need to force anything. Just allow. And gently inquire into the nature of this experience. This loneliness, let's say.

Gently explore:

What self-talk is present?
What are you saying to yourself about this experience?

And then see through this self-talk . . . nothing you
need to judge or reject.
It's transparent. Simply move *through* it . . .

What emotions are present?
What feelings are here?
And then see *through* these emotions and feelings . . .
nothing you need to judge or reject.
Simply swim through them . . .
They are empty.

Now consciously explore what's happening in the body.

What sensations are present?

Is there anything to these sensations other than
vibration?
Gently, without judgment, explore this vibration.
Let the vibration simply be vibration.
Move through it in your mind's eye.

Notice how you know this self-talk, these emotions,
these sensations.

Surrender the self-talk to the vastness of this awareness.
Surrender emotion to this presence.

Surrender sensation to being.

Like a dense cloud, expanding, opening, becoming
translucent, releasing into the vastness of the open
sky.Self-talk, emotion, sensation, all vibration in
vast awareness.

Turn toward, move into and through this vibration,
not as if you are separate from it . . . more like the way
a drop of water moves into a pond . . .

the way a river flows toward and into the sea.

Move toward, in, through,

release.

Surrender anything that would imply that you are separate from this vibration.

Surrender it to presence . . . to luminous being.

Surrender it to the sea.

This sea, shining with countless drops of water.

These drops, all shining with the sea.

There can be no drop without this water.

Even if the drop is colored by something—filled with algae, let's say—the same suchness that is *water* still shines through.

The same suchness, the same being, shines through what the mind labels "loneliness."

Any experience like loneliness is simply activity of the mind coloring the vastness of being, but not other than it.

What beautiful and complex creatures we are!

We have the capacity to attend to the coloring or what is being colored!

We can attend to the experience the conditioned mind labels "loneliness"—the self-talk, the emotion— or we can surrender to what's always shining *through* the loneliness.

We can surrender to what's often in the background of our experience, seemingly hidden.

We can release into being.

In moving toward, we go into the coloring

and into what's colored.

We go into the heart of all things.

We go into the heart of who we are.

We go into infinite being, which is everywhere and nowhere all at once.

How is infinite being nowhere?

Because it doesn't exist in a place.

It doesn't exist in time.

It isn't bound by matter.

You don't exist in a place.

You don't exist in time.

You aren't bound by matter.

Everything that is and everything that isn't is shining with this same being.

Therefore there is nothing to annihilate . . . nothing to hold at bay . . .

nothing to judge and no one to judge it.

All can be released to being.

In being.

As being.

Rest in being and find this being in all things.

Know this being in all things.

Love this being in all things.

FROM THE ABSOLUTE TO THE RELATIVE

How does what we experience in meditation—our knowing of the absolute, the oneness of our being—translate to our experience on the ground? How do we *actually* reconcile the felt truth of oneness with the world that is entrenched in the relative experiences of separateness, our conditioning, and othering?

I've been learning the answers to these questions through my work with Presence Collective and Peace in Schools. In fact, years ago, Peace in Schools inspired these questions. For me, outcomes of Peace in Schools have been beacons of what can be accomplished when we create systems from the heart of knowing and bring this knowing to bear on the relative plane.

For me, Peace in Schools is yet another example of how acts of being ripple outward. This organization is the first place that required me to deeply confront that mindfulness practice does not automatically equal a full, heart-centered, inclusive, trauma-informed approach for all it serves. Mindfulness practice, like anything, often reflects the collective conditioning that it exists within. (For example, structures arising in white supremacist dominant culture reflect white supremacist dominant culture.)

Longing to reconcile the needs of the diverse population of high school students (as opposed to a self-selected group of people who find practice on their own) exposed the ways this disconnect existed in the world at large. It revealed to me what's missing in a conditioned collective approach that does not reflect the whole.

This is how the rippling happens. Peace in School's work and commitment to wholeness, for example, affects the students; the students influence the program's creation—for they are not simply seen as who is being served but as integral collaborators. The unfolding and evolution of the program creates the questions. The organization commits to answering the questions. Deep investigations lead to further inquiry. Further embracing and affecting others, creating more questions, and on and on. This spiral is the result of pausing and ensuring that our approach is, to the best of our ability, truly investigating, exploring, and encompassing the whole; truly seeing all beings and the being of us all. As you read through the next section, I invite you to explore ways this can apply in your life.

From the beginning at Peace in Schools, it was incredibly important to me that we focus on what's underneath what the world calls "bad behavior." Paramount, in fact. Great schoolteachers have been doing this forever, but many education systems haven't centered it structurally. Peace in Schools puts healthy compassionate relationship at the center of the classroom, curricula, and community.

A philosophical approach that consciously implements "power with" strategies is also paramount. Such an approach recognizes the screen behind the movie but also doesn't deny the real pain that can exist within the movie.

So many teens—especially teens marginalized by dominant culture—are labeled "problem students." Often this labeling is the result of unrecognized implicit bias. Once so labeled, these students are often written off. Authorities respond to their behavior, to how they present themselves, through various forms of punishment rather than through connection and curiosity. We forget to ask what is happening for them, what happened *to* them. We look only at the outcome, ignoring the process. We only see the *what*, not the *how*.

By only focusing and engaging with the acting out, what's under the behavior is forgotten. In this forgetting we've abandoned our deepest knowing as well as the deepest truth of our true nature. We abandon being.

The result? More ripples of trauma. More identification with various aspects of the personality. Survival strategies are strengthened. For a teen, it may be the survival strategy of being tough and unaffected by punishment. For the teacher, it may be the strategy of divorcing themselves from feeling as a way to cope and get through a job that can be overwhelming.

When we take a turning-toward approach with our students, our children, our coworkers, whomever we are in relationship with, we commit to seeing their wholeness, no matter their behavior. We commit to engaging with this wholeness, to reflecting it back to them.

The word *emotion* derives from the Latin *emovēre*, a word that suggests energy in motion. In a turning-toward approach we commit to allowing emotion and all other temporary experience to move through. We look past, or *through*, the outer layer of things. We focus on what's real. We see what's not broken, no matter how much apparent brokenness appears to be manifesting on the surface.

When interacting with students, as a way to keep what's underneath at the forefront of awareness rather than fall into conditioned *power-over* educational techniques, Peace in Schools uses a motto:

Connection over control.

Remembering this in any relationship is paramount to witnessing and seeing wholeness. You could apply it to being in relationship with your partner, your child, *yourself*!

When we don't address what's happening under the surface, we get stuck in punitive behaviors and systems. Punitive systems are full of dams. They provide lots of places for energy to get stuck. Blocks are created. Another way I see trauma manifest, put simply, is energy that can't move. When we *turn toward*, we have the opportunity to cease identifying with what's been blocking the movement of energy. Constriction can be surrendered because we realize that even constriction is shining with reality. Seeing the ultimate truth of reality in all of our relative experience, *turning toward* allows us to remember, return to, and embody our inherent freedom.

When emotion isn't getting stuck anywhere, when it's free to move, it leaves no trace—no trace in the body, mind, energetic system. Why does this matter? Because the ego hides out in the traces, and when we are identified with the ego, we suffer.

In movement there is freedom.
In freedom there is movement.

TURNING TOWARD OUR STUDENTS AT PEACE IN SCHOOLS

In the same way we invite young people to move toward their experience rather than away, our Peace in Schools facilitators are trained to turn toward whatever is arising in the moment. The capacity to be spontaneous and responsive to the moment is at the top of the job description. Most importantly, though, is their dedication to seeing the true nature of those they work with.

Students are deeply affected by the presence of a caring adult who is committed to *turning toward*, to knowing the truth of experience and keeping an eye on the truth of experience. To being in touch with what doesn't change—in themselves and the students. To surrendering what veils reality. To showing up for each student unconditionally.

In "The Science of Resilience: Why Some Children Can Thrive Despite Adversity," Bari Walsh of Harvard's Graduate School of Education addresses an important question: "When confronted with the fallout of childhood trauma, why do some children adapt and overcome, while others bear lifelong scars that flatten their potential?"

Walsh's response: "A growing body of evidence points to one common answer: Every child who winds up doing well has had at least one stable and committed relationship with a supportive adult." She went on to say that, according to a new report from the National Scientific Council on the Developing Child, a multidisciplinary collaboration chaired by Harvard's Jack Shonkoff, "The power of that one strong adult relationship is a key ingredient in resilience—a positive, adaptive response in the face of significant adversity."

We can be this adult for our young people. But to be this adult for them, we have to be this adult for ourselves.

Dr. Christopher Willard is a psychologist, educational consultant, and author of *How We Grow Through What We Go Through*, *Growing Up Mindful*, *Alphabreaths*, and many other books for parents, professionals, and children. He teaches at Harvard and is on the advisory board of Peace in Schools. In a recent conversation on this topic, Chris shared this with me:

> "The number one predictor of resilience is the adult, and a close second is finding meaning in something larger.
>
> The easiest way to create stressed-out miserable kids is to surround them with stressed-out miserable adults, but the best way to create mindful, present, and compassionate kids is to surround them with mindful, present, compassionate adults. Through the coregulation of their nervous systems, a well-regulated adult who has dealt with their own trauma and history can then lend that regulation to the child, who in turn practices and internalizes that skill for themselves, then hopefully for their own classmates, family, and community in a positive ripple."

Here's what stands out to me about our conversation:

Focusing on what's real is contagious. Transformation ripples.

ACCEPTING WHAT IS REAL IS NOT
THE SAME AS RESIGNATION

It can be extremely difficult to focus on what's real if we are busy rejecting, denying, or avoiding what is. Once we feel established in our understanding of who we truly are, we have the opportunity to find the truth in all things as we move through the world. If we are caught in resisting acceptance of what is, however, we simply cannot surrender to this seeing. We forget the screen. We live the movie.

Acceptance is a doorway that allows us to not get stuck in dams and dead ends but to see our inherent wholeness. Only then can we stand in truth rather than reactivity, holding space for each person by recognizing their being from our being—by, in fact, realizing that this being is the same.

First, however, I want to point out one important distinction between acceptance and resignation. *Resignation* is an act of giving up, checking out. When we are in resignation, we are living in denial, resistance, or avoidance. This resignation could be the fallout of a turning-away approach gone awry, a form of confusion resulting from the belief that we have to reject experience. An identification with powerlessness is an understandable reaction to this belief. Resignation arises out of and leads to further suffering.

People often assume acceptance is the same thing as resignation, but it isn't. Surrender is a daughter of *acceptance*. It's an activity born of acceptance. It's a letting go within the borderless container of awareness. Acceptance means not living in denial, seeing clearly and fully acknowledging what is, living on life's terms. When acceptance is our ground, surrendering to life becomes possible. In acceptance we are willing to be with what is, even if it's not what we want. Why? Because

Awareness itself is inherently accepting

and we are awareness itself.

250

Embracing surrender as a practice allows us to move through life from a heart-centered perspective. The primary reason we move away from acceptance and instead resist, deny, or avoid is that we do not want to experience pain or discomfort. But if we don't have a way to *be* with pain or discomfort, we might fall into the powerlessness of resignation. This conditioned survival strategy, of course, doesn't work. It just creates more suffering. (To paraphrase the meditation teacher Shinzen Young, Pain x Resistance = Suffering.) Remember, however, that acceptance is a quality of your very nature. It's who you are, not something you have to *do*. Embracing surrender as a practice can help us return to this remembrance, and we don't have to apply effort simply because we're calling it a practice. Consider how the maple surrenders her leaves, how the snake surrenders his skin. Clouds surrender rain to the infinite expanse of the sky.

A Practice: Focusing on the Reality of What Is

Pause now and feel into your own experience.

Bring the attention into your body.

Breathe.

Explore, with your CARE journal if you'd like:

How have both acceptance and resignation manifested in your life?

How has it been when you've been trying to accept something versus remembering that you are the open space, the open awareness, that accepts what is, naturally? When you lean into how it's only when identified with the conditioned mind that you *strive* for the very thing you are?

What shifts in your world when you *turn toward* what is, embracing it fully? When you surrender the temptation to reject, deny, avoid, or resign?

What shifts when you focus on the reality of whatever is arising? When you keep your eye on the heart of what is?

ACCEPTANCE IS DIFFERENT THAN ACQUIESCING

For deep transformation in collective human consciousness, it is also helpful to
see the difference between *acceptance* and *acquiescing*. Picture Justin, the bully
on the playground, handing over the ball he stole from his classmate Charlie,
but only because an adult said it was the right thing to do. Can you see the
teacher looming over him forcing the exchange? Maybe Justin hands it over
based on the pressure. Maybe because the teacher just threatened to take away
Justin's recess tomorrow. But steam is building inside Justin. Perhaps even steam
that has greater force the next time the lid blows.

You can know real transformation has occurred when Justin realizes that
it hurts his heart to steal from Charlie, when Justin has been supported with
the kind of inner curriculum that allows him to recognize his own experience
of empathy—a swelling of compassion upon seeing empty-handed head-hung
Charlie crying.

We can know real change has occurred when Justin, unprompted, surrenders what wasn't his in the first place and reaches out to Charlie to apologize
because he knows that he loves his classmate. And he wants everyone to be able
to have fun on the playground—together. When he surrenders the survival
strategy of the bully because he realizes how much it hurts—him *and* others—
and he doesn't want to hurt anymore. When he realizes that he, like all eight
billion of us, simply longs to be happy. When he becomes self-aware enough to
let go of anything and everything that would stand in the way of our collective
well-being.

While I'm being playful with the image, this isn't just airy-fairy Pollyanna
talk. If this can happen in a classroom, which I've seen, it can happen in our society. What's required? Getting to the root of things. Heart surgery that releases
constriction, not simply new rules and laws.

May we collectively remove the thorns in our shared heart
while remembering that, fundamentally, every thorn
is made of the same thing
we are.

**May we turn toward, surrender, and allow every thorn
to be devoured in the light of our shared being.
Devoured by Love.**

There is nothing to fear.

Given that we are not all treated equally within society, we can turn toward how we each contribute to this lack of equity in various ways. To create equitable communities, and therefore an equitable society, we can turn toward truth while surrendering what veils our direct experience of oneness.

We can surrender our collective fear of difference, our conditioned resistance to diversity, our shared habit of being attached to a materialist model.

And, as with so much in this book, there's nuance here. It feels important to name both relative and absolute truths. There's more going on than simply a conditioned tendency to be fearful of the world we live in; or fearful of diversity because we are afraid of what we don't understand, what we can't relate to, or what feels foreign to us. Particularly for those who are marginalized, this fear can be linked to physical survival.

There's a very particular relative reality that I think is important to acknowledge. Consider the history of the lived experience of violence against BIPOC who were simply minding their own business when harmed. Kenneth Bourne, a Philadelphia-based social worker who is Black, recently told me that what struck him most about my book *A Kids Book About Mindfulness* was the invitation to focus on the sky. "Growing up in Philly, we're not taught to look up often. We will always check our sides or behind us, but you never look up," he says. That is based on a relative plane reality that I did not experience growing up.

And, to refer to an earlier example from my life, if I find a stalker in my kitchen, uninvited, I can get a restraining order and learn invaluable lessons such as to avoid putting your home address on your professional website. I can take action that protects me on the relative plane. I can also do this while practicing not getting paralyzed by fear, while not running the story that all men are "out to get me," while remembering the ultimate truth of our shared being.

Don't forget, this isn't about right and wrong. "Getting stuck in fear means I'm a bad spiritual person," and the like. This is about freedom. This is about recognizing when the conditioned mind takes an experience and tries to run with it, creating tremendous suffering within. This is about presence rather than spinning, stillness rather than running. This is about the inner stillness that has nothing to do with the circumstances of our lives.

JOYOUS BELONGING

The work of Radical Dharma does a brilliant job supporting folks in recognizing that those who identify with dominant culture do not "win" in a system of inequity; that, in fact, there is tremendous suffering for those "on top" in grasping to this distortion. It's an expensive position. To stay "on top," those there must divorce themselves from feeling and from our shared humanity. Shared being must be forgotten. In the midst of such efforting, there is contraction. And in the contraction, what's missed is the cultural richness that is outside the conditioned norm—a norm that is only defined as "normal" by dominant culture.

Some time ago, a beloved friend invited me to be in a procession—but not just any procession. This procession was in New Orleans, where second-line parades are the descendants of the city's famous jazz funerals. There are dozens of different second-line parades put on throughout the year, usually on Sunday afternoons, often in the French Quarter. The processions range in size, level of organization, and traditions, but they always include a brass band, jubilant dancing in the street, members decked out in bright colors, hats, parasols. On this day, the band leader, in a freshly pressed suit, wore miniature stuffed crows on his shoulders. Decorating the band alone, there were more brightly colored feathers than I could count.

When I pause, I can still call to mind the exuberance of the brass horns, the humidity in the air, the sound of our shoes on hot pavement, the unified rhythm of the crowd as we made our way, dancing, from neighborhood to neighborhood. A traveling block party proclaiming joy, inviting those on the sidelines to join. And they did. Without hesitation, they did. Black, brown, white—didn't matter. All responded to the call to be together, to celebrate, to love.

While this tradition has African American roots, and I was one of the few white people at the beginning of the procession, all were welcome. *Real* welcoming. *Deep* welcoming. *Joyous* belonging. All this in the name of celebrating a beloved's birthday, and not even a decade one at that! Needless to say, when I was growing up, this is not how birthdays were celebrated, and certainly this is not what funerals felt and looked like!

Dancing with my friends, I found myself overcome with the aliveness of life itself. Life dancing through me, through us, our river of shared song flooding the streets. My heart swelling with the beauty of it all. My disintegrating new sandals, not a concern. Joyful tears merging with sweat. Time, forgotten.

THE COST OF MONOCULTURE

Monoculture is the practice of growing a single crop on rotation year after year. The costs of this are many: pests can easily feed on row after row of their favorite food; pesticides have to be used, which kills pollinators; the natural balance of the soil is upset as nutrients are robbed; the plants are weakened year after year; more chemicals are added; biodiversity decreases. This cycle repeats and only reinforces itself.

There's more. The chain of events goes on. You get the idea.

Culture is the same way. A single, homogeneous culture without diversity or little variation is often not a healthy collective. It's not reflective of the magnificence of life's natural multifariousness. It's not whole. Homogeneity doesn't reflect inherent wholeness, which excludes nothing. Imbalance arises. And that lack of diversity has a cost—a high cost.

In surrendering the collective conditioning to gravitate toward homogeneity, we see that awareness, which is inherently accepting, naturally embraces the vast variations of consciousness that arise. We see that, in fact, the variety of forms that arise are an outpouring of possibility on behalf of consciousness itself.

The ego, individual or collective, is a dam in the river of infinite possibility.

SPEAKING OF COSTS

We forget that money is an invention. We devised it 4,500 years ago to facilitate the sharing of resources and goods. It was an ingenious creation. It allowed a shoemaker to exchange more easily with a farmer or baker. For quite a long time now, though, money has been widely used to marginalize. It is a form of—and a means to extend and expand—power. In many cases it's become a mechanism of control. Money and our ability to produce it has come to define our place in society. Dominant culture regards us as consumers or human capital as opposed to citizens.

Within conditioned dominant culture, we've assigned more value to money than human life. We've made it more important than the natural world. All this creation reflects the conditioned lie of scarcity. The fable that *more is better*. The grasping for power. A grasping that results in things like war, famine, disease, displacement, white supremacy, and climate crisis.

THE MIND OF SCARCITY, THE LIE OF SCARCITY

I want to acknowledge the relative reality of someone experiencing scarcity as in, let's say, not enough food to eat. Such a circumstance is not simply a state of mind. I would never blame someone's hunger on their belief system. Here I'm focusing on the *mind of scarcity*. In my years of teaching, I see the mind of scarcity as the most pervasive pattern of thought and expectation moving human activity. We all experience scarcity as a mindset. Those who have many properties and bank accounts can still get deeply identified with the mental experience of scarcity—oftentimes more than people who only have enough for today. This mindset is at the root of much suffering as it arises on behalf of the belief that we are separate, that there is not enough, that competition is required.

> To live as an enlightened collective,
> we must surrender the lie of scarcity,
> the fable that more is better,
> and our conditioned grasping for power.
>
> We must be unwilling to abandon
> the peace of our true nature,
> for anything.
>
> To realize freedom together,
> we must value our shared being
> above all else.

OUR SACRED DUTY

Our journey began on the progressive "not this, not that" path; seeing the damage of identifying with the inner critic, learning how to recognize unmet needs, and the various ways we reinforce our felt sense of separation in an attempt to meet those needs. We focused on how to be compassionate, recognizing we are all looking for the same thing:

Love.
Connection.
Belonging.

These steps can be deeply fruitful places of exploration and learning. But we are more than the activity of the conditioned mind, more than our suffering, more than our learnings!

To begin realizing freedom together, we must see through the faulty appearances of the ego. We must know the truth of our being as pure consciousness with no divisions, no separations. It is then that we can fully heed the sacred call to act on behalf of our understanding.

We are the absolute shrouded in human experience. In knowing and experiencing this reality, we have a blessed opportunity—a sacred duty—to reconcile our worldly, often difficult, relative existence with who we truly are. To create a world that reflects the truth of our oneness, we must move from the heart of the absolute as we turn toward the difficulties of the relative plane. We must see that the relative plane is made of the absolute, not separate from it. We have a sacred duty to not only recognize truth within ourselves but also share and communicate this love and understanding in the world. This is how acts of being come to be.

Knowing the absolute in our personal practices reminds us we are more than the content of our lives. We can first see, then accept, all parts of ourselves from this understanding of who we truly are, most importantly the parts of ourselves we have been conditioned to judge as "unacceptable." Loving these parts of ourselves unconditionally is a surrendering of sorts, fragments surrendered to the whole. Because this is the heart of who we are: whole, unchanging, absolute, Love itself.

Collective practice also requires truly seeing the "unacceptable" parts of society, then bringing truth, compassion, and Love to bear on what we find there: addressing the wholeness underneath, returning to the wholeness, tending to the wholeness, acting from the wholeness.

Truly *turning toward* the pain of the world can be an uncomfortable practice. We turn toward the pain because we know it's all part of our complete knowing of truth. By doing this we can heal and move beyond the paralysis that can be a conditioned by-product of the "not this, not that" approach. *Turning toward* allows us to move into the world with empowerment, resilience, and the strength to continue to come back to difficulties that come our way.

It can be helpful to remember that acknowledging and accepting the experiences of the relative world doesn't tarnish the truth of the absolute. In fact, truly seeing and accepting inequities and difficulties that are the truth of the relative world is the only way we can start to bring our direct experience of unity to the pain of the world. This holding of both truths—our absolute knowledge and our relative pain—allows for all to become visible, to be brought out of the shadows of "othering" or "Oh, that's just too much for any one person to deal with." It's what is needed before true change can occur.

RECONCILING PARADOX

From here we can hold the absolute truth that we are one while also holding the truth that we are not all having the same experience, bearing the same burdens, or feeling the same pains on the relative plane. We can be with and turn toward the complexity of this. We can turn toward paradox, to various truths:

The truth of identity and the truth that identity is illusory.
The truth of a gradual path and the truth of a direct approach.
The truth that the body is illusory and that this body is how and where we create acts of being.
The truth of a negating approach and the truth of a turning-toward approach.

The truth of the relative and the truth of the absolute.

Through acceptance, through Love, all is reconciled.

When we are unable to hold these paradoxes, to be with the complexity of them, to know the truth of all things, we identify with one side of a duality. Ultimately, as discussed in chapter seven, we identify as a subject with the world as the object. This is where suffering lives. And this suffering plays out in lots of ways.

For example, if you are identified with the relative world—only able to see the relative world, the material world, the world where we appear as separate—then the only change you can make in this world is *from* separation. If you are focusing on the absolute from a dualistic perspective, as if it is separate from relative existence, you might lose touch with your agency, your capacity, to act on the injustices of our relative world. The trap of this perspective: there *is no world*, therefore there's nothing to change. If you're caught in this trap, you might miss the call for sacred duty should it knock on your door.

True acceptance is generous. It has breadth and room for all that is—and all that isn't! From acceptance we say yes to what is—yes to ourselves in the most limited way we are conditioned to see ourselves and yes to the vastest understanding of who we truly are. We say yes to the world as it is, with all of its hardship and struggle, and we say yes to what the world could be. We say yes to our capacity to create the world we want to live in—together.

How do we know what this world of possibility looks like? It's simply a mirror, a reflection of the heart of who we are. It takes form through the vessels of truth, love, and beauty. It shines with the truth of our shared being.

We must allow our practices to become a universal yes to what is.
Saying yes isn't resignation or acquiescence. It is not defeat.
We cannot change what we cannot accept.

If we can hold paradox, it allows us to not deny the truth of any aspect of reality.

But how do I practice holding paradox?

You don't have to. You *are* what holds paradox. Plus, you learn to find the true nature in experience through finding the true nature in experience!

Collective Practice: Being That Which Blesses

PRACTICE 1: CELEBRATION OF JOY

Choose one thing in your life that ignites joy. Pick something you've not engaged in fully because you've believed that it's indulgent or isn't in keeping with your practice. Consciously embrace it. Consciously engage. Move toward. What if all of it was practice? Bring your life fully into your practice versus your practice into your life. Leave nothing out. What do you notice about doing this?

If you are working with a group, share your findings, your experience. Play with how you do this. This could involve a talent show of sorts! (Though be very mindful not to fall into a conditioned definition of talent. Perhaps "Celebration of Joy!" would be a better title? Let your group run with it.)

PRACTICE 2: ALTAR OF AWARENESS

On your own or with a group, create an Altar of Awareness. This is your altar. It will look however you want it to look.

What do you wish to surrender to it? Make a ritual out of it, perhaps even a ceremony. Create a place for letting go. (Not to be confused with getting rid of.) You may wish to give specific form to this, such as writing down things you wish to let go of, then burning them at the altar. Trust yourself and be empowered to create what is yours to create.

We've focused a lot in this journey on undoing—undoing conditioned assumptions, beliefs, and judgments that manifest personally and collectively. We move now even more fully into creating, into embodied acts of being.

Allow yourself or your group as a whole to release into the practice of honoring. Honor everything, even the pain that comes when we acknowledge that change is coming upon us. Honor the nervousness, loneliness, despair, rage. Honor our common humanity. Honor loss. Honor exhaustion and slowness. Rather than the temptation to push or change this experience, honor it. Honor the emotional fatigue we might feel as we try to create change in our world. Move toward it. *Know* the truth in it. *Feel* the truth in it. *Be* the truth in it. Allow this also to be a place of blessings. *Everything is welcome.*

PRACTICE 3: BEING THAT WHICH BLESSES

Offering blessings is a practice.
Release into the opportunity to know yourself as that which blesses.

On your own or as a group, create an opportunity for sending blessings out into the world.

Again and again

may we return

to what is holy.

What is whole.

May we find it

everywhere.

Chapter Twelve

Return to Service

Loving and Living Truth in the World

Zen is not just personal practice, and our enlightenment
is not just personal attainment. When we attain
enlightenment, everything should be enlightened.

—Shunryu Suzuki

Picture a mother cat with a large litter. Say, seven little kittens. One is running one way. One is running after another. One is hurt. One is crying. One is scratching another. One is scared. One is joyfully bounding about. Even though we might want to run away if we had seven kids chaotically running around, this mother doesn't. When the kittens are in distress, she tends to them. When they are in danger, she takes the scruff of their necks into her mouth and carries them to safety. Picture a mother cat that is truly *here*.

Or perhaps picture the archetype of the divine mother. What keeps her *here*, staying with the chaos of the world?

Love.

Every time we don't run away from what is difficult in our lives and our practices, Love is tethering us to what is.

In the name of Love, the unconditional, divine mother moves step by step into deeper relationship with what is. (Though she wouldn't describe it as being "in relationship" given that she doesn't perceive herself as separate from what is.) She practices asking questions, finds out what's going on, holds, tends to, caresses. Each child, or kitten, the same. With Love, in Love, she moves closer. She moves *in*.

The same process can happen within.

Healing happens through unconditional attention.
Attention is a form of Love.
All parts of you deserve your loving attention.
They cannot be healed by anyone else.

These dreamed characters within you all have particular wounds. No one—not your partner, not the best therapist on the planet, not the wisest spiritual teacher—can know better than you what these parts of you need. It can feel like you want the attention of a therapist, or a teacher, or your partner, and that may be so, but true healing, true resolution of the wounds, happens through the vehicle of your loving attention.

Attention, a reaching arm of awareness.
You, the light of liberation.

When we truly embody this truth, we become masters of our own lives. We know that no one can make us feel anything. No one can control where we put our attention. When we embody this, we take full responsibility for our life experience.

My first Zen teacher's teacher used to say, "You are as much of a pain in the ass when you take offense as when you give offense." Here, we take responsibility for all of it: taking offense, giving offense—all of it. We take responsibility for our lives.

This is not the same thing as saying no one else has any responsibility or that you should roll over in the face of injustice and "just work on yourself." I want to be crystal clear about this. It's through the kind of care we are talking about here, this kind of taking responsibility, that the mother cat may realize that she needs to move her kittens into another den. Perhaps one that is safer for them. Perhaps an environment that is more reflective of the unconditional love she embodies and offers. Perhaps boundaries are put in place. She is empowered to respond to the moment as needed. As the teacher, embodiment coach, and writer Prentis Hemphill says, "Boundaries are the distance at which I can love you and me simultaneously." Don't allow the conditioned mind to grab hold of this lesson. This is about being empowered to realize:

> **You hold the keys to your freedom.**
> **No one can take them from you.**
>
> **In taking full responsibility for our lives,**
> **we become a service to ourselves,**
> **we are a service to others,**
> **we are a service to the world.**

IN SERVICE TO RELATIONSHIP AND NO RELATIONSHIP

Relationship—with others, with community, with systems, with ourselves— is at the heart of our existence on the relative plane. All relationships shift when we discover who we truly are—in fact, when we remember who we've always been. When we return to it. Conscious community, truth, wholeness, inquiry, unconditional love, belonging, unity, presence, oneness, embodiment, surrender, and service—all various pathways of returning to who we truly are. To what we truly are. All are openings and invitations for acts of being.

> **When we act from being,**
> **when we serve from the heart of who we are,**
> **our world reflects it.**
> **In service, Love, truth, and beauty**
> **shine at the forefront of experience**
> **rather than hide in the shadows, veiled.**

Remember, in absolute truth there are no relationships—no separate self that serves and no separate self being served. We are all the same consciousness that is in service to itself. When we stabilize in the direct experience of who we truly are—Love itself—service becomes the physical embodiment of this Love.

Love, overflowing with itself, manifests as acts of being in our relative world. Love fills the void of need through acts of itself.
We transform our world through Love, by Love.

When we learn to stabilize in this knowing, it offers the empowerment necessary to face the harshness that exists in our relative world where separation has a particular reality. It can give us the strength to create the world that's a reflection of the knowing that we are one. With systems that recognize the humanity of all, the rights of all, the being of all. Systems that prioritize justice and collective well-being through environments of CARE—and through Love.

FROM THE ABSOLUTE TO THE RELATIVE

How many of us can relate to, in one moment, having clear understanding of the reality of oneness, and in the next, finding ourselves emotionally activated, perhaps in relationship with, say, a partner. (I'm fresh out of a session with our marriage counselor, y'all, so just to be clear, this is real talk. There is nothing theoretical about it.)

I went into our counseling session knowing and naming that part of me was nervous about what I intended to bring to the table, about giving voice to a particular experience. I could see the conditioning that would cause me to sugarcoat my words in the name of making sure "my partner was taken care of; that he didn't get hurt." The desire not to be hurtful is sincere and deep. There's something else at play too. It's *also known as* trying to keep him from getting angry so I don't have to be with the discomfort of my own fear of rejection.

Even knowing this about myself, even within a larger context of knowing that my husband and I share the very same being, the conditioned pattern still arose. We both got triggered. And with this there was sadness, grief, pain.

I chose this example because there's nothing that would fall in the category of severe trauma happening here. It was a temporary, typical feeling of *other than*. A few more threads ripped from a tear that's age-old and that every human being knows: the tear of *feeling* outside presence, believing ourselves to be cut off, separate.

Picture such an experience as a ripple. If we're speaking about consciousness, picture it as a vibration of consciousness that takes the form of a little wave in a lake, expanding outward in concentric circles. Conditioned patterns that play out, like the one with my husband, rippling wider and wider. Perhaps touching other people and circumstances in its wake.

Often in meditation practice we have this sense that peace comes from the water being still. So, with great sincerity on our cushions, we give our attention to the stillness. Or perhaps we even visualize the ripples moving outward until they dissipate, not taking them personally while we witness them vanish. Nothing wrong with any of this.

Although for so many of us—for most of us, I daresay—this same pattern in the water is bound to arise again. Different content but the same process of triggering, rippling, expanding.

And, to underline, there's nothing wrong with the same process arising again. It will arise again, until it doesn't.

Our conditioned processes, our wounds,
will arise again and again until they're healed.
We can count on this.
In the name of ending suffering,
we can even say thank you for this.

Thank you? Really?

Indeed. We can be grateful, because if our intention is to know our inherent freedom in all moments and in all circumstances, it does not support our intention to leave any stone on our path unturned. It's not helpful to attempt to withhold the light of conscious awareness from anything. It's not useful to compartmentalize, to vault off, to hide things under rugs and rocks, to avoid the lessons life freely offers.

And here's the fun part: ultimately, as we learned from Huìnéng and his verse on the bodhi tree, these stones are empty. On one level, there isn't anything to turn over. No thing to take off a shelf or out of a box. Nothing to unlock. And there's no *one* to do the turning, the unwrapping, the opening, or the learning either!

If you are a person for whom the light of this truth has come on so fully that there's been no trace of suffering in the body-mind since, then this next part isn't for you. I'm going to trust, however, that you wouldn't have picked up this book if that were the case. And certainly you might not still be reading it!

For most of us, fleeting moments of feeling cut off from being arise again and again—even after we recognize ourselves as consciousness. Yes, we can rest in the stillness, the infinite vastness of our true nature and, as we do so, the ripples need not only move in one direction. They need not only roll outward.

Remember, as conditioned creatures, we make up time.

In truth it is always now.
And now is not a moment in time.
Now is all there is.

In this now, we are moving about like dreamed characters in this illusory world. The construct of time is happening inside the dream. Identity is happening inside the dream. Suffering is happening inside the dream.

You might wonder, *even great and unjust suffering*?

Even great and unjust suffering.

Consciousness gives rise to and animates the dream of existence.
The dream is made of consciousness, happening inside consciousness.
There is nowhere else it could exist.

When traumas great and small create ripples, the ripples are experienced by the dreamed character within the dream. We can engage with these ripples in the same way that time can move forward and backward in a dream.

A Practice: Rolling Experience Backward

Picture a place in your life where you have a wound—not too big. Maybe there's something fresh and current to work with? Some hurt that arises again and again. Say, the feeling of being abandoned, or the fear of being rejected, or of not being loveable.

What's an experience that starts the ripples?

It all begins with with a thought. Something arises, some little experience—like something my husband said in our therapy session—that an aspect of the personality makes meaning out of. Visualize a place where you get triggered or an experience where the ripples begin, now.

Next, notice all the thoughts, beliefs, and feelings that follow. That ripple outward.

Pause.

Notice, without judgment, if you are simply reading along like a witness in another room, removed. Or if you are actually following the prompts. There's no right or wrong in whatever you see. This could potentially be rich to explore, depending on what you find.

What's happening in the body, mind, and energetic system as these ripples expand?

Yes, the ripples are happening in vast consciousness. In awareness. You can rest the attention in awareness. You can allow the ripples to dissipate, not taking them personally, not getting identified with them. (They always dissipate eventually. Remember: Emotion is energy in motion. Emotions will roll and dissolve into the still lake of awareness if allowed. Such is the law of impermanence.)

You can also picture these ripples rolling backward. (The only place that any of this is happening is in the mind anyway, so why not?) This backward rippling is another version of turning toward: moving in and through.

Picture all the thoughts, beliefs, and feelings coming home, drawing back, returning to presence, to being. Rather than rippling outward, creating further suffering, imagine a rippling inward. Visualize the fragmented aspects of the personality returning to wholeness. Their vehicle is Love.

One way to heal the trauma of separation is to reverse engineer it.

The light of awareness is our guide.

It can be tempting, especially as we become accustomed to resting the attention in infinite consciousness, to leave behind the messages, and specifically the learnings, in the ripples. We sometimes attempt to skim over the information in the triggers, the lessons in the places of rub or tension in our lives, the gold in the rough edges of experience. It can be tempting to long for transcendence over the content.

Again, on the deepest level of truth, there is no separate self that is learning and nothing to learn. While this is so, it is also the case that a huge impetus for incarnation on this relative plane of existence is to learn something, to work something out. The dream of incarnation is ignited through the urge, the call, to learn and to feel.

We can appreciate the learning. Move into the feeling. We can be grateful and allow ourselves to receive the very thing we're here for. There's a rightness of being in this.

Life is teaching us in every moment.

> We are always being provided
>
> with the very thing we need
>
> to support our liberation.

REVERSE-ENGINEERING TRAUMA

Usually in speaking about reverse engineering, we are referring to disassembling, examining, or analyzing to discover how something is structured, often in order to produce something similar. In this case, we're exploring this reversing process such that the light of awareness has penetrated so deeply and so fully within our movement into experience, into the wound, that there's nothing left of it other than luminous being itself.

Let's stay with the example of a tiff with my husband. The trigger only arises when something that experiences itself as *other than* arises, when the illusion of separation appears. If I try to write this off or brush it aside—"Oh, any reactivity is just the ego"—it's likely to come back. If I try to transcend it (but it's simply code for *avoid it*), it's likely to come back. If I pretend not to see it, it's likely to come back. If I give over to it completely through fully identifying with it, it's likely to come back.

In this particular reversing practice (though *practice* can be a misleading word in that for some it might imply more efforting than is required), we are simply moving step by step, consciously, back into the wound of separation. We are gently, reverently, lovingly picking up the pieces that have been dropped along the way as we've experience ourselves as separate. We are gathering what has veiled pure being, what has led to feeling cut off from presence. We are lovingly ushering everything home.

Our longing and searching for happiness, for wholeness, for belonging, has arisen out of our knowing of happiness, wholeness, and belonging. To realize freedom together we consciously and lovingly return.

On a personal level, this can look like returning to repetitive thought or memory that creates suffering, and rather than trying to let it go or transcend it, shepherding the thought home. On a collective level, we start by bearing witness to our collective wounds, together, from the knowing of who we truly are. Then we allow what has been—grief, trauma, pain—to be devoured by Love. In presence. Together.

It may sound like this takes a lot of work, but it doesn't. All that's required is loving attention, commitment to liberation, and awareness. All these things, while sometimes veiled, are inherent and can't be taken from us, so all is in our favor. We don't have to effort our way through this.

Picture a clenched fist.
It actually takes effort to keep the fist gripped.
The releasing of the hand happens with the releasing of effort.

The freedom is felt in the letting go.
The liberation is in the release.

COLLECTIVE REVERSE ENGINEERING

This approach in practice can have profound societal effects. As Resmaa Menakem says, "In America, nearly all of us, regardless of our background or skin color, carry trauma in our bodies around the myth of race." We aren't going to heal such collective wounds through touting "We're all one" and deluding ourselves that we can avoid the ripple effects of this collective trauma.

In reverse engineering we're moving back through our collective
distortions with the light of conscious awareness. We're allowing what's
been festering in the dark to be healed by Love, through Love.

Again, simply saying "We're all one" won't heal the wound of separation. We have to acknowledge where the hatred, greed, and delusion have arisen. We have to go back into the burning building. But first we have to acknowledge the building is burning and take proper precautions. We can use our contemplative tools to help us remember we are the absolute in the face of inequity, domination, violence, and trauma. If we enter these buildings from a place of identification, a place of believing we're separate, we won't be able to put out any fires. In fact, we'll only douse them with gasoline.

**Realizing freedom together isn't just about collectively realizing that we
are one.**
It's about having our actions—and systems—reflect this understanding.
It's about bringing the absolute truth to bear on relative circumstances.

When I get triggered in a session with our couples counselor, it's my job to
clean this up, to bring the truth of my understanding to this wound, this distortion—to shepherd the hurt home to Love. In the same way, it's our job, collectively,
to understand and know our shared being, and to bring this understanding into
the undoing of what we've created by choosing distortion over truth.

To leave no stone unturned.
And to leave no one behind.

We lovingly move in and through our very wounds to do this. The healing
happens through the same tunnel in which the wounds were inflicted, just in
a different direction and now with the accompaniment of Love and the understanding of truth.

I've experienced this many times. Years ago, Peace in Schools was up against
severe school district budget cuts and our semester-long course was on the
chopping block. At a series of school board meetings, students, educators, and
parents advocated publicly for our program to stay intact. I'll always remember
Kai, a junior who had taken my class many times, taking the stand. I had no idea
what he would say. The room fell silent as he described all the hardships in his
life, and he followed that with this:

"Mindful Studies didn't save my life. It gave me the tools to save myself."

More recently I experienced this process unfold organically through a Presence Collective retreat. Cofacilitated with jylani ma'at—friend, meditation
teacher, and president of our board—it was the first retreat most of us had been
to in person since the onset of the pandemic. Individual and collective hardship
was palpable in the room our first evening. It had been a challenging few years
for all of us.

The ages of the participants ranged from late twenties through late sixties. The gathering was 50 percent BIPOC, and the group reflected various socioeconomic and religious backgrounds. I could only dream then of what was alive in the group by the last day: intimate friendships formed, unconscious biases named and challenged, the truth of our shared being recognized.

We tasted the beginnings of something incredibly important. The intimacy and the collective experience of unity was profound. Together, we savored the relief of undoing—personal beliefs and collective beliefs—individually and as a group. We shared the joy of *seeing through* and the freedom that comes from *moving toward* rather than away. After the retreat, jylani and I agreed that we were blessed to bear witness to and participate in this transformative unfolding. And that's how it is as we move collectively. That's how it is as we love.

We've got all the contemplative technologies we need to meet this moment. Dismantling and undoing unjust systems is critical, and all the tools offered throughout this book can support us as we bring the light of conscious awareness to our movements for peace, justice, and unity.

**We can undo the habit of believing ourselves to be something we are not.
We can undo the systems that arise from this distortion.
We can realize freedom together.**

We're all served when, for the benefit of ourselves and others, we each commit to noticing when we're identified with the mind of scarcity and limitation, when the voice of self-hate is our guide, when our actions are arising on behalf of a felt sense of being separate—from ourselves, from each other, from the planet, from life. We're all served when we each commit to returning to presence, to the experience of shared being, together.

**In every moment, we can ask, does this thought, feeling, action arise
on behalf of truth, Love, understanding?
Or does it arise on behalf of an illusory self that feels cut off from being?
If so, we can redirect. In doing so, we take full responsibility for our lives.**

In my experience, it's not enough to simply see patterns, conditioned beliefs, and assumptions—to recognize them as veils of truth—and have the attention stay there. If we stay fixated on the veils, we will remain in the dark. The curtains are drawn back through loving attention, through the collective healing of wounds. If we stay fixated on the veils, we keep reinforcing things that only exist within human consciousness, within the identification, within the dream.

True liberation does not happen inside human consciousness.
It does not happen inside the dream.

For true collective liberation, we must go beyond drawing back what blocks the light.

We must see both the movie and the screen. It can be tempting to exclusively focus on cutting apart what veils. But true liberation doesn't come from tearing everything down (although this can be a valuable step along the way).

We've had our fair share of *against* infused with hate.
We need the vision of *toward* infused with Love.

At some point, for true liberation, we must touch and know ourselves as awareness itself—inherently creative, unborn and undying, infinite consciousness.

Love is consciousness.
Realizing freedom together comes from knowing ourselves as Love.
Love, required for rebuilding.

Love, the spark of creation.

THE PRACTICALITY OF UNCONDITIONAL LOVE

The educator and contemplative Barnaby Willett has been an invaluable co-visionary in the formation of Peace in Schools. He helped grow the nonprofit to be a national leader in mindfulness education. Recently he wrote,

"Poppy Schoenberg and David Vago run the Contemplative Neuroscience and Integrative Medicine Laboratory at Vanderbilt University. In a 2018 journal article, they presented a cutting-edge framework on how brain science might evolve to capture the complexity, impact, and nuance of contemplative practices. I was struck by their developmental model, which placed attentional and embodied practices as the foundational stage, insight and non-dual approaches as the middle stage, and unconditional love as the highest stage of contemplative actualization.

This validated everything I learned firsthand from teaching high school students with Peace in Schools: that when you talk and educate about unconditional love with humans, that's what resonates most deeply in their own being. It's what they say matters most to them too. It's a profound thing to be in a room full of high school students, all of us in a circle, having just finished an activity in which we explore a deep expression of unconditional love, and feel the whole room united by that shared value.

Teens have a reputation of being challenging. And rightly so, they're challenging the messed-up system created by adults as they find their identities. One of my students, Maddi, said she was cynical about the idea of love before she joined the class. But when you get an amazing variety of students all sharing in the direct experience of unconditional love in a high school classroom, you start to believe that the world of human beings might be able to realize the fullness of its potential."

This is what is possible for us, friends:
To realize the fullness of human potential.

And, in truth, this doesn't happen in a hierarchical way. It's spherical. It's not a line.

This realization happens
through Love,
in Love,
as Love.

It has always deeply moved me to hear teens and educators speak about Love, especially in settings in which it can be considered almost taboo by dominant culture. At the end of the short film *Into Light*, made by Wavecrest Films, Jared, unprompted, said this about his experience of his Mindful Studies class:

> "It's not just as simple as taking a breath, but it almost is. There's a lot of different steps you can take, but what it comes down to is realizing that you are worthy of love. And that was beautiful."

This is how the healing of our collective occurs—through this Love. And we cannot wholeheartedly create new structures together without healing.

We're all seeking love and acceptance. We all long to be happy. At the end of the day, we're not actually very complex creatures.

I've been leading New Year's retreats and workshops for adults for more than fifteen years. These retreats always focus at some point on conscious intention— intention that arises from Love and understanding, that supports us in aligning our thoughts and actions with our deepest recognition of truth. At one point in the retreat, I always offer a meditation that supports folks in getting in touch with their heart's deepest desire. While there is usually some variation in the content, the underlying longing is always the same:

We all long to be happy.
We all long to be free.
We all long to belong
and know ourselves
as beloved.

A middle school counselor, Rebecca Cohen, who has attended our Peace in Schools trainings for educators, shared a story of love, practice, and education and gave me permission to include it here:

> "It wasn't until I started doing mindfulness work that I gave myself permission . . . to understand that telling a student that you

love them . . . I get a little teary . . . is not unprofessional. That is the one permission that I've given [myself]. I often will sit with a student and tell them, 'I love you' and 'How can I help you?'

I was out doing something on the playground at the end of the pandemic and I had a student who walked through the gym of my school and called me over and took out this crumpled paper and handed it to me. It said

Dear Rebecca, thank you for everything. Thank you for being there for me this year . . . dah, dah, dah . . . I love you.

I mean, really? A sixth-grade boy is telling you they love you? But that's because I had opened that up and told him over and over that he was important to me, that he mattered, and that I loved him. And I think that those connections in a school . . . during those times in school that can be really hard . . . to know that there's someone in the building that loves you, and has told you that, changes everything."

Jeremy, Rebecca's husband and an elementary school principal, chimed in: "And that's true for our teachers too." By learning to allow for love, he has learned that you have to accept all of a person's life, not just the part in front of you—in his case, teachers. He went on to say,

"I say to my staff all the time, 'I just love you guys. I can't believe the work you're doing.' There are a lot of teachers at my school and I really love . . . I love them. They're so committed, and the work is really hard. And I know, frequently, I'll have teachers who are having some really hard stuff happening in their lives. And I have to help them. Part of my role is to help them.

In the same way that for a first grader I would catch off the bus and help him get from where he was with what happened [difficulties at home in the morning before school] to where we are right now, and how to be ready for that . . . I have to do the same for teachers, who are parents who sometimes have really hard things happening. They're sons and daughters of aging parents, and sometimes really hard things are happening with that. They are spouses, or . . . in the middle of divorces, and have really, really complicated lives—*and* we need them to show up at school for the kids. . . .

Part of what I'm trying to do as the school leader is help my teachers say, 'All that stuff is happening in my life. *And* I can be here now for these kids. And I don't have to pick. I can do both. Because when I'm at home, I can also be really present with that experience . . . and not be at school.' Because that's another problem that teachers have, right? Teachers bring their school home with them all the time and they never stop working . . . actually . . . presence solves all those things.

Presence can help you be just where you are. And when you're doing school, do school. And when you're working on your own relationships, or you're with your family, or with your kids, or with your aging parents, then be there with them."

"It's true!" Rebecca exclaimed with exuberance, "When you're playing, play. When you're eating, eat!"

Jeremy has supported over 90 percent of the staff in his school in taking mindfulness trainings, including those offered by Peace in Schools. "As a school leader, I see my role as reducing barriers," he stated. Jeremy makes a practice of asking, "What's in the way of teachers being the best they can be? Sometimes it's just structural." But as he looked into it, he learned more. He explained that "ultimately you have to start with the adults, because if the adults can't regulate themselves, the kids don't stand a chance."

Rebecca and Jeremy's experience speaks directly to the power of realizing collective transformation. Structural change happens in the borderless container of presence. It happens through Love. Transformation occurs through adults being supported in letting go of the conditioning that blocks Love, students being supported in knowing and expressing Love, teachers being supported in prioritizing presence. Evolution is an entire staff committing to valuing presence and Love, doing so together—not in an airy-fairy way but in a grounded fashion that becomes woven into the structure of the system.

LIFE PURPOSE

People often ask me about purpose in life. I've heard Rupert Spira speak to this question, and here is a version of what that inspired in me.

Let's be simple about it. What if our purpose was to:

1. Recognize our true nature, what we authentically are (implying discernment regarding what we are not).

2. Express this truth. Communicate it. Create and build on its behalf. Even *celebrate* our true nature through our bodies and minds.

Again, if this book ended up in your hands, then you too care about systems: the undoing of systems that arise on behalf of the primary distortion of dominant culture and the creation of systems that arise on behalf of Love and truth. For this creation to occur, our thoughts and actions must be aligned with our deepest understanding, the greatest Love.

The nature of Love is to express itself, to take form.
The expression of Love is Love.

LIVING A LIFE OF SERVICE

There is a reason that "Be the change you want to see in the world" has become a cliché. It took hold in our collective psyche because it's true. It lands. It resonates.

One aspect of creating Peace in Schools that has been enlivening for me has been creating opportunities for meaningful employment for others. Within dominant culture, it's become all too commonplace for work simply to be something required for survival yet totally removed from deeper meaning or purpose.

We tend to wither without purpose.

It has been profoundly beautiful to watch the impact that transformative education has on our youth. And no less beautiful to then see the impact on administrators, educators, and parents—to be present to the ripples.

Fundamentally, everything is vibration. So the vibration of trauma ripples, but so does the vibration of Love. All various modulations of consciousness within consciousness.

When it's someone's primary job to embody unconditional love and presence, the effect is powerful. I've witnessed this through the teachers at Peace in

Schools. It's been humbling to watch our staff rise to the occasion of this kind of embodiment, again and again.

My first Zen teacher's teacher once said, "You will do for the love of others what you would not do for yourself." Before Peace in Schools even existed, as I trained practitioners to become facilitators, I always offered this sentiment to those who were wary of taking this seat. I often still do. It can provide wind for the sails.

When Janice Martellucci came to my meditation class with her mother, in a new shiny Sacramento, California, yoga studio, I can assure you she did not know that twelve years later she'd be the executive director of a nonprofit with a $1.3 million budget; an organization that has the motto "Liberate mind and heart." Certainly, neither did I. It's been profoundly meaningful to me to see Janice refine her capacity to embody practice over the years, to know her as a student, to watch her practice flourish through countless private consultations and retreats, to know her as one of our teachers, to know her as a leader.

What has struck me most is not limited to one person, though, or to any one role that any one person has taken on in the organization. It goes beyond Peace in Schools. This is about seeing what has the opportunity to flourish when we focus our attention on serving truth, embodying our understanding and living it in the world. I've witnessed this take countless shape and form.

Remember this from chapter one?

The quality of our lives is dramatically affected by the focus of our attention.

Something shifts in our lives when the primary focus of our attention is on serving Love and truth. So what impresses me about Janice's trajectory is not relegated to the content of it. One need not be running a nonprofit to live a life in alignment with your deepest love and understanding. For some of us, this will take the form of being an artist. For some of us, we will, in fact, have jobs that the conditioned mind might label mundane but that have deep meaning based on the quality of presence we bring to them. As you've heard me say many times now, it's not about the *what*. It's all in the *how*.

This is about the *process* of serving Love and truth, of getting out of the way and allowing life to live through you. This direct experience then informs our actions. And this cannot help but change what we build in the world and how we build it.

> Service is a natural by-product of Love.
> When we recognize ourselves as Love,
> when we recognize ourselves as one body,
> one heart, one being,
> we cannot help but be of service to *this*.
> Love overflows with itself through us.

Through Love we become servants of spirit, or consciousness, or God, or whatever you are inspired to call it. This becomes an orientation rather than whatever the conditioned mind says we "should be doing"; rather than fulfilling the ego, a deeply impossible task that will never lead anywhere other than suffering.

> The illusion of a self that is separate from life
> cannot experience true fulfillment.
> Fulfillment shines
> in its absence.

LIBERATION IN ANY FORM

I was standing in our office speaking to one of our largest donors about the current school budget crisis. The writing was on the wall. Our program was likely to be cut by the district. He turned to me and asked me what we would do if the district didn't renew our funding. I didn't hesitate.

"We'll do something else," I said. "We'll serve somewhere else. We have an amazing team full of folks who are deeply committed to supporting people in ending suffering, and there is no shortage of suffering in the world. Who knows, perhaps we'll end up serving people in hospice, or maybe prisons."

It wasn't until I saw the surprise on the donor's face that I realized that according to dominant culture's standard, my response was an odd one, especially when delivered to a donor. I got it that what was expected might have been something like, "We set out to change public education, and there is nothing outside that goal." This would be said, of course, with ambition and drive, perhaps even the tone of aggressive determination. But when our drive is to serve Love and liberation, the form takes second place. In fact, on one level, it's somewhat irrelevant.

Don't get me wrong. I get lit up by seeing the system of education transform—a classroom, a school, a district, a state. But it truly is simply a form. It's the form I fell into when tending to my commitment to serve my deepest understanding, and to serve Love. My heart was similarly ignited when offering a private consultation to an adult who wept about being in love with the experience of being alive, when just one year prior, his addiction to cocaine almost killed him. Literally.

Liberation in any form is liberation.

For you, it will likely be something different than me. And this is how true system change can happen—each of us serving Love and understanding in the areas we're in, in the ways that are ours to do. You don't have to be a leader. You don't have to be smart. You don't have to be well educated. You don't have to be wealthy. We all share the same being. To serve the truth of this being is a choice. It's a choice that has to do with the attention. It's a choice that has to do with Love. It's a choice that has to do with releasing all that blocks Love, surrendering what gets in the way—personally and collectively.

When we realize our true nature on the most absolute level, a natural byproduct of this recognition is to dream of a society, a world, that reflects this recognition.

To create it we must dream it.
To dream it we must know it.

You cannot long for something you have never tasted.

How will Love take shape through your body-mind?

In this world, there are countless manifestations of Love expressing itself, and these expressions have nothing to do with our egos. In fact, these expressions are infinite. When awake, we see them everywhere.

Love is in the lip of a potter's freshly thrown teabowl.
It's in the curl of a rusty autumn leaf.
It's in the high-pitched call of the indigo bunting.

Love is in the stench of a decaying seal on the beach.
It's in the delight of Dōgen the dog who rolls in the seal's perfume,
then proudly parades it like a new gown for the queen!

Love is in the mother's voice as she speaks up in a school board meeting.
It's in the hands of the nurse as he turns his bedridden patient.
It's in the activist's creation of an environment of CARE.
It's in the painter's final dash of cerulean blue.

Love is in all of this.
Love *is* all of this.

There is
only This.

How will Love move in you, through you?
How will you serve it?
How will you serve the deepest truth of unity—the unity of being?

SERVING LOVE AND TRUTH

In terms of ending suffering, again, things can get sticky if we think we're serving *an-other*—that is, if I identify myself as the helper and see you as the one being helped, or the other way around. Can you see how this keeps the subject/object relationship in place?

True service occurs in the collapse of the subject/object relationship.
When there's no one to serve and no one to do the serving,
there is only enlightened activity.

In Buddhism, there is emphasis on the bodhisattva vows. They are an expression of the desire to realize enlightenment for the sake of others, to put the collective foremost in our mind, beyond the illusion of a separate self separately attaining a separate enlightenment. These vows are a profound way to direct the attention, to orient ourselves on this relative plane of existence.

In truth, though,
there are no sentient beings to save.
And no one to save them!

Knowing this, let's get to work, together. Let's bring all the collective loving attention we can muster to seeing through the countless systems we've created that are not reflections of Love and truth, together. Let's dismantle them not because we are acting to get rid of a part of ourselves but to infuse all parts of ourselves and our society with Love, in presence, focusing together on the potential for collective transformation. Let's cry, grieve, sing, burn to the ground and dance on what hasn't worked, what doesn't reflect or honor our oneness. Let's dream up, in this collective dream, systems that honor our shared being, reflect truth, prioritize justice and collective well-being—systems that celebrate our shared humanity, together.

Freedom is who we are, not what we attain.
There is no separate self.
Therefore, there is no collective.

So let's do this.
As a collective.
Together.

A Contemplation: How Shall We Serve?

Rest in the stillness of being.

Know yourself as presence.

Visualize what you think of as *an-other*.

See the unborn mind in what you are conditioned to
call *an-other*.

Zoom out.
See others, too, as presence.

Know their inherent freedom.

Don't try to fix them. Or change them. Don't try to
free them.

Don't fall for the story that the freedom of others is
not inherent.

On the relative plane, there is deep inequity, and the
expressions of deep inequity go on and on in this
world. This contemplation is not suggesting that there
is not a very particular reality to this. There is.

You might want to cry, or yell. You might want to curl
up in a ball, or run. Feel this.

Move *into* this. Into the reality of this—the true
nature of this—whatever this is.
Move into the being of this.

And, here's an invitation:
What shifts when you don't allow the recognition of
these systems and forms of inequity to convince you
that we are not the same being? When you recognize

these appearances, no matter how seemingly separate, as not separate?

What shifts when you remember that you are not broken?

That others are not broken?

That the world is not broken?

What shifts when you remember that you don't need to be saved?

Or that you don't need to save?

Forms that create and express inequity arise out of delusion.

We can see *through* the delusion.

We can remember what's true.

We can create from here.

We can allow our vision of collective freedom

to be collective remembering of the unity of being.

Let's surrender our attention to this, together.

Let's surrender as a collective.

From here, what shall we build?

How shall we serve?

How will we Love?

Collective Practice

Our lives.

Acknowledgments

"It is important that I tell you their names, that you know
that I have never achieved anything alone."

– Ta-Nehisi Coates

C ollective—the word appears in this book more often than most. This book would have never come to be without collective support, without collective guidance. There are many people I'd like to personally thank, more than I'll be able to in this format. First, a collective acknowledgment that is important to me to name.

To me, it is an honor to be published. One that I don't take lightly. Who gets published in the US is in no way reflective of the deep collective wisdom that takes various forms in our world. I also want to clearly name that my greatest learnings around race have come from Black, Indigineous, People of Color. I have done my best to uplift their voices throughout.

My beloved readers, your feedback shaped the book, and shaped me. Rev. angel Kyodo williams and David Perrin, your responses to draft one were not only invaluable, but they required me to stand on my own two feet, to ground more deeply in the heart of who I am, why I am here, and to trust myself. I will forever be grateful for this. Michelle Cassandra Johnson, you never wavered in your commitment to reflect my heart back to me, you believed in me. Thank you for your medicine. Zakiya Rhodes, you stood next to me through the storms of this writing process every single step of the way. You were so much more than my friend who was willing to be a personal sensitivity reader. You were a rock of unconditional stability, and all your coaching came through the arms of unconditional love. You never took your eye off who I truly am, and for this I am eternally grateful.

Jen Cai, your sweat is in this book, and your attention to detail and commitment to a healthy birth was invaluable. Ive Shipman, not only did you provide profound and important feedback, this book has the name it does because of you. Thank you for the form your love took. It was transformational. To my Sounds True sensitivity reader, thank you for helping me see things I hadn't.

Barry Boyce, aka Gandalf, thank you for reading every word many times and helping to sort out knotty questions. You were more than a cheerleader in the dark; you were the voice of reason in the biggest storms. You got the wtf phone calls, and the celebratory ones. You always picked up, always had something to give, and gently placed your hands on my shoulders, turning me in the right direction, more times than I can count. It was a privilege to have you as a developmental editor as I navigated new waters for the first time. Thank you.

Rupert Spira, my practice and therefore teaching have been so deeply impacted by your teachings that it's common for me to have an experience of not knowing where your offerings end and my offerings begin. It would be awkward to reference you throughout every meditation or way of framing an experience that appears the way it does in part due to your influence. Rupert, your teachings have shaped me. But more than that, the way you've embodied the teachings, *how* you've lived through example, has transformed me. Your friendship, your love, your care, your encouragement has had an unconditional quality that has taken seed in my heart and has completely shifted how I engage with others I share practice with. Thank you.

I feel grateful for the entire team at Sounds True and to Gareth Esersky and the Carol Mann Agency for believing in this project. Jennifer Yvette Brown, I had no idea that working with an editor could be such an intimate and joyful process. This book wouldn't be what it is without your wisdom, expertise, guidance, and care. Laurel Szmyd and Emily Wichland, thank you for your meticulous attention to detail; and Jennifer Miles, thank you for the lovely cover design. Terri Bennett and Jennifer Anderman, hallelujah for your willingness to be such terrific transcribers! Justin Michael Williams, bless you for opening the way for this book to be born. Stephanie Domet, thank you for swooping in and tending to last minute clean-up with grace. Thank you for your flame-like encouragement.

Anna Forsline, your work was invisible to many, but I'll always know the importance of your contribution. You were a pillar of support and your dedication was steadfast. Rashid Hughes and jylani ma'at, thank you for the conversations, the musings, the pebbles you dropped in the soup. The flavor would not be as rich without you. Charlie Chapman and Heather Shaw, thank you for having my back. Onward and upward!

Morgan Perry, your hand appears on most pages of this book. Your structural support was not only invaluable, but through your help I became a better writer. And I needed your tenacity. Thank you for all you gave and for teaching me how to make the perfect margarita in the process. Barnaby Willett, you were a muse in the trees, embodying the whispers of the imaginal realm and loving me unconditionally without stumble. You never got ruffled by anything on the surface of the water. Thank you. David Zimmerman, my sangha brother, it has been a tremendous pleasure to banter with you about emptiness, Zen, and nuances in this book that perhaps few would have delightfully geeked out about as we did!

Jim Anderson, Julia Conner, and Emily Davis, thank you for knowing the artist in me and for your relentless dedication to beauty—in me, in us, in the world. Deborah Eden Tull, I bow to our dharmic sisterhood. Also a bow to India Arie; your songs can be heard in so many pages of this book. You were part of my morning prayer.

I was blessed to find refuge in many stunning places throughout the process of writing this book, and this was made possible only because of community. So much gratitude for all who helped house me—for not only honoring my need for solitude but helping me create it. Tom Dancer and Nita Forde, surely staying in a rural North Carolina cabin used as a wagon wheel fix-it-shop in the late 1800s infused the words in mysterious ways I'll, thankfully, never be able to name. Nita, you gave of your heart to support in a way that few know how to. I am eternally grateful and I bow to you. Latifa Till, having your beautiful home to myself was an immeasurable gift. Your love and care, for more years than I wish to count, has never waivered. Gasshō. Kerry Keeler and Betsy Oakes, I'll never be able to separate the final inspirations of this book with the beautiful space they arose out of. Nityananda, it was in the cabin you offered that I realized that writing is one way that I get to be alone with Spirit. Elaine Michaelides, thank you. Krista Hornish and Bethany Roth, what would this book have become without Bongo the cat and Maggie the super-mutt beaming love my way as I wrote? Your unconditional support has imprinted deeply in my heart.

This book also never would have come to be without the support of the entire team at Peace in Schools, including every teen who has been part of our program. While the views in this book are entirely my own and I take full responsibility for them, my experience within Peace in Schools has nurtured my understanding in incalculable ways. I cannot list all the past and present employees by name here, nor every teen, but please know that you have not been forgotten and that you are appreciated. Everyone involved in the org knows that there's been a book for me to write for years, hanging in the wings, waiting. Janice Martelluci and Amanda Morse, it's through your visioning and restructuring support that I've gotten out of the organizational weeds and have been able to turn toward my next child, all while not leaving my first born. I bow to your practices and to your hearts of service. Geri Stewart and Carl Reinhold, your steadfastness to the deepest truth has been imperative on our board. Stuart Moore, you've been a life-line—because of you, we are. Sam Hendricks, my life changed when we met in a coffee shop on SE Division and your eyes lit up upon hearing my wild idea. Maggie Steele, our conversations over the years seeded deep inquiry in me; they ignited a call for reconciliation. Much of this reconciliation is now in the form of this book. Thank you. Dr. Sarà King, thank you for being a crucible for transformation.

Claire Wings and Walter Mckitchen, Wola and Ramada, I sing gratitude into the universe at the top of my lungs for all the ways that you lit up what is beyond this body-mind—the wisdom, the Love. A deep bow to the invisible voice of my ancestors and the knowing beyond.

Another deep bow to *The Heart of Who We Are Sangha*, who has become family to me, to your practices and your commitment. And to the board of Presence Collective—Rashid, jyalni, Dave, and Grace Song—I am blessed to be in collaboration with you. It is a deep joy to be your playmate.

My dearest Moma, thank you for the love that never waivers. In the face of life's greatest difficulties you supported me and this project. In the midst of physical pain, you'd pause, ask me about my book, and demand detailed answers. You've always supported me. Even when you didn't understand me, you've always supported me. How can I express my gratitude for the way you have given me life?

And lastly my beloved Vineet, I admire you. You opened yourself to supporting this project as a seva of sorts, and I recognize that this meant having to keep your eye fixed on what is larger than you in difficult moments—as well as pick up *way* more than your fair share of dog poop. This book wouldn't have been possible without your love. You have seen me through every twist and turn like no one else, and I am grateful for your dedication to this project, but more importantly, your dedication to my heart. I'm so grateful you were willing to go on this ride with me, Vineet. Your love and constant encouragement nourished me. Thank you for keeping me laughing, especially when it felt like there was little to laugh about. Thank you for all you give and for being who you are. I love you.

I end with the words that Michelle Cassandra Johnson started us off with, and I thank you, dear reader, for your engagement. As you well know by now, I value the way in which we're in this together. "May we all come back to the profound and unchangeable truth that we are divine beings with a divined purpose rooted in love at this time and in this place."

Resources

To include a comprehensive listing of the potential resources in this area could run to dozens of pages, so I've decided to include a manageable list—one that is reflective of work that has touched either me or my closest friends and colleagues directly. There are wonderful resources not listed here, and anything not included does not represent a judgment on my part.

ADDITIONAL RESOURCES FROM CAVERLY

Caverly is dedicated to supporting your practice of liberation and offers a wide and growing range of resources. Visit www.caverlymorgan.org for the latest on retreats, online courses, meditation groups, and other offerings Caverly is leading.

Presence Collective

> A 501(c)3 nonprofit

> A community of cross-cultural contemplatives committed to personal and collective transformation, creating spaces for wisdom exchange and belonging.

> https://www.presencecollective.org

Peace in Schools

> A 501(c)3 nonprofit dedicated to transformative mindfulness education.

> https://www.peaceinschools.org/

Morgan, Caverly. *A Kid's Book About Mindfulness.*

MINDFULNESS IN EDUCATION

Books:

Ergas, Oren. *Reconstructing "Education" Through Mindful Attention.*

Hammond, Zaretta, and Yvette Jackson. *Culturally Responsive Teaching and the Brain: Promoting Authentic Engagement and Rigor Among Culturally and Linguistically Diverse Students.*

Hanh, Thich Nhat. *Happy Teachers Change the World.*

Himelstein, Sam. *A Mindfulness-Based Approach to Working with High-Risk Adolescents.*

Srinivasan, Meena. *Teach Breathe Learn.*

Organizations and Innovators:

Inward Bound Mindfulness Education

https://ibme.com

Mindful Life Project

http://mindfullifeproject.org/about/

Dr. Angel Acosta

https://www.drangelacosta.com/

Dr. Christopher Willard

https://www.drchristopherwillard.com

RACE EDUCATION:

Books:

Baldwin, James. *The Fire Next Time.*

DiAngelo, Robin. *White Fragility: Why It's So Hard for White People to Talk About Racism.*

Hannah-Jones, Nikole. *The 1619 Project: A New Origin Story.*

Metzl, Jonathan. *Dying of Whiteness.*

Oluo, Ijeoma. *So You Want to Talk About Race.*

Wilkerson, Isabel. *Caste: The Origins of Our Discontents.*

RACE AND DHARMA

Books:

Johnson, Michelle Cassandra. *Finding Refuge: Heart Work for Healing Collective Grief.*

Johnson, Michelle Cassandra. *Skill in Action: Radicalizing Your Yoga Practice to Create a Just World.*

King, Ruth. *Mindful of Race: Transforming Racism from the Inside Out.*

Magee, Rhonda V. *Inner Work of Racial Justice: Healing Ourselves and Transforming Our Communities Through Mindfulness.*

Owens, Lama Rod. *Love and Rage: The Path of Liberation Through Anger.*

williams, Rev. angel Kyodo, Lama Rod Owens, Jasmine Syedullah. *Radical Dharma: Talking Race, Love, and Liberation.*

Yang, Larry. *Awakening Together: The Spiritual Practice of Inclusivity and Community.*

TRAUMA

Books:

Harris, Nadine Burke. *The Deepest Well.*

Hübl, Thomas. *Healing Collective Trauma: A Process for Integrating Our Intergenerational and Cultural Wounds*

Levine, Peter A. *Waking the Tiger: Healing Trauma.*

Menakem, Resmaa. *My Grandmother's Hands: Healing Racial Trauma in Our Minds and Bodies.*

Treleaven, David A. *Trauma-Sensitive Mindfulness: Practices for Safe and Transformative Healing.*

Van der Kolk, Bessel. *The Body Keeps the Score: Mind, Brain and Body in the Transformation of Trauma.*

Films:

The Wisdom of Trauma, featuring Dr. Gabor Maté. Directed by Maurizio and Zaya Benazzo. Science and nonduality, 2021. https:// thewisdomoftrauma.com/

COMPASSION

Books:

Bays, Jan Chozen, and Heng Sure. *Jizo Bodhisattva: Modern Healing & Traditional Buddhist Practice.*

Germer, Christopher K. *The Mindful Path To Self-Compassion: Freeing Yourself From Destructive Thoughts And Emotions.*

Huber, Cheri, and June Shiver. *There Is Nothing Wrong with You: Regardless of What You Were Taught to Believe.*

Neff, Kristin. *Self Compassion: The Proven Power of Being Kind to Yourself.*

ZEN

Books:

Blofeld, John, and P'ei Hsiu. *The Zen Teaching of Huang Po: On the Transmission of Mind.*

Dogen, Eihei (Author), Kazuaki Tanahashi (Editor, Translator), Robert Aitken (Translator). *Moon in a Dewdrop: Writings of Zen Master Dogen.*

Hanh, Thich Nhat. *The Heart of the Buddha's Teaching: Transforming Suffering into Peace, Joy, and Liberation.*

Reps, Paul, and Nyogen Senzaki. *Zen Flesh, Zen Bones: A Collection of Zen and Pre-Zen Writings.*

Suzuki, Shunryū. *Zen Mind, Beginner's Mind: Informal Talks on Zen Meditation and Practice.*

Uchiyama, Kosho (Author), Tom Wright (Translator), Jisho Warner (Translator). *Opening the Hand of Thought: Foundations of Zen Buddhist Practice.*

Wadell, Norman (Translator). *Unborn: The Life and Teachings of Zen Master Bankei, 1622–1693.*

EMPTINESS AND THE HEART SUTRA

Analyo, Bhikku. *Emptiness and Compassion.*

Armstrong, Guy. Emptiness: *A Practical Guide for Meditators.*

Brunnhölzl, Karl. *The Heart Attack Sutra: A New Commentary on the Heart Sutra.*

Tanahashi, Kazuaki and Joan Halifax. *The Heart Sutra: A Comprehensive Guide to the Classic of Mahayana Buddhism.*

NON-DUALITY

Books:

Atmananda, Shri, Nitya Tripta. *Notes on Spiritual Discourses of Shri Atmananda.*

Godman, David. *Be As You Are; Teachings of Ramana Maharshi.*

Klein, Jean. *I Am.*

Lucille, Francis. *Eternity Now.*

Maharaj, Sri Nisargadatta, Sudhaker S. Dikshit (Editor), Maurice Frydman (Translator). *I Am That: Talks with Sri Nisargadatta Maharaj.*

Spira, Rupert. *The Ashes of Love: Sayings on the Essence of Non-Duality.*

Spira, Rupert. *You Are the Happiness You Seek: Uncovering the Awareness of Being.*

Bibliography

INTRODUCTION

Maharshi, Ramana, and Ram Dass. *Abide as the Self: The Essential Teachings of Ramana Maharshi*. Inner Directions, 2002. (DVD)

Williams, angel Kyodo, Lama Rod Owens, Jasmine Syedullah. *Radical Dharma: Talking Race, Love, and Liberation*. North Atlantic Books, 2016.

CHAPTER 1

Huber, Cheri. *That Which You Are Seeking Is Causing You to Seek*. Keep It Simple Books, 1990.

Thich Nhat Hanh. "The Next Buddha May Be a Sangha." Inquiring Minds, Spring 1994 (Vol. 10, No. 2).

CHAPTER 2

Siegel, Daniel J. *Mind: A Journey to the Heart of Being Human*. W. W. Norton & Company, Inc., 2016.

Stone, Jon R. *The Routledge Dictionary of Latin Quotations the Illiterati's Guide to Latin Maxims, Mottoes, Proverbs and Sayings*. New York: Routledge, 2005.

CHAPTER 3

Gray, Terence James Stannus (Wei Wu Wei). *Ask the Awakened: The Negative Way*. Routledge & K. Paul, 1963.

Williams, Justin Michael. "Ending Racism: How to Change the World in One Generation." August 28, 2020. Accessed 10/6/21. https://www.justinmichaelwilliams.com/blog/endingracism.

CHAPTER 4

Brown, C. Brené. *I Thought It Was Just Me: Women Reclaiming Power and Courage in a Culture of Shame*. New York: Gotham Books, 2007.

Coates, Ta-Nehisi. *Between the World and Me*. Spiegel & Grau, 2015.

Kempton, Sally. "Cutting Loose." *Esquire Magazine*, July 1970, 57.

Krishnamurti, Jiddu. *The Only Revolution*. Harper & Row, 1970.

CHAPTER 5

Bethell, Christina D., Narangerel Gombojav, and Robert C. Whitaker. "Family Resilience and Connection Promote Flourishing Among US Children, Even Amid Adversity." *Health Affairs* 38, no. 5 (2019): 729–37.

Bethell, Christina, Jennifer Jones, Narangerel Gombojav, Jeff Linkenbach, and Robert Sege. "Positive Childhood Experiences and Adult Mental and Relational Health in a Statewide Sample." *JAMA Pediatrics* 173, no. 11 (2019).

Bethell, Christina D., Michele R. Solloway, Stephanie Guinosso, Sandra Hassink, Aditi Srivastav, David Ford, and Lisa A. Simpson. "Prioritizing Possibilities for Child and Family Health: An Agenda to Address Adverse Childhood Experiences and Foster the Social and Emotional Roots of Well-Being in Pediatrics." *Academic Pediatrics* 17, no. 7 (2017): S36-S50.

Bethell, Christina, Narangerel Gombojav, Michele Solloway, and Lawrence Wissow. "Adverse Childhood Experiences, Resilience and Mindfulness-Based Approaches." *Child and Adolescent Psychiatric Clinics of North America* 25, no. 2 (2016): 139–56.

hooks, bell. "Toward a Worldwide Culture of Love." *Shambhala Sun*, July 2006.

King, Ruth. *Mindful of Race: Understanding and Transforming Habits of Harm*. Boulder, CO: Sounds True, 2018.

King, Sará. "The "Science of Social Justice": An Interdisciplinary Theoretical Framework Grounded in Neuroscience, Education, and Anthropology Towards Healing Intergenerational Trauma," *Journal of Contemplative Inquiry* 9, no. 1 (2022).

Lorde, Audre. *Sister Outsider: Essays and Speeches*. Trumansburg, NY: Crossing Press, 1984.

Neff, Kristin D., and Roos Vonk. "Self-Compassion Versus Global Self-Esteem: Two Different Ways of Relating to Oneself." *Journal of Personality* 77, no. 1 (2009): 23–50.

Stevens, Jane Ellen, Aces Too High News, May 13, 2013. https://acestoohigh.com/2013/05/13/nearly-35-million-u-s-children-have-experienced-one-or-more-types-of-childhood-trauma/.

Treleaven, David. https://davidtreleaven.com/david-tsm/, accessed 9/8/21.

Van der Kolk, Bessel A. *The Body Keeps the Score: Brain, Mind, and Body in the Healing of Trauma*. New York: Viking, 2014.

Zhang, Jia Wei, and Serena Chen. "Self-Compassion Promotes Personal Improvement from Regret Experiences via Acceptance." *Personality and Social Psychology Bulletin* 42, no. 2 (2016): 244–58.

CHAPTER 6

Berensohn, Paulus. *Finding One's Way with Clay: Pinched Pottery and the Color of Clay*. Simon & Schuster, 1972.

Bethell, Christina. "Identifying, Preventing, and Treating Childhood Trauma: A Pervasive Public Health Issue that Needs Greater Federal Attention," Testimony to the House Committee on Oversight and Reform, July 11, 2019.

Merton, Thomas. *The Way of Chuang Tzu*. New York: New Directions Books, 2010.

Selassie, Sebene. Belonging & Imagination, https://www.sebeneselassie.com/blog/belonging-amp-imagination, accessed 12/15/21.

CHAPTER 7

Brown, Adrienne Maree. *We Will Not Cancel Us: And Other Dreams of Transformative Justice*. Edinburgh: AK Press, 2020.

Gupta, Sameer Das. *Advanced History of Buddhism: Monasteries and Temples.* Cyber Tech Publications, 2008.

King, Ruth. *Mindful of Race: Understanding and Transforming Habits of Harm.* Boulder, CO: Sounds True, 2018.

Manuel, Zenju Earthlyn. *The Way of Tenderness: Awakening Through Race, Sexuality, and Gender.* Boston: Wisdom Publications, 2015.

Waddell, Norman (translator). *Unborn: The Life and Teachings of Zen Master Bankei, 1622–1693.* Farrar, Straus and Giroux, 2020.

CHAPTER 8

Haskel, Peter, Mary Farkas, and Yoshito Hakeda. *Bankei Zen: Translations from the Record of Bankei.* New York: Grove Press, 1984.

CHAPTER 9

Aksapāda. *Tao of Dogen: Abstracted Zen Lessons from the Father of Sōtō Zen Buddhist School.* Independently published, 2018.

CHAPTER 10

Frydman, Maurice (translator). *I AM THAT: Dialogues of Sri Nisargadatta Maharaj, 1973.* online edition. http://www.maharajnisargadatta.com/I_Am_That.pdf.

hooks, bell. *The Will To Change: Men, Masculinity, and Love.* New York: Washington Square Press, 2004.

CHAPTER 11

Miles, Justin F. *Space: The Problem And The Promise Of Hiphop.* a gathering together Literary Journal. Spring 2021. https://www.agatheringtogether.com/space-the-problem-and-the-promise-of-hiphop/.

Morgan, Caverly. *A Kids Book About Mindfulness.* Portland, OR: *A Kids Book About,* 2020.

Walsh, Bari. "The Science of Resilience: Why Some Children Thrive Despite Adversity." Harvard's Graduate School of Education, March 23, 2015. https://www.gse.harvard.edu/news/uk/15/03/science-resilience.

Young, Shinzen. *Natural Pain Relief: How to Soothe and Dissolve Physical Pain with Mindfulness*. Boulder, CO: Sounds True, 2011.

CHAPTER 12

Into Light. Wavecrest Films, 2018. http://wavecrestfilms.com.

Pascal, Blaise, W. F. Trotter (translator). *Pensées*. United States: Dover Publications, 2018.

Menakem, Resmaa. *My Grandmother's Hands*. Las Vegas: Central Recovery Press, 2017.

Suzuki, Shunryu. "Using Various Stones." Talk given at Tassajara Zen Mountain Center, Carmel Valley, CA, September 8, 1967. From http://www.shunryusuzuki2.com/Detail1?ID=181m, accessed 6/30/22.

About the Author

Caverly Morgan is a meditation teacher, author, nonprofit leader, and visionary. She is the founder of the nonprofit Presence Collective—a community of cross-cultural contemplatives committed to personal and collective transformation. She is also the founder and Lead Contemplative of Peace in Schools—a nonprofit that created the nation's first for-credit mindfulness class in public high schools.

Caverly blends the original spirit of Zen with a modern nondual approach. Her practice began in 1995 and has included eight years of training in a silent Zen monastery. She has been teaching contemplative practice since 2001.

Caverly is the author of *A Kids Book About Mindfulness*. She leads online classes, workshops, and meditation retreats internationally. She lives in Portland, Oregon, with her husband, Vineet, and their two dogs, Sweetpea and Dōgen.

About Sounds True

Sounds True is a multimedia publisher whose mission is to inspire and support personal transformation and spiritual awakening. Founded in 1985 and located in Boulder, Colorado, we work with many of the leading spiritual teachers, thinkers, healers, and visionary artists of our time. We strive with every title to preserve the essential "living wisdom" of the author or artist. It is our goal to create products that not only provide information to a reader or listener but also embody the quality of a wisdom transmission.

For those seeking genuine transformation, Sounds True is your trusted partner. At SoundsTrue.com you will find a wealth of free resources to support your journey, including exclusive weekly audio interviews, free downloads, interactive learning tools, and other special savings on all our titles.

To learn more, please visit SoundsTrue.com/freegifts or call us toll-free at 800.333.9185.